ZANE GREY ON FISHING

Fishing Books by Zane Grey

An American Angler in Australia

Tales of the Angler's Eldorado, New Zealand

Tales of Fishes

Tales of Fishing Virgin Seas

Tales of Freshwater Fishing

Tales of Southern Rivers

Tales of Swordfish and Tuna

Tales of Tahitian Waters

By Terry Mort

The Reasonable Art of Fly Fishing

ZANE GREY
ON FISHING

ZANE GREY

Edited and with an Introduction by
TERRY MORT

Foreword by Loren Grey

THE LYONS PRESS

Guilford, Connecticut

An imprint of The Globe Pequot Press

The Lyons Press is an imprint of The Globe Pequot Press

10 9 8 7 6 5 4 3 2 1

Designed by Compset, Inc.

Library of Congress Cataloging-in-Publication Data

Grey, Zane, 1872–1939.
    Zane Grey on fishing / edited by Terry Mort.
        p. cm.
    ISBN 1–58574–871–4 (alk. paper)
    1. Fishing stories, American. I. Mort, Terry. II. Title.
        PS3513.R6545 A6 2003
        813'.52—dc21

Contents

Contents

Foreword

It seems ironic that though Zane Grey's stature as a writer of consequence has increased recently, his fame as a Western author has more than correspondingly diminished. In the years between 1910 and 1930 he was the most famous writer of that era and his name was a household word both here in the United States and in some European countries as well, despite the critics of his day regularly denigrating his work as being superficial and trashy. Despite this, he played a major role in defining America's perception of the West and indeed, of ourselves, as well. The reason for Grey's diminished fame was not his fault, but was due mainly to a dramatic decline in reading for pleasure in all forms, primarily because of the competing forms of entertainment, mostly television. Though Grey's stature has grown in academia as a serious writer in recent years, his fame has not—except in one pursuit that has enlarged immensely in the past few years, and that is sport fishing. Deep-sea angling has burgeoned enormously all over the globe and it's safe to say that every serious deep-sea aficionado knows of Zane Grey. This is not just because of his pioneering deep-sea tackle and his many world records, but his extensive writing in the field.

I have always felt that writing about Dad's fishing exploits were more fun for him than the serious composing of his novels. In his fishing tales, he manages to convey much of the similar excitement and thrills that are present in his Western books. Though at one time he held 16 all-tackle deep-sea world records, he seemed to derive as much enjoyment from the thrills of vainly trying to capture a six-pound small-mouthed bass in Lackawaxan Creek as he did in subduing his 1040 lb. blue marlin, the first grander ever caught off Tahiti in 1930. His fishing adventures ranged not only from hunting for bass and trout in the Ohio and Pennsylvania rivers, but stalking the wily bonefish off the flats in Florida, fly-fishing for steelhead in the Umpqua Rivers of Oregon, to trout fishing in the mighty Tongariro River in New Zealand, and stalking mighty gamefish in the waters of Catalina, Mexico, Tahiti and New Zealand.

This volume contains a representative collection of many of Zane Grey's adventures and documents and illustrates vividly, as I alluded to before, how he could become as enthralled about trying to land a six-pound small-mouth bass, the "Lord of Lackawaxen Creek," as he called it, to battling thousand-pound marlin and sharks off Tahiti and Australia. Each story is told with the fervor and excitement that unquestionably afford him the title of one of the master storytellers of all time.

Loren Grey, Woodland Hills, California

Introduction

How did Zane Grey think of himself—as a writer who fished or a fisherman who wrote? Hard to say. They were his twin passions, and each supported the other. Not all of his books dealt with angling, of course. Most were historical novels or Westerns, and many were best sellers. His most famous novel, *Riders of the Purple Sage,* sold an astonishing one million copies when it came out in 1912. After struggling through the early years, suffering rejection from publishers, he finally achieved the commercial success that made him world famous and wealthy.

That allowed him to go fishing. And go he did. Few if any anglers have logged so many miles and spent so much time at sea or alongside a stream. And, being a writer, he wrote about what he did and what he saw and about the incredible varieties of fish he searched for and the wild or exotic places that lured him. For a man with his restless temperament and appetite for adventure, it would seem to be a perfect blending of vocation and avocation. And many believe that his books and articles on fishing are his best work, for his fiction is sometimes conventional and ornate, but his angling stories by comparison are fresh and unadorned.

He was born in 1872 in Zanesville, Ohio, a town named for his pioneer ancestor, Ebenezer Zane. His mother named him Pearl Zane Gray, but he dropped the Pearl for obvious reasons and then later changed the spelling of his last name to the more aristocratic-looking Grey. And certainly his feeling for words served him well there. Could there be a better name for a writer of adventure stories than 'Zane Grey?' His father, a dentist, was a cold and conventional man who detested Zane's interest in fishing—and writing—but could do nothing about it, although he tried. He insisted that his son follow him into the profession, and so Zane went to the University of Pennsylvania, where he played baseball and studied dentistry. After getting his degree he went to New York where he opened his practice and spent his evenings writing stories that no one wanted to publish and his leisure time playing pro baseball for the Orange (NJ) Athletic Club. He also began going to Lackawaxen, Pennsylvania to escape the noxious air and crowds of the city and to fish in the beautiful upper Delaware where Lackawaxen Creek joins the main river and where bass and trout were plentiful.

There in 1900 he met his future wife, Dolly, a woman who was eleven years younger and who would become his chief support and agent and business manager. Dolly believed in him, understood his yearnings to abandon dentistry and to become a writer. She suffered with him through the early disappointments and the bitter rejections. She helped him publish his first novel with her modest legacy when no publisher would take it, and later when he achieved commercial success, she managed the enterprise that Zane Grey had become. She negotiated with publishers to extract the maximum royalties and edited his prolific output. She was essential to his success. And yet, she once described herself as "the alone-est person I ever met," for ZG would leave her at home to look after things while he went off to fish, sometimes in the company of young women. If there's a heroine in ZG's own story, it would seem to be Dolly. They had three children, Romer, Loren and Betty, and in the fishing stories the two boys appear now and then as apprentice anglers.

Most often, though, Zane Grey was accompanied by his brother, R.C. They were close companions as boys and remained so throughout their lives. Time and again ZG refers wistfully to his boyhood days and attributes his fishing, in part, to the need to recover the feelings he had when he and R.C. ignored their father's angry strictures and went off to the streams and rivers. "Fishing keeps men boys longer than any other pursuit!"

His other companions on these trips were friends, like Captain Laurie Mitchell, an English sportsman he met in Nova Scotia, or men who worked for him, such as Captain Sid Boerstler. Captain Sid ran ZG's fishing boats and also oversaw the renovation of ZG's great yacht, *Fisherman*. ZG bought the 190-foot schooner in Nova Scotia and had her refitted so that he and his entourage could search in comfort for 'virgin seas.' And there were other assistants, men like Peter Williams, a New Zealand whaler and fisherman, whose steady and dependable knowledge of all things nautical made many of ZG's great triumphs possible. The stories are sprinkled with these characters, for ZG liked the company of such men. He admired their competence and courage. "All my life I have envied country boys, backwoodsmen, native fishermen, and the hardy men who eke out a living from the deep. For they see most of nature's wonders. They are always there, daybreak and sunset, and they catch the most and biggest fish."

But it was not just catching fish that mattered. What mattered was going and seeing and simply *being* in the wild. Fishing took him to out-of-the-way places that civilization had not ruined and helped him refine his skills of observation. It was a means to many ends. "To capture the fish is not all of the fishing."

And so, although a gamefish might be the quarry, it was not an adversary so much as a partner, albeit unwilling, in an aesthetic and emotional and physical experience. Fishing was a battle without an enemy (except for sharks, which he hated.) ZG was always intent on giving his quarry a fair chance. He disliked all methods in which the object was simply to acquire the fish. He could be bitterly disappointed when he lost a fish, but he would not resort to methods he considered unfair just to capture it. He wanted "to do things properly," to use a Hemingway phrase. He raised a stir in New Zealand when he criticized the local practice of hooking a gamefish and then letting the fish drag the boat until it died or could be harpooned. This sort of thing was wrong, and he said so. When it came to a great fish the idea was to "stop him and fight him."

This concern for fair treatment extended also to using the proper equipment. Just as it was unseemly to use heavy tackle to haul a light fish to the boat, so it was wrong to use tackle that was too light. That sort of fight almost always ended in breaking off the fish that would then swim away trailing line and leader. Nor would ZG countenance the use of treble hooks, which he said caused foul hooking. ZG knew tackle. He worked with Hardy Brothers of London to design and manufacture the "Hardy Zane Grey," a heavy reel made for heavy fish, and he wrote extensively about the need to match the tackle to the fish, not only because it was effective but also because it was the proper thing to do.

The angling ethics of that time were different, of course. ZG generally kept the fish he caught. Now and then he would release one, and he writes occasionally about the desirability of releasing fish that are unharmed. He was an early advocate of releasing small marlin caught off Catalina, California, where he was a member of the prestigious Tuna Club. And he frequently expressed contentment, when a particularly game fish got away, or regret at the end of a successful fight. "It gave me a pang—that I should be the cause of the death of so beautiful a thing."

It may seem ironic to modern anglers, who usually release their fish, that ZG could go into genuine raptures about the beauties of a fish and then hang it up for photographs afterwards. But that was a different time. And the fact that ZG released any fish at all was remarkable in that day, when most anglers killed all their fish and often just discarded them afterwards. As he writes in *Gulf Stream Fishing*, " . . . tons of good food and gamefish are brought in only to be thrown to the sharks. I mention this here to give it wide publicity. It is criminal in these days and ought to be stopped." The fish ZG kept were not wasted, at least.

He was also ahead of most of the other anglers of the day in his attitude toward the environment and conservation. Like Teddy Roosevelt he gloried in the wilderness and detested anyone bent on despoiling it, for whatever reason. Both men understood that the wilderness and the oceans were not invulnerable, that the numbers of fish and game were not inexhaustible and the wilderness, once gone, was gone for good.

But neither he nor TR would have had any patience with today's extreme 'environmentalists' who regard fishing and hunting as barbaric anachronisms. Both men would have been perplexed and irritated by such ideas. For them, the wilderness and the sea were places where men tested themselves against the elements and against their own inner doubts and physical limitations. Nature was not something to be conquered or subdued or exploited. Rather, it was the context in which people could develop and become more fully human—sometimes by dramatic hunting or fishing encounters, sometimes by just sitting quietly and looking around. "How cool and fresh and shady and redolent of cedar that deep canyon! Then the beauty of Deer Creek and its environment gave me a sense of sheer, wild, exquisite joy."

ZG was unusually sensitive to the beauties of nature, and he felt thrilled and cleansed and restored by them. He went fishing, in part, for that reason: "How often fishing leads a man to find beauty otherwise never seen!" And he was as responsive to miniatures as he was to panoramas; he took as much pleasure in birds or aquatic insects or fields of wild flowers as he did in dramatic sunsets at sea or the vast western mountain ranges. He could be quite happy wading in a quiet freshwater steam casting for bass or trout.

But it was not a kind of passive Thoreauvian contentment that he looked for. Not always. He wanted excitement, too, and he went to sea to look for it. He knew the ocean and what it could do. "An old familiar dread of the ocean mounted in me again." He understood that nature was not in the least benign and that the oceans and the wilderness were utterly indifferent, and that, too, stimulated him. He went in search of great fish in order to connect himself with them, literally, because they were wild and lived in wild, daunting places where man was not at home and therefore must become more alert, more intensely alive. The danger of fishing for giant swordfish that could attack and sink a small boat both frightened and aroused him, and he thought of those great battles as tests of his strength and skill and fortitude. And many of the rivers he fished were turbulent and hazardous. And they were remote. Just getting to them was itself an adventure in those times.

While some might regard all this as macho egotism, ZG's motives were more complex. Far from imposing his will on nature in general and a fish in particular, ZG went fishing to escape what he called the "plague of himself." Often troubled by black moods, he went into nature to be distracted, to forget himself. " . . . I was out to see and learn, and I was not preoccupied with my own ideas." This hardly seems like egotism. Of course, afterwards, there was the thrill of success and the pride of capture, and there was ego involved then, to be sure. He was proud of his achievements and numeous angling records. But there was always more to it than that.

* * *

Although ZG did not invent the Western novel, he did refine it and popularize it and, essentially, establish the genre. *Riders of the Purple Sage* features the lone hero, Lassiter, riding out of the wilderness to come to the aid of rancher Jane Withersteen. Hardly the wilting Victorian heroine, Jane would pass muster in a gathering of independent women today; she ran the outfit, after all. But she was outnumbered by her enemies, and Lassiter came along to even the odds. This is the knight errant armed with six-shooters. Laconic. Self-sufficient. Intolerant of abuses. Chivalrous. Individualistic. Courageous in the face of violence. Adept. Iconic.

The critics more or less dismissed Zane Grey's Westerns. Some said the stories relied on conventional plots and cliches. 'Villains, varmints and virgins,' as one critic called them. Other critics looking for literary fiction in which the protagonist is enmeshed in grim and gritty reality—and is, more often than not, defeated by it—did not find it in Zane Grey's work. It was therefore not to their taste, and they berated it. Such criticism hurt ZG, of course. But he was not about to change. "Reality is death to me. I can't stand life as it is." So he wrote about the West as he imagined it was, or as it should have been. He understood that one person's cliche is another's archetype.

Not all literati of his day dismissed him, though. None other than Ernest Hemingway admired his work, especially the fishing stories. Hemingway carried the books aboard *Pilar* and gave other copies as presents. Most likely Hemingway regarded ZG as a role model of sorts—the writer as hero of his own life. And it seems more than coincidental that ZG's story about going 83 days without a fish followed on the 84th by an encounter with a huge marlin that is subdued after a long battle, tied to the boat and then attacked by sharks, which are beaten off with gaffs and boathooks, should turn up a few decades later in Hemingway's *The Old Man and the Sea*. Hemingway said that the book was based on a true story he heard in Cuba, but he must also have remembered reading something similar before that.

Toward the end of his life ZG suggested to Hemingway that they go together on an extended fishing trip. They would film the trip and distribute it commercially. Hemingway declined, saying he thought ZG was trying to capitalize on Hemingway's fame—a reaction that Hemingway's biographer, Carlos Baker, dismissed as the 'silliest of surmises.' But it was probably the right decision, although for the wrong reason. The two authors, both so intensely competitive, might not have been comfortable sharing a fishing boat or a trout stream. Possibly, Hemingway sensed that.

ZG liked to take pictures of his exploits. Both he and R.C. were always "diving" for their cameras when the other was hooked to a fish. And quite often among his entourage there was a professional photographer or cinematographer. ZG was active in the early movie business. In fact, over one hundred films have been made from his books. *Riders* has been made four different times. When he moved to California he established his own production company to exploit this new medium.

But there is something more to this interest than just record keeping or movie making. ZG seems to have had an intensely visual imagination. His stories are filled with descriptions of color, of contour, of line and shadow. He seems dazzled by visual stimuli, and he responds to them more like a painter or photographer than a writer of prose. Often he wishes he had the ability to paint what he sees. He tries to do it in words but frequently admits his failure to do justice to the varieties of nature, whether birds, or flowers, or mountains or rivers or fish, great and small. Perhaps that is why he seems fascinated by the camera.

There is also the possibility that photographs and movies allowed ZG to be literally the hero of his own films. It was perhaps a bit of vanity, but he could afford it. He made and spent tremendous amounts of money. He had a house in Lackawaxen and another in Catalina, both favorite places to fish. His excursions to Tahiti, where he had a permanent camp for several years, New Zealand, Australia, Nova Scotia, Mexico as well as his trips to Oregon for steelhead—all were complete with an entourage of friends and assistants. No expense was spared. The *Fisherman* was equipped with a couple of thirty-foot launches that the anglers used to scour the seas for gamefish. At the end of the day they would return either to the comfort of the yacht or to the camp along the beach. These trips lasted months, and there is at least one passage in which ZG laments the fact that this year's fishing in Tahiti is over, because he has to get to New Zealand . . . to fish. For someone who thought he was a chronically unlucky angler, this seems a fortunate sort of life. And he generally had a cameraman along to record it.

Yet always he worked. He wrote prolifically, and there were times when the writing was not only a passion but a necessity, because ZG suffered from the occasional vicissitudes of the market and, particularly, the Depression. Some years he earned $400,000, but others a tenth of that. But, despite these market gyrations, there was always another book to write, one that Dolly would edit and sell while he went in search of more adventures, more fish. He died in 1939, but his inventory of manuscripts was so extensive that his publishers could release one new title a year until 1963. All told, he wrote 89 books.

In compiling this volume I tried to pick stories that illustrated Zane Grey's travels and the variety of fishing he enjoyed. Some of the pieces are excerpts from longer narratives; others are standalone stories. I also tried to choose stories that illustrated his way of thinking and the quality of his writing. As with any author, his work is not uniformly excellent. But he had many more good days than bad, and the difficulty was deciding what to leave out. The occasional purple passages and old-fashioned figures of speech are nothing in the larger context of his writing. For what it's worth, the more I read him—and the more carefully I read him—the better I liked him, as a writer and as a man. He had his warts, personally and professionally, but he was not unique in that.

Once taking a break from steelhead fishing on the Rogue River he was asked about his opinions on writing:

We arrived at length at the subject of angling books. Marvelous to realize, I actually have more fishing books than fishing rods. I was asked why I so obviously thought the English fishing books superior to the American.

"I suppose because the English anglers write better," was my reply.

Was he including his own books in the comparison? Maybe. Maybe the old doubts or the old criticisms were bothering him just then. Or maybe he was just being modest, as befitted a man who achieved such enormous success. It's hard to know. But if ZG sincerely thought his work did not belong with the classics of angling literature, these stories prove him wrong.

—Terry Mort
Dec. 3, 2002

I

Lackawaxen

Surely the best virtue of fishermen is their hopefulness.

I have caught a good many Delaware bass running over six pounds, and I want to say that these long, black and bronze fellows, peculiar to the swift water of this river, are the most beautiful and gamy fish that swim.

Old familiar places haunt me more than the new ones. Camps and streams and lakes and shores, with long acquaintance, become dear. The thought of saying farewell to them hurts, even though another visit some day is sure. And to say good-bye forever—that is losing something beloved. I am always divided between the thrilling call of new places and the haunting memory of the old.

The Lord of Lackawaxen Creek

Winding among the Blue Hills of Pennsylvania there is a swift amber stream that the Indians named Lack-a-wax-en. The literal translation no one seems to know, but it must mean, in mystical and imaginative Delaware, "the brown water that turns and whispers and tumbles." It is a little river hidden away under gray cliffs and hills black with ragged pines. It is full of mossy stones and rapid riffles.

All its tributaries, dashing white-sheeted over ferny cliffs, wine-brown where the whirling pools suck the stain from the hemlock roots, harbor the speckled trout. Wise in the generation, the red-spotted little beauties keep to their brooks; for, farther down, below the rush and fall, a newcomer is lord of the stream. He is an archenemy, a scorner of beauty and blood, the wolf-jawed, red-eyed, bronze-backed black bass.

A mile or more from its mouth the Lackawaxen leaves the shelter of the hills and seeks the open sunlight and slows down to widen into long lanes that glide reluctantly over the few last restraining barriers to the Delaware. In a curve between two of these level lanes there is a place where barefoot boys wade and fish for chubs and bask on the big boulders like turtles. It is a famous hole for chubs and bright-sided shiners and sunfish. And, perhaps because it is so known, and so shallow, and so open to the sky, few fishermen ever learned that in its secret stony caverns hid a great golden-bronze treasure of a bass.

In vain had many a flimsy feathered hook been flung over his lair by fly-casters and whisked gracefully across the gliding surface of his pool. In vain had many a shiny spoon and pearly minnow reflected sun glints through the watery windows of his home. In vain had many a hellgrammite and frog and grasshopper been dropped in front of his broad nose.

Chance plays the star part in a fisherman's luck. One still, cloudy day, when the pool glanced dark under a leaden sky, I saw a wave that reminded me of the wake of a rolling tarpon; then followed an angry swirl, the skitter of a frantically leaping chub, and a splash that ended with a sound like the deep chung of water sharply turned by an oar.

Big bass choose strange hiding places. They should be looked for in just such holes and rifts and shallows as will cover their backs. But to corral a six-pounder in the boys' swimming-hole was a circumstance to temper a fisherman's vanity with experience.

Thrillingly conscious of the possibilities of this pool, I studied it thoughtfully. It was a wide, shallow bend in the stream, with dark channels between submerged rocks, suggestive of underlying shelves. It had a current, too, not noticeable at first glance. And this pool looked at long and carefully, colored by the certainty of its guardian, took on an aspect most alluring to an angler's spirit. It had changed from a pond girt by stony banks to a foam-flecked running stream, clear, yet hiding its secrets, shallow, yet full of labyrinthine watercourses. It presented problems which, difficult as they were, faded in a breath before a fisherman's optimism.

I tested my leader, changed the small hook for a large one, and selecting a white shiner fully six inches long, I lightly hooked it through the side of the upper lip. A sensation never outgrown since boyhood, a familiar mingling of strange fear and joyous anticipation, made me stoop low and tread the slippery stones as if I were a stalking Indian. I knew that a glimpse of me, or a faint jar vibrating under the water, or an unnatural ripple on its surface, would be fatal to my enterprise.

I swung the lively minnow and instinctively dropped it with a splash over a dark space between two yellow sunken stones. Out of the amber depths started a broad bar of bronze, rose and flashed into gold. A little dimpling eddying circle, most fascinating of all watery forms, appeared round where the minnow had sunk. The golden moving flash went down and vanished in the greenish gloom like a tiger stealing into the jungle. The line trembled, slowly swept out and straightened. How fraught that instant with a wild yet waiting suspense, with a thrill potent and blissful!

Did the fisherman ever live who could wait in such a moment? My arms twitched involuntarily. Then I struck hard, but not half hard enough. The bass leaped out of a flying splash, shook himself in a tussle plainly audible, and slung the hook back at me like a bullet.

In such moments one never sees the fish distinctly; excitement deranges the vision, and the picture, though impressive, is dim and dreamlike. But a blind man would have known this bass to be enormous, for when he fell he cut the water as a heavy stone.

The best of fishing is that a mild philosophy attends even the greatest misfortunes. To be sure this philosophy is a delusion peculiar to fishermen. It is something that goes with the game and makes a fellow fancy that he is a stoic, invulnerable to the slings and arrows of outrageous fortune.

So I went on my way upstream, cheerfully, as one who minded not at all an incident of angling practice; spiritedly as one who had seen many a big bass go by the board. The wind blew softly on my face; the purple clouds, marshaled aloft in fleets, sailed away into the gray distance; the stream murmured musically; a kingfisher poised marvelously over a pool, shot downward like a streak, to rise with his quivering prey; birds sang in the willows and daisies nodded in the field; misty veils hung low in the hollows; all those attributes of nature, poetically ascribed by anglers to be the objects of their full content, were about me.

I found myself thinking about my two brothers, Cedar and Reddy [R.C.] for short, both anglers of long standing and some reputation. It was a sore point with me and a stock subject for endless disputes that they just never could appreciate my superiority as a fisherman. Brothers are singularly prone to such points of view. So when I thought of them I felt the incipient stirring of a mighty plot. It occurred to me that the iron-mouthed old bass, impregnable of jaw as well as of stronghold, might be made to serve a turn. And all the afternoon the thing grew and grew in my mind.

Luck favoring me, I took home a fair string of fish, and remarked to my brothers that the conditions for fishing the stream were favorable. Thereafter, morning on morning my eyes sought the heavens, appealing for a cloudy day. At last one came, and I invited Reddy to with me. With childish pleasure, that would have caused weakness in any but an unscrupulous villain, he eagerly accepted. He looked over a great assortment of tackle and finally selected a five-ounce Leonard bait rod carrying a light reel and fine line. When I

thought of what would happen if Reddy hooked that powerful bass, an unholy glee fastened upon my soul.

We never started out that way together, swinging rods and
pails, but old associations were awakened. We called up the
time when we had left the imprint of bare feet on the country
roads; we lived over many a boyhood adventure by a running
stream. And at last we wound up on the never threadbare
question as to the merit and use of tackle.

"I always claimed," said Reddy, "that a fisherman should
choose his tackle for a day's work after the fashion of a hunter
in choosing his gun. A hunter knows what kind of game he's
after and takes a small or large caliber accordingly. Of course a
fisherman has more rods than there are calibers of guns, but
the rule holds. Now today I have brought this light rod and
thin line because I don't need weight. I don't see why you've
brought that heavy rod. Even a two-pound bass would be a
great surprise up this stream."

"You're right," I replied, "but I sort of lean to possibilities.
Besides, I'm fond of this rod. You know I've caught a half a
dozen bass from five to six pounds with it. I wonder what
you'd do if you hooked a big one on that delicate thing."

"Do?" ejaculated my brother. "I'd have a fit! I might handle a big bass in deep water with this outfit, but here in this
shallow stream with its rocks and holes I couldn't. And that is
the reason so few big bass are taken from the Delaware. We
know they are there, great lusty fellows! Every day in season
we hear some tale of woe from some fisherman. 'Hooked a
big one—broke this—broke that—got under a stone.' That's
why no five- or six-pound bass are taken from shallow, swift,
rock-bedded streams on light tackle."

When we reached the pool I sat down and began to fumble with my leader. How generously I let Reddy have the first cast! My iniquity carried me to the extreme of bidding him steal softly and stoop low. I saw a fat chub swinging in the air; I saw it alight to disappear in a churning commotion of the water, and I heard Reddy's startled, "Gee!"

Hard upon his exclamation followed action of striking swiftness. A shrieking reel, willow wand of a rod wavering like a buggy whip in the wind, a sound as of a banjo string snapping, a sharp splash, then a heavy sullen souse; these, with Reddy standing voiceless, eyes glaring on a broken rod and limp trailing line, were the essentials of the tragedy.

Somehow the joke did not ring true when Reddy waded ashore calm and self-contained, with only his burning eyes to show how deeply he felt. What he said to me in a quiet voice must not, owing to family pride, go on record. It most assuredly would not be an addition to the fish literature of the day.

But he never mentioned the incident to Cedar, which omission laid the way open for my further machinations. I realized that I should have tried Cedar first. He was one of those white-duck-pants-on-a-dry-rock sort of fishermen, anyway. And in due time I had him wading out toward the center of that pool.

I always experienced a painful sensation while watching Cedar cast. He must have gotten his style from a Delsartian school. One moment he resembled Ajax defying the lightning, and the next he looked like the fellow who stood on a monument, smiling at grief. And not to mention pose, Cedar's execution was wonderful. I have seen him cast a frog a mile—but the frog had left the hook. It was remarkable to see him catch his hat and terrifying to hear the language he used at such an ordinary angling event. It was not safe to be in his vicinity, but if this was unavoidable, the better course was to face him, because if you turned your back an instant, his flying hook would have a fiendish affinity for your trousers, and it was not beyond his powers to swing you kicking out over the stream. All of which, considering the frailties of human nature and fishermen, could be forgiven; he had, however, one great fault impossible to overlook, and it was that he made more noise than a playful hippopotamus.

I hoped, despite all these things, that the big bass would rise to the occasion. He did rise. He must have recognized the situation of his life. He spread the waters of his shallow pool and accommodatingly hooked himself.

Cedar's next graceful move was to fall off the slippery stone on which he had been standing and to go out of sight. His hat floated downstream; the arched tip of his rod came up, then his arm, and his dripping shoulders and body. He yelled like a savage and pulled on the fish hard enough to turn a tuna in the air. The big bass leaped three times, made a long shoot with his black dorsal fin showing, and then, with a lunge, headed for some place remote from here. Cedar plowed after him, sending the water in sheets, and then he slipped, wildly swung his arms, and fell again.

I was sinking to the ground, owing to unutterable sensations of joy, when a yell and a commotion in the bushes heralded the appearance of Reddy.

"Hang on, Cedar! Hang on!" he cried, and began an Indian war dance.

The few succeeding moments were somewhat blurred because of my excess of emotion. When I returned to consciousness Cedar was wading out with a hookless leader, a bloody shin, and a disposition utterly and irretrievably ruined.

"Put up a job on me!" he roared.

Thereafter during the summer each of us made solitary and sneaking expeditions, bent on the capture of the lord of the Lackawaxen. And somehow each would return to find the other two derisively speculative as to what caused his clouded brow. Leader on leader went to grace the rocks of the old bronze warrior's home. At length Cedar and Reddy gave up, leaving the pool to me. I fed more than one choice shiner to the bass and more than once he sprang into the air to return my hook.

Summer and autumn passed; winter came to lock the Lackawaxen in icy fetters; I fished under Southern skies where lagoons and moss-shaded waters teemed with great and gamy fish, but I never forgot him. I knew that when the season rolled around, when a June sun warmed the cold spring-fed Lackawaxen, he would be waiting for me.

Who was it spoke of the fleeting of time? Obviously he had never waited for the opening of the fishing season. But at last the tedious time was like the water that has passed. And then I found I had another long wait. Brilliant June days without a cloud were a joy to live, but worthless for fishing. Through all that beautiful month I plodded up to the pool, only to be unrewarded. Doubt began to assail me. Might not the ice, during the spring break-up, have scared him from the shallow hole? No. I felt that not even a rolling glacier could have moved him from his subterranean home.

Often as I reached the pool I saw fishermen wading down the stream, and on these occasions I sat on the bank and lazily waited for the intruding disturbers of my peace to pass on. Once, the first time I saw them, I had an agonizing fear that one of the yellow-helmeted, khaki-coated anglers would hook my bass. The fear, of course, was groundless, but I could not help human feelings. The idea of that grand fish rising to a feathery imitation of a bug or a lank dead bait had nothing in my experience to warrant its consideration. Small, lively bass, full of play, fond of chasing their golden shadows, and belligerent and hungry, were ready to fight and eat whatever swam into their ken. But a six-pound bass, slow to reach that weight in swift running water, was old and wise and full of years. He did not feed often, and when he did he wanted a live fish big enough for a good mouthful. So, with these facts to soothe me I rested my fears and got to look humorously at the invasions of the summer-hotel fishers.

They came wading, slipping, splashing downstream, blowing like porpoises, slapping at the water with all kinds of artificial and dead bait. And they called to me in a humor actuated by my fishing garb and the rustic environment.

"Hey, Rube! Ketchin any?"

I said the suckers were bitin' right pert.

"What d'you call this stream?"

I replied, giving the Indian name.

"Lack-a-what? Can't you whistle it? Lack-awhacken? You mean Lack-afishin'"

"Lack-arotten," joined in another.

"Do you live here?" questioned a third.

I modestly said yes.

"Why don't you move?" Whereupon they all laughed and pursued the noisy tenor of their way downstream, pitching their baits around.

"Say, fellows," I shouted after them, "Are you training for the casting tournament at Madison Square Garden or do you think you're playing lacrosse?"

The laugh that came back proved the joke on them, and that it would be remembered as part of the glorious time they were having.

July brought the misty, dark, lowering days. Not only did I find the old king at home on these days, but just as contemptuous of hooks and leaders as he had been the summer before. About the middle of the month he stopped giving me paralysis of the heart; that is to say, he quit rising to my tempting chubs and shiners. So I left him alone to rest, to rust out hooks and grow less suspicious.

By the time August came the desire to call on him again was well-nigh irresistible. But I waited, and fished the Delaware, and still waited. I would get him when the harvest moon was full. Like all the old moss-backed denizens of the shady holes, he would come out then for a last range over the feeding shoals. At length a morning broke humid and warm, almost dark as twilight, with little gusts of fine rain. Of all days this was the day! I chose a stiff rod, a heavy silk line, a stout brown leader, and a large hook. From my bait box I took two five-inch red catfish, the little 'stone-rollers' of the Delaware, and several long shiners. Thus equipped I sallied forth.

The walk up the tow path, along the canal with its rushes and sedges, across the meadows white with late-blooming daisies, lost nothing because of its familiarity. When I reached the pool I saw in the low water near shore several small bass scouting among the schools of minnows. I did not want these pugnacious fellows to kill my bait, so, procuring a hellgrammite from under a stone, I promptly caught two of them and gave the other a scare he would not soon forget.

I decided to try the bass with one of his favorite shiners. With this trailing in the water I silently waded out, making not so much as a ripple. The old familiar oppression weighed on my breast; the old familiar boyish excitement tingled through my blood. I made a long cast and dropped the shiner lightly. He went under and then came up to swim about on the surface. This was a sign that made my heart leap. Then the water bulged, and a black bar shot across the middle of the long shiner. He went down out of sight, the last gleams of his divided brightness fading slowly. I did not need to see the little shower of silver scales floating up to know that the black bar had been the rounded nose of the old bass and that he had taken the shiner across the middle. I struck hard, and my hook came whistling at me. I had scored a clean miss.

I waded ashore very carefully, sat down on a stone by my bait pail, and meditated. Would he rise again? I had never known him to do so twice in one day. But then there had never been the occasion. I bethought me of the 'stone-rollers' and thrilled with certainty. Whatever he might resist, he could not resist one of those little red catfish. Long ago, when he was only a three- or four-pounder, roaming the deep eddies and swift rapids of the Delaware, before he had isolated himself to a peaceful old age in this quiet pool, he must have poked his nose under many a stone, with red eyes keen for one of those dainty morsels.

My excitement thrilled itself out to the calm assurance of the experienced fisherman. I firmly fashioned on one of the catfish and stole out into the pool. I waded farther than ever before; I was careful but confident. Then I saw the two flat rocks dimly shining. The water was dark as it rippled by, gurgling softly; it gleamed with lengthening shadows and glints of amber.

I swung the catfish. A dull flash of sunshine seemed to come up to meet him. The water swirled and broke with a splash. The broad black head of the bass just skimmed the surface; his jaws opened wide to take in the bait; he turned and flapped a huge spread tail on the water.

Then I struck with all the power the tackle would stand. I felt the hook catch solidly as if in a sunken log. Swift as flashing light the bass leaped. The drops of water hissed and the leader whizzed. But the hook held. I let out one exultant yell. He did not leap again. He dashed to the right, then the left, in bursts of surprising speed. I had hardly warmed to the work when he settled down and made for the dark channel between the yellow rocks. My triumph was to be short-lived. Where was the beautiful spectacular surface fight I expected of him? Cunning old monarch! He laid his great weight dead on the line and lunged for his sunken throne. I held him with the grim surety of the impossibility of stopping him. How I longed for deep, open water! The rod bent, the line strained and stretched. I removed my thumb, and the reel sang one short shrill song. Then the bass was as still as the rock under which he had gone.

I had never dislodged a big bass from under a stone, and I saw herein further defeat; but I persevered, wading to different angles and working all the tricks of the trade. I could not drag the fish out, nor pull the hook loose. I sat down on a stone and patiently waited for a long time, hoping he would come out of his own accord.

As a final resort, precedent to utter failure, I waded out. The water rose to my waist, then to my shoulders, my chin and all but covered my raised face. When I reached the stone under which he had planted himself I stood in water about four feet deep. I saw my leader and tugged upon it and kicked under the stone, all to no good.

Then I calculated I had a chance to dislodge him if I could get my arm under the shelf. So down I went, hat, rod and all. The current was just swift enough to lift my feet, making my task most difficult. At the third trial I got my hand on the sharp corner of the stone and held fast. I ran my right hand along the leader, under the projecting slab of rock, till I touched the bass. I tried to get hold of him but had to rise for air.

I dove again. The space was narrow, so narrow that I wondered how so large a fish could have gotten there. He had gone under sidewise, turned, and wedged his dorsal fin, fixing himself as solidly as the rock itself. I pulled frantically till I feared I would break the leader.

When I floundered up to breathe again, the thought occurred to me that I could rip him with my knife and, by taking the life out of him, loosen the powerful fin so he could be dragged out. Still, much as I wanted him, I could not do that. I resolved to make one more fair attempt. In a quick determined plunge I secured a more favorable hold for my left hand and reached under with my right. I felt his whole long length, and I could not force a finger behind him anywhere.

The gill toward me was shut tight like a trap door. But I got a thumb and forefinger fastened to his lip. I tugged till a severe cramp numbed my hand; I saw red and my head whirled; a noise roared in my ears. I stayed until one more second would have made me a drowning man, then rose gasping and choking.

I broke off the leader close to the stone and waded ashore. I looked back at the pool, faintly circled by widening ripples. What a great hole and what a grand fish! I was glad I did not get him and knew I would never again disturb his peace.

So I took my rod and pail and the two little bass, and brushed the meadow daisies, and threaded the familiar green-lined towpath toward home.

II

Southern California

It is a favorite opinion of ours that nothing in the "fish line" ever comes easy and that only by long patience and endless endurance do we ever get results. We have had good luck at times, of course, but we have always been hard luck fishermen. And sometimes it goes against the grain.

Presently I felt a strong electrifying tug. What a shock it gave me! He let go. A deep whirling eddy appeared back of my bait. I waited in stinging hope. He did not come back. Perhaps the hook had stuck him. I bewailed my luck, my miserable fisherman's luck, my four-multiplying, triple-expansion, T.N.T.-voltage, ivory-tipped luck.

Two Fights with Swordfish

My first day at Avalon, 1916, was likely to be memorable among my fishing experiences.

The weather (August 2nd) was delightful—smooth, rippling sea, no wind, clear sky and warm. The Sierra Nevada Mountains shone dark above the horizon.

A little before noon we passed my friend, Lone Angler, who hailed us and said there was a big broadbill swordfish off in the steamer-course. We steered off in that direction.

There were sunfish and sharks showing all around. Once I saw a whale. The sea was glassy, with a long, heaving swell. Birds were plentiful in scattered groups.

We ran across a shark of a small size and tried to get him to take a bait. He refused. A little later Captain Dan espied a fin, and upon running up we discovered the huge, brown, leathery tail and dorsal of a broadbill swordfish.

Captain Dan advised a long line so that we could circle the fish from a distance and not scare him. I do not remember any unusual excitement. I was curious and interested. Remembering all I had heard about these fish, I did not anticipate getting a strike from him.

We circled him and drew the flying fish bait so that he would swim near it. As it was, I had to reel in some. Presently we had the bait some twenty yards ahead of him. Then Captain Dan slowed down. The broadbill wiggled his tail and slid out of sight. Dan said he was going for my bait. But I did not believe so. Several moments passed. I had given up any little hope I might have had when I received a quick, strong, vibrating strike—different from any I had ever experienced. I

19

suppose the strangeness was due to the shock he gave my line when he struck the bait with his sword. The line paid out unsteadily and slowly. I looked at Dan and he looked at me. Neither of us was excited or particularly elated. I guess I did not realize what was actually going on.

I let him have about one hundred and fifty feet of line.

When I sat down to jam the rod-butt in the socket I had awakened to possibilities. Throwing on the drag and winding in until my line was taut, I struck hard—four times. He made impossible any more attempts at this by starting off on a heavy, irresistible rush. But he was not fast, or so it seemed to me. He did not get more than four hundred feet of line before we ran up on him. Presently he came to the surface to thresh around. He did not appear scared or angry. Probably he was annoyed at the pricking of the hook. But he kept moving, sometimes on the surface, sometimes beneath. I did not fight him hard, preferring to let him pull out the line, and then when he rested I worked on him to recover it. My idea was to keep a perpetual strain on him.

I do not think I had even a hope of bringing this fish to the boat.

It was twelve o'clock exactly when I hooked him, and a quarter of an hour sped by. My first big thrill came when he leaped. This was a surprise. He was fooling around, and then, all of a sudden, he broke water clear. It was an awkward, ponderous action and looked as if he had come up backward, like a bucking bronco. His size and his long, sinister sword amazed and frightened me. It gave me a cold sensation to realize I was hooked to a huge, dangerous fish. But that in itself was a new kind of thrill. No boatman fears a marlin as he does the true broadbill swordfish.

My second thrill came when the fish lunged on the surface in a red foam. If I had hooked him so he bled freely, there was a chance to land him! This approach to encouragement, however, was short-lived. He went down, and if I had been hooked to a submarine I could scarcely have felt more helpless. He sounded about five hundred feet and then sulked. I had the pleasant task of pumping him up. This brought sweat upon me and loosened me up. I began to fight him harder. And it seemed that as I increased the strain, he grew stronger and a little more active. Still there was not any difference in his tactics. I began to get a conception of the vitality and endurance of a broadbill in contrast with the speed and savageness of his brother fish, the marlin, or roundbill.

At two o'clock matters were about the same. I was not tired, but certainly the fish was not tired, either. He came to the surface just about as much as he sounded. I had no difficulty at all in getting back the line, at least all save a hundred feet or so. When I tried to lead him or lift him—then I got his point of view. He would not budge an inch. There seemed nothing to do but to let him work on the drag, and when he had pulled out a hundred feet of line we ran up on him and I reeled in the line. Now and then I put all the strain I could on the rod and worked him that way.

At three o'clock I began to get tired. My hands hurt. And I concluded I had been rather unlucky to start on a broadbill at the very beginning.

From that time he showed less frequently, and, if anything, he grew slower and heavier. I felt no more rushed. And along about this time I found I could lead him somewhat. This made me begin to work hard. Yet, notwithstanding, I had no hope of capturing the fish. It was only experience.

Captain Dan kept saying: "Well, you wanted to hook up with a broadbill! Now, how do you like it?" He had no idea I would ever land him. Several times I asked him to give an opinion as to the size of the swordfish, but he would not venture that until he had gotten a good close view of him.

At four o'clock I made the alarming discovery that the great B-Ocean reel was freezing, just as my other one had frozen on my first swordfish the year previous. Captain Dan used language. He threw up his hands. He gave up. But I did not.

"Dan, see here," I said. "We'll run up on him, throw off a lot of slack line, then cut it and tie it to another reel!"

"We might do that. But it'll disqualify the fish," he replied.

Captain Dan, like all the boatmen at Avalon, has fixed ideas about the Tuna Club and its records and requirements. It is all right, I suppose, for a club to have rules, and not count or credit an angler who breaks a rod or is driven to the expedient I had proposed. But I do not fish for clubs or records. I fish for the fun, the excitement, the thrill of the game, and I would rather let my fish go than not. So I said:

"We'll certainly lose the fish if we don't change reels. I am using regulation tackle, and to my mind the more tackle we use, provided we land the fish, the more credit is due us. It is not an easy matter to change reels or lines or rods with a big fish working all the time."

Captain Dan acquiesced, but told me to try fighting him a while with the light drag and the thumb-brake. So far only the heavy drag had frozen. I tried Dan's idea, to my exceeding discomfort; and the result was that the swordfish drew far away from us. Presently the reel froze solid. The handle would not turn. But with the drag off the spool ran free.

Then we ran away from the fish, circling and letting out slack line. When we came to the end of the line we turned back a little, and with a big slack we took the risk of cutting the line and tying it on to another reel. We had just gotten this done when the line straightened out. I wound in about twelve hundred feet of line and was tired and wet when I had gotten in all I could pull. This brought us to within a couple of hundred feet of our quarry. Also it brought us to five o'clock. Five hours! . . . I began to have queer sensations—aches, pains, tremblings, saggings. Likewise misgivings!

About this period I determined to see how close to the boat I could pull him. I worked. The word "worked" is not readily understood until a man has tried to pull a big broadbill close to the boat. I pulled until I saw stars and my bones cracked. Then there was another crack. The rod broke at the reel seat! And the reel seat was bent. Fortunately the line could still pay out. And I held the tip while Dan pried and hammered the reel off the broken butt on to another one. Then he put the tip in that butt, and once more I had to reel in what seemed miles and miles of line.

Five-thirty! It seemed around the end of the world for me. We had drifted into a tide rip about five miles east of Avalon, and in this rough water I had a terrible time trying to hold my fish. When I discovered that I could hold him—and therefore that he was playing out—then there burst upon me the dazzling hope of actually bringing him to gaff. It is something to fight a fish for more than five hours without one single hope of his capture. And now, suddenly, to be fired with hope gave me new strength and spirit to work. The pain in my hands was excruciating. I was burning all over; wet and slippery and aching in every muscle. These next few minutes seemed longer than all the hours. I found that to put the old strain on the rod made me blind with pain. There was no fun, no excitement, no thrill now. As I labored I could not help marveling at the strange, imbecile pursuits of mankind. Here I was in an agony, absolutely useless. Why did I keep it up? I could not give up, and I concluded that I was crazy.

I conceived the most unreasonable hatred for that poor swordfish that had done nothing to me and that certainly would have been justified in ramming the boat.

To my despair the fish sounded deep, going down and down; Captain Dan watched the line. Finally it ceased to pay out.

"Pump him up!" said Dan.

This was funny. It was about as funny as death.

I rested awhile and meditated upon the weakness of flesh. The thing most desirable and beautiful in all the universe was rest. It was so sweet to think of that I was hard put to keep from tossing the rod overboard. There was something so desperately trying and painful in this fight with a broadbill. At last I drew a deep, long breath, and, with a pang in my breast and little stings all over me, I began to lift on him. He was at the bottom of the ocean. But there are the ethics of a sportsman!

Inch by inch and foot by foot I pumped up this live and dragging weight. I sweat[ed], I panted, I whistled, I bled— and my arms were dead, and my hands raw and my heart seemed about to burst.

Suddenly Captain Dan electrified me.

"There's the end of the double line!" he yelled.

Unbelievable as it was, there the knot in the end of the short six feet of double line showed at the surface. I pumped and reeled inch by inch.

A long dark object showed indistinctly, wavered as the swells rose, then showed again. As I strained at the rod so I strained my eyes.

"I see the leader!" yelled Dan, in great excitement.

I saw it, too, and I spent the last ounce of strength left in me. Up and up came the long, dark, vague object.

"You've got him licked!" exclaimed Dan. "Not a wag left in him!"

It did seem so. And that bewildering instant saw the birth of assurance in me. I was going to get him! That was a grand instant for a fisherman. I could have lifted anything then.

The swordfish became clear to my gaze. He was a devil- ish-looking monster, two feet thick across the back, twelve feet long overall, and he would have weighed at the least over four hunderd pounds. And I had beaten him! That was there to be seen. He had none of the beauty and color of the round- bill swordfish. He was dark, almost black, with huge dorsal and tail, and a wicked broad sword fully four feet long. What terrified me was his enormous size and the deadly look of him. I expected to see him rush at the boat.

Watching him thus, I reveled in my wonderful luck. Up to this date there had been only three of these rare fish caught in twenty-five years of Avalon fishing. And this one was far larger than those that had been taken.

"Lift him! Closer!" called Captain Dan. "In two minutes I'll have the gaff in him!"

I made a last effort. Dan reached for the leader.

Then the hook tore out.

My swordfish, without a movement of tail or fin, slowly sank—to vanish in the blue water.

* * *

After resting my blistered hands for three days, which time was scarcely long enough to heal them, I could not resist the call of the sea.

We went off Seal Rocks and trolled about five miles out. We met a sand-dabber who said he had seen a big broadbill back a ways. So we turned around. After a while I saw a big, vicious splash half a mile east, and we made for it. Then I soon espied the fish.

We worked around him awhile, but he would not take a barracuda or a flying fish.

It was hard to keep track of him, on account of rough water. Soon he went down.

Then a little later I saw what Dan called a marlin. He had big flippers, wide apart. I took him for a broadbill.

We circled him, and before he saw a bait he leaped twice, coming about half out, with belly toward us. He looked huge, but just how big it was impossible to say.

After a while he came up, and we circled him. As the bait drifted round before him—twenty yards or more off—he gave that little wiggle of the tail sickle, and went under. I waited. I had given up hope when I felt him hit the bait. Then he ran off, pretty fast. I let him have a long line. Then I sat down and struck him. He surged off, and we all got ready to watch him leap. But he did not show.

He swam off, sounded, came up, rolled around, went down again. But we did not get a look at him. He fought like any other heavy swordfish.

In one and a half hours I pulled him close to the boat, and we all saw him. But I did not get a good look at him as he wove to and fro behind the boat.

Then he sounded.

I began to work on him, and worked harder. He seemed to get stronger all the time.

"He feels like a broadbill, I tell you," I said to Captain Dan.

Dan shook his head, yet all the same he looked dubious.

Then began a slow, persistent, hard battle between me and the fish, the severity of which I did not realize at the time. In hours like those time has wings. My hands grew hot. They itched, and I wanted to remove the wet gloves. But I did not and sought to keep my mind off what had been half-healed blisters. Neither the fish nor I made any new moves, it all being plug on his part and give and take on mine. Slowly and doggedly he worked out toward the sea, and while the hours passed, just as persistently he circled back.

Captain Dan came to stand beside me, earnestly watching the rod bend and the line stretch. He shook his head.

"That's a big marlin, and you've got him foul-hooked," he asserted. This statement was made at the end of three hours and more. I did not agree. Dan and I often had arguments. He always tackled me when I was in some situation as this—for then, of course, he had the best of it. My brother Rome [R.C.] was in the boat that day, an intensely interested observer. He had not as yet hooked a swordfish.

"It's a German submarine!" he declared.

My brother's wife and the other ladies with us on board were inclined to favor my side; at least they were sorry for the fish and said he must be very big.

"Dan, I could tell a foul-hooked fish," I asserted. "This fellow is too alive—too limber. He doesn't sag like a dead weight."

"Well, if he's not foul-hooked, then you're all in," replied the captain.

Cheerful acquiescence is a desirable trait in anyone, especially an angler who aspires to things, but that was left out in the ordering of my complex disposition. However, to get angry makes a man fight harder, and so it was with me.

At the end of five hours Dan suggested putting the harness on me. This contrivance, by the way, is a thing of straps and buckles, and its use is to fit over an angler's shoulders and to snap on the rod. It helps him lift the fish, puts his shoulders more into play, rests his arms. But I had never worn one. I was afraid of it.

"Suppose he pulls me overboard with that on!" I exclaimed. "He'll drown me!"

"We'll hold on to you," replied Dan, cheerily, as he strapped it around me.

Later it turned out that I had exactly the right view concerning this harness, for Dustin Farnum was nearly pulled overboard and—But I have not enough space for that story here. My brother Rome wants to write that story, anyhow, because it is so funny, he says.

On the other hand, the fact soon manifested itself to me that I could lift a great deal more with said harness to help. The big fish began to come nearer and also he began to get mad. Here I forgot the pain in my hands. I grew enthusiastic. And foolishly I bragged. Then I lifted so hard that I cracked the great Conroy rod.

Dan threw up his hands. He quit, same as he quit the first day out, when I hooked the broadbill and the reel froze.

"Disqualified fish, even if you ketch him—which you won't," he said dejectedly.

"Crack goes thirty-five dollars!" exclaimed my brother. "Sure is funny, brother, how you can decimate good money into the general atmosphere!"

If there really is anything fine in the fighting of a big fish, which theory I had begun to doubt, certainly Captain Dan and Brother R.C. did not know it.

Remarks were forthcoming from me, I am ashamed to state, that should not have been. Then I got Dan to tie splints on the rod, after which I fought my quarry some more. The splints broke. Dan had to bind the cracked rod with heavy pieces of wood and they added considerable weight to what had before felt like a ton.

The fish had been hooked at eleven o'clock and now it was five. We had drifted or been pulled into the main channel, where strong currents and a choppy sea made the matter a pretty serious and uncomfortable one. Here I expended all I had left in a short and furious struggle to bring the fish up, if not to gaff, at least so we could see what he looked like. How strange and unfathomable a feeling this mystery of him gave rise to! If I could only see him once, then he could get away and welcome. Captain Dan, in anticipation of a need of much elbow room in that cockpit, ordered my brother and the ladies to go into the cabin or up on top. And they all scrambled up and lay flat on the deck-roof, with their heads over, watching me. They had to hold on some, too. In fact, they were having the time of their lives.

My supreme effort brought the fish within the hundredth foot length of line—then my hands and back refused any more.

"Dan, here's the great chance you've always hankered for!" I said. "Now let's see you pull him right in!"

And I passed him the rod and got up. Dan took it with the pleased expression of a child suddenly and wonderfully come into possession of a long-unattainable toy. Captain Dan was going to pull that fish right up to the boat. He was! Now Dan is big—he weighs two hundred; he has arms and hands like the limbs of a Vulcan. Perhaps Dan had every reason to believe he would pull the fish right up to the boat. But somehow I knew that he would not.

My fish, perhaps feeling a new and different and mightier hand at the rod, showed how he liked it by a magnificent rush—the greatest of the whole fight—and he took about five hundred feet of line.

Dan's expression changed as if by magic.

"Steer the boat! Port! Port!" he yelled.

Probably I could not run a boat right with perfectly fresh and well hands, and with my lacerated and stinging ones I surely made a mess of it. This brought language from my boatman—well, to say the least, quite disrespectable. Fortunately, however, I got the boat around and we ran down on the fish. Dan, working with long, powerful sweeps of the rod, got the line back and the fish close. The game began to look great to me. All along I had guessed this fish to be a wonder; and now I knew it.

Hauling him close that way angered him. He made another rush, long and savage. The line smoked off that reel. Dan's expression was one of utmost gratification to me. A boatman at last cornered—tied up to a whale of a fish!

Somewhere out there a couple of hundred yards the big fish came up and roared on the surface. I saw only circling wake and waves like those behind a speedy motorboat. But Dan let out a strange shout, and up above the girls screamed, and brother Rome yelled murder or something. I gathered that he had a camera.

"Steady up there!" I called out. "If you fall overboard, it's good night! . . . For we want this fish!"

I had all I could do. Dan would order me to steer this way and that—to throw out the clutch—to throw it in. Still I was able to keep track of events. This fish made nineteen rushes in the succeeding half-hour. Never for an instant did Captain Dan let up. Assuredly during that time he spent more force on the fish than I had in six hours.

The sea was bad, the boat was rolling, the cockpit was inches deep under water many a time. I was hard put to stay at my post; and what saved the watchers above could not be explained by me.

"Mebbe I can hold him now—a little," called Dan once, as he got the hundred foot mark over the reel. "Strap the harness on me!"

I fastened the straps around Dan's broad shoulders. His shirt was as wet as if he had fallen overboard. Maybe some of that wet was spray. His face was purple, his big arms bulging, and he whistled as he breathed.

"Good-bye, Dan. This will be a fitting end for a boatman," I said, cheerfully, as I dove back to the wheel.

At six o'clock our fish was going strong and Dan was tiring fast. He had, of course, worked too desperately hard.

Meanwhile the sun sank and the sea went down. All the west was gold and red, with the towers of Church Rock spiring the horizon. A flock of gulls was circling low, perhaps over a school of tuna. The white cottages of Avalon looked mere specks on the dark island.

Captain Dan had the swordfish within a hundred feet of the boat and was able to hold him. This seemed hopeful. It looked now just a matter of a little more time. But Dan needed a rest.

I suggested that my brother come down and take a hand in the final round, which I frankly confessed was liable to be hell.

"Not on your life!" was the prompt reply. "I want to begin on a little swordfish! . . . Why that—that fish hasn't waked up yet!"

And I was bound to confess there seemed to be a good deal of sense in what he said.

"Dan, I'll take the rod—rest you a bit—so you can finish him," I offered.

The half-hour Dan recorded as my further work on this fish will always be a dark and poignant blank in my fishing experience. When it was over twilight had come and the fish was rolling and circling perhaps fifty yards from the boat.

Here Dan took the rod again, and with the harness on and fresh gloves, went at the fish in grim determination.

Suddenly the moon sailed out from behind a fog bank and the sea was transformed. It was as beautiful as it was lucky for us.

By Herculean effort Dan brought the swordfish close. If any angler doubts the strength of a twenty-four-thread line, his experience is still young. That line was a rope, yet it sang like a banjo string.

Leaning over the side, with two pairs of gloves on, I caught the double line, and as I pulled and Dan reeled, the fish came up nearer. But I could not see him. Then I reached the leader and held on as for dear life.

"I've got the leader!" I yelled. "Hurry, Dan!"

Dan dropped the rod and reached for his gaff. But he had neglected to unhook the rod from the harness, and as the fish lunged and tore the leader away from me there came near to being disaster. However, Dan got straightened out and anchored in the chair and began to haul away again. It appeared we had the fish almost done, but he was so big that a mere movement of his tail irresistibly drew out the line.

Then the tip of the rod broke off short just even with the splints, and it slid down the line out of sight. Dan lowered the rod so most of the strain would come on the reel, and now he held on like grim death.

"Dan, if we don't make any mistakes, we'll get that fish!" I declared.

The sea was almost calm now, and moon-blanched so that we could plainly see the line. Despite Dan's efforts, the swordfish slowly ran off a hundred feet more of line. Dan groaned. But I yelled with sheer exultation. For, standing up on the gunwale, I saw the swordfish. He had come up. He was phosphorescent—a long gleam of silver—and he rolled in the unmistakable manner of a fish nearly beaten.

Suddenly he headed for the boat. It was a strange motion. I was surprised—then frightened. Dan reeled in rapidly. The streak of white gleamed closer and closer. It was like white fire—a long, savage, pointed shape.

"Look! Look!" I yelled to those above. "Don't miss it! . . . Oh, great!"

"He's charging the boat!" hoarsely shouted Dan.

"He's all in!" yelled my brother.

I jumped into the cockpit and leaned over the gunwale beside the rod. Then I grasped the line, letting it slip through my hands. Dan wound in with fierce energy. I felt the double end of the line go by me, and at this I let out another shout to warn Dan. Then I had the end of the leader—a good strong grip—and, looking down, I saw the clear silver outline of the hugest fish I had ever seen short of shark or whale. He made a beautiful, wild, frightful sight. He rolled on his back. Roundbill or broadbill, he had an enormous length of sword.

"Come, Dan—we've got him!" I panted.

Dan could not, dare not get up then.

The situation was perilous. I saw how Dan clutched the reel, with his big thumbs biting into the line. I did my best. My sight failed me for an instant. But the fish pulled the leader through my hands. My brother leaped down to help us—alas, too late!

"Let go, Dan! Give him line!"

But Dan was past that. Afterward he said his grip was locked. He held, and not another foot did the swordfish get. Again I leaned over the gunwale. I saw him—a monster—pale, wavering. His tail had an enormous spread. I could no longer see his sword. Almost he was ready to give up.

Then the double line snapped. I fell back in the boat and Dan fell back in the chair.

Nine hours!

Tuna at Avalon, 1919

The 1919 season for tuna at Avalon was the best for many years. What it might have been if the round-haul net-boats had not haunted the channel, taking thousands of tons of tuna, no one could conjecture. Tuna were never before seen there in such numbers, both large and small.

But no matter how wonderful the fishing, it was spoiled by the [commercial] net-boats. These round-haul boats have nets half a mile long and several hundred feet deep. When they surround a school of tuna it is seldom that any escape. If the tuna are very large, over one hundred pounds, then a great many of them are destroyed. Sometimes the weight of a large school is so great that the netters cannot handle it. In which case they take on board all that they can dispose of and let the rest sink. Some of the tons of tuna go to the canneries at San Pedro, and a good many go to the fertilizer plants. . . . One day this year I counted sixteen round-haul net-boats within a half a mile of Avalon Bay, and some of them were loaded so heavily that they sank in the water nearly to their gunwales, and the others were hauling their nets as fast as power and muscle could do it. . . .

No wonder I was sick with anger and disgust and bade the tuna good-bye.

During the season I caught a good many tuna, more, in fact, than ever before. Captain Danielson averred that it was the best season I ever had at Catalina. This was owing to my catches of blue-button tuna. The Tuna Club of Avalon recognizes only fish that weigh over one hundred pounds [hence, the blue-button award given by the club]. I may say that it took me five years to catch my first blue-button fish. In 1919 my big tuna weighed 117 pounds, 114, 111, 109, and 109. My brother R.C. caught one of 117 pounds. Apparently this looks like remarkably good luck. But when I think of all the bad luck I had, the good seems small in proportion.

I have no idea how many very large tuna I hooked and lost on twenty-four-thread line [roughly 72-pound test] during July and August. But there must have been at least twenty-five. I had exceptionally good luck in locating schools of large tuna. Captain Dan and I were always roaming the sea, peering for the white spouts of water on the horizon.

One day when we had guests aboard and they were fishing, I put out a bait on my light tackle and trolled it close behind the boat. Immediately there came a splash and a heavy pull. I had hooked a big tuna on my light outfit. The others, of course, had to reel in. My fish made the long fast diving run that is usually so destructive to tackle. But he stopped short of two hundred yards, and so for the moment I saved him. Captain Dan buckled a belt on me, and I stood up, with the rod in the belt socket, and began to work on that fish. Work meant to pull and lift all the rod would stand, then lower it quickly and wind the reel. It is fun for only a little while! My ambition, of course, was to land a hundred-pound tuna on light tackle—something which had not yet been done. So I was in deadly earnest. So was Captain Dan. This fish was so loggy and rolly that we decided he was a yellow-fin tuna of very large size. There are two kinds of tuna, yellow-fin and blue-fin.

My brother and our guests made considerable fun of me as I heroically struggled with that tuna. I would lift him and wind him up a hundred feet or so, and then he would take that line away from me. It happened so often that it must have looked funny. All of a sudden my tuna started to sound. He did not run. He just plugged down and down and down. The reel screamed—zee—zee—zee! This procedure grew alarming. Two hundred yards—three hundred yards—-three fifty, and finally four hundred yards of line he took straight down. This was the deepest I ever had any fish sound up to that date. Captain Dan stood beside me, watching the reel. He shook his head at every zee. My rod lay in the hollow of my left elbow and the tip was double straight down. The zee-zee-zee grew markedly shorter in time and farther apart. Tremendous pressure of water on that tuna had begun to tell. Most remarkable about this incident was the fact that the nine-thread line [roughly 27-pound test] had not broken. It resembled a very tight, wet banjo string. Finally the tuna stopped. I had half an inch of thickness of line left on the reel spool. Then I began to work, carefully lifting and winding. Inch by inch! And after a while, foot by foot. This was harder work than heavy tackle. It took an hour to pump that tuna back up to his original position. I was as wet as if I had fallen overboard.

For two more hours I heaved and wound, gaining and losing in about the same proportion. What spurred me on was a certainty that little by little the tuna was weakening. But it was so little! The others on board stopped making a game of me. They began to realize that this was a fight seldom recorded in the annals of angling. Besides, I must have been an object to excite wonder and pity, perhaps awe. My tuna hung around near the boat, sometimes rising toward the surface, to one side or the other, but mostly straight down. That is what makes a tuna fight so laborsome.

The very thing I feared he began again. He started down. Zee-zee-zee! Slower this time. Captain Dan left the wheel and stood beside me, watching the reel. I laid the rod over my left arm and watched, too. Zee-zee-zee! It was terrible to see all that hard-earned line slip off and off and off. I would lose him this time. That was inevitable. Zee-zee-zee! He plugged down. I could feel him banging the leader with his tail. Slower and slower the line paid off. It seemed ages in going. I began to see red. I wanted him to hurry and break off. But more than that I hoped desperately that he would stop. How short and slow and squeaky the zees! At last he got out as much line as he had taken on the first occasion. There were four hundred and fifty yards on the reel. Captain Dan threw up his hands and groaned: "Good night! It's all off!"

I suppose he meant the fight was all off. Assuredly the tuna was still on. Zee-zee-zee!

I bade him a mute and despondent farewell. But the line still held. It seemed to me that the thing which had to snap was in my head. I was nearly crazy. The making of angling history is sometimes so painful. Zee-zee-zee! Slower and slower. Then, incredibly, when a couple of more zees would have pulled all the line out and broken it, the tuna stopped. The strain eased. He could not stand the pressure of the water. He had started back. I wound and wound and wound that reel until I thought my arm would fall dead at my side. With a small reel it takes a great deal of winding to get in even a little line. This time it took perhaps a half an hour to get all the line back. My tuna did not come readily all the time. He rested occasionally.

But I got him up, closer than ever before. He lazily rose to the surface about sixty feet or so from the boat. I heard him break water, but as the light was bad I could not see him. R.C. was on top of the deck. Captain Dan leaped up on the stern. They both saw the tuna. How strangely silent and tense they were! But I was too much exhausted and riveted to my post to have any thrills left. The tuna rolled around out there. He was a beaten fish. I realized it.

"Easy now," warned Captain Dan. "He's licked. Pull him along easy."

Then all of a sudden the reel stuck tight. The handle would not turn. The line would not run out. I could not tell Captain Dan. I was speechless. But he saw it. Quick as a flash he grasped a screwdriver and began to loosen the screws in the reel plate. How swiftly he worked! I heard him pant. My tuna was lolling around out there. Once I saw his saberlike tail, and the sight of it would have paralyzed me if I had not already been paralyzed.

Captain Dan got some of the screws loose. The spool grew less tight. One moment more and he would have the friction eased! But in that moment my tuna decided to loll and roll a little farther off, and he snapped the line. Five hours!

Some time afterward, when I was in condition to stand shocks, Captain Dan and R.C. both told me that they had seen the tuna, that he had been a beaten fish and would have weighed at least a hundred and fifty pounds.

Tuna fishing has many poignant moments. . . .

III

Florida

In my experience as a fisherman the greatest pleasure has been the certainty of something new to learn, to feel, to anticipate, to thrill over. An old proverb tells us that if you wish to bring back the wealth of the Indias you must go out with its equivalent. Surely the longer a man fishes the wealthier he becomes in experience, in reminiscence, in love of nature, if he goes out with the harvest of a quiet eye, free from the plague of himself.

Then I saw a couple of bonefish. They shone like silver, were singularly graceful in build, felt heavy as lead and looked game all over. I made the mental observation that the man who had named them bonefish should have had half that name applied to his head.

The morning was hot and still—a very delightful opportunity for sand flies and mosquitoes, which they made the most of. I fought them with one hand while I held my rod with the other. Under the circumstances it would have been difficult then to substantiate arguments as to the good time I was having. Some things are hard to explain. Fishing is a condition of mind wherein you cannot possibly have a bad time.

Bonefish

Five years ago I had never heard of a bonefish. The first man who had ever spoken to me about this species said to me, very quietly with serious intentness: "Have you had any experience with bonefish?" I said no and asked him what kind that was. His reply was enigmatical. "Well, don't go after bonefish unless you can give up all other fishing." I remember I laughed. But I never forgot that remark, and now it comes back to me clear in its significance. That fisherman read me as well as I misunderstood him.

Later that season I listened to talk of inexperienced bonefishermen telling me what they had done and heard. To me it was absurd. So much fishing talk seems ridiculous, anyway. And the expert fishermen, wherever they were, received the expressive titles: "Bonefish Bugs and Bonefish Nuts!" Again I heard arguments about tackle rigged for these mysterious fish and these arguments fixed my vague impression. By and by some bonefishermen came to Long Key, and the first sight of a bonefish made me curious. I think it weighed five pounds— a fair sized specimen. Even to my prejudiced eye that fish showed class. So I began to question the bonefishermen.

At once I found this type of angler to be remarkably reticent as to experience and method. Moreover, the tackle used was amazing to me. Stiff rods and heavy lines for little fish! I gathered another impression, and it was that bonefish were related to dynamite and chain lightning. Everybody who would listen to my questions had different things to say. No two men agreed on tackle or bait or ground or anything. I enlisted the interest of my brother R.C., and we decided, just to satisfy curiosity, to go out and catch some bonefish. The complacent, smug conceit of fishermen! Fortunately it is now past tense. If I am ever conceited again, I hope no one will read my stories.

My brother and I could not bring ourselves to try for bonefish with heavy tackle. It was preposterous. Three-four-five-pound fish! We had seen no larger. Bass tackle was certainly heavy enough for us. So in the innocence of our hearts and the assurance of our vanity we sallied forth to catch bonefish.

That was four years ago. Did we have good luck? No! Luck has nothing to do with bonefishing. What happened? For one solid month each winter we had devoted ourselves to bonefishing with light tackle. We stuck to our colors. The space of this whole volume would not be enough to tell our experience—the amaze[ment], the difficulty, the perseverance, the defeat, the wonder, and at last the achievement. The season of 1918 we hooked about fifty bonefish [on light tackle] and we landed fourteen of them. I caught nine and R.C. caught five. R.C.'s eight-pound fish justified our contention and crowned our efforts.

To date, in all my experience, I consider this bonefish achievement the most thrilling, fascinating, difficult and instructive. This is a broad statement, and I hope I can prove it.

I am prepared to state that I feel almost certain, if I spent another month bonefishing, I would become obsessed and perhaps lose my enthusiasm for other kinds of fish.

Why?

There is a multiplicity of reasons. My reasons range from the exceedingly graceful beauty of a bonefish to the fact that he is the best food fish I ever ate. That is a wide range. He is the wisest, shyest, wariest, strangest fish I ever studied; and I am not excepting the great *Xiphias gladius*—the broadbill swordfish. As for the speed of the bonefish, I claim no salmon, no barracuda, no other fish celebrated for swiftness of motion, is in his class. A bonefish is so incredibly fast that it was a long time before I could believe the evidence of my own eyes. You see him; he is there perfectly still in the clear, shallow water, a creature of fish shape, pale green and silver, but crystal-like, a phantom shape, staring at you with strange black eyes; then he is gone. Vanished! Absolutely without your seeing a movement, even a faint streak! By peering keenly you may discern a little swirl in the water. As for the strength of a bonefish, I actually hesitate to give my impressions. No one will ever believe how powerful a bonefish is until he has tried to stop the rush and heard the line snap. As for his cunning, it is utterly baffling. As for his biting, it is almost imperceptible. As for his tactics, they are beyond conjecture.

I want to append here a few passages from my notebooks, in the hope that a bare, bald statement of fact will help my argument. . . .

Day before yesterday R.C. and I went up to the Long Key point and rowed in on the mangrove shoal where once before I saw so many bonefish. The tide was about one quarter in, and there was a foot of water all over the flats. We anchored at the outer edge and began to fish. We had made elaborate preparations in the way of tackle, bait, canoe, etc., and it really would have been remarkable if we had any luck. After a little while I distinctly felt something at my hook, and upon jerking I had one splendid surge out of a good, heavy bonefish. That was all that happened in that place.

It was near flood tide when we went back. I stood up and kept a keen watch for little muddy places in the water, also bonefish. At last I saw several fish, and there we anchored. I fished on one side of the boat, and R.C. on the other. On two occasions, feeling a nibble on his line, he jerked, all to no avail. The third time he yelled as he struck, and I turned in time to see the white thresh of a bonefish. He made a quick dash off to the side and then came in close to the boat, swimming around with short runs two or three times, and then, apparently tired, he came close. I made ready to lift him into the boat, when, lo and behold, he made a wonderful run of fully three hundred feet before R.C. could stop him. Finally he was led to the boat and turned out to be a fish of three and a half pounds. It simply made R.C. and me gasp to speak of what a really large bonefish might be able to do. There is something irresistible about the pursuit of these fish, and perhaps this is it. We changed places, and as a last try anchored in deeper water, fishing as before. This time I had a distinct tug at my line, and I hooked a fish. He wiggled and jerked and threshed around so that I told R.C. that it was not a bonefish, but R.C. contended it was. Anyway, he came to the boat rather easily until we saw him and he saw us, and then he made a dash similar to R.C.'s fish and he tore out the hook. This was the extent of our adventure that day, and we were very much pleased.

Next morning we started out with a high northeast trade wind blowing. Nothing could dampen our ardor.

It was blowing so hard up at No. 2 viaduct that we decided to stay inside. There is a big flat there cut up by channels, and it is said to be a fine ground for bonefish. The tide was right and the water was clear, but even in the lee of the bank the wind blew pretty hard. We anchored in about three feet of water and began to fish.

After a while we moved. The water was about a foot deep, and the bottom clean white marl, with little patches of vegetation. Crabs and crab holes were numerous. I saw a small shark and a couple of rays. When we got to the middle of a big flat, I saw the big, white, glistening tails of bonefish sticking out of the water. We dropped anchor and, much excited, were about to make casts when R.C. lost his hat. He swore. We had to pull up anchor and go get that hat. Unfortunately this scared the fish. Also, it presaged a rather hard luck afternoon. In fishing, as in many other things, if the beginning is tragedy all will be tragedy, growing worse all the time. We moved around up above where I had seen these bonefish, and there we dropped anchor. No sooner had we got our baits overboard than we began to see bonefish tails at quite some distance. The thing to do, of course, was to sit right there and be patient, but this was almost impossible for us. We moved again and again, but we did not get any nearer the fish. Finally I determined that we would stick in one place. This we did, and the bonefish began to come around. When they would swim close to the boat and see us, they would give a tremendous surge and disappear, as if by magic. But they always left a muddy place in the water. The speed of these fish is beyond belief. I could not cast where I wanted to; I tried again and again. When I did get my bait off at a reasonable distance, I could feel crabs nibbling at it. These pests robbed us of many a good bait. One of them cut my line in two. They seemed to be very plentiful, and that must be why the bonefish were plentiful, too. R.C. kept losing bait after bait, which he claimed was the work of crabs, but I rather believed it to be the work of bonefish. It was too windy for us to be able to tell anything about the pressure of the line. It had to be quite a strong tug to be felt at all. Presently, I felt one, and instead of striking at once I waited to see what would happen. After a while I reeled in to find my bait gone. Then I was consoled by the proof that a bonefish had taken the bait off for me. Another time three bonefish came along for my bait and stuck their tails up out of the water and were evidently nosing around it, but I felt absolutely nothing on the line. When I reeled in the bait was gone.

We kept up this sort of thing for two hours. I knew that we were doing it wrong. R.C. said bad conditions, but I claimed that these were only partly responsible for our failure. I knew that we moved about too much, that we did not cast far enough and wait long enough, and that by all means we should not have cracked bait on the bottom of the boat, and particularly we did not know when we had a bite! But it is one thing to be sure of a fact and another to be able to practice it. At last we gave up in despair, and upon paddling back toward the launch we saw a school of bonefish with their tails in the air. We followed them around for a while, apparently very much to their amusement. At sunset we got back to the launch and started for camp.

This was a long, hard afternoon's work for nothing. However, it is my idea that experience is never too dearly bought. I will never do some things again, and the harder these fish are to catch, the more time and effort it takes—the more intelligence and cunning—all the more will I appreciate success if it ever does come. It is in the attainment of difficult tasks that we earn our reward. There are several old bonefish experts here in camp, and they laughed when I related some of our experiences. Bonefishermen are loath to tell anything about their methods. This must be a growth of the difficult game. I had an expert bonefisherman tell me that when he was surprised while fishing on one of the shoals, he always dropped his rod and pretended to be digging for shells. And it is a fact that the bonefish guides at Metacumbe did not let anyone get a line on their methods. They will avoid a bone-fishing-ground while others are there, and if they are surprised there ahead of others, they will pull up anchor and go away. May I be preserved from any such personal selfishness and reticence as this! One of these bonefish experts in camp told me that in all his years of experience he had never gotten a bonefish bite. If you feel a tug, it is when the bonefish is ejecting the hook. Then it is too late. The bonefish noses around the bait and sucks it in without any apparent movement of the line. And that can be detected first by a little sagging of the line or by a little strain upon it. That is the time to strike. He also said that he always broke his soldier crabs on a piece of lead to prevent the jar from frightening the fish.

Doctor B. tells a couple of interesting experiences with bonefish. On one occasion he was fishing near another boat in which was a friend. The water was very clear and still, and he could see his friend's bait lying upon the sand. An enormous bonefish swam up and took the bait, and Doctor B. was so thrilled and excited that he could not yell. When the man hooked the fish it shot off in a straight-away rush, raising a ridge upon the water. It ran the length of the line and freed itself. Later Doctor B.'s friend showed the hook that had been straightened out. They measured the line and found it to be five hundred and fifty-five feet. The bonefish had gone the length of this in one run, and they estimated that he would have weighed not less than fifteen pounds.

On another occasion Doctor B. saw a heavy bonefish hooked. It ran straight off shore, and turning, ran in with such speed that it came shooting out upon dry land and was easily captured. These two instances are cases in point of the incredible speed and strength of this strange fish.

* * *

It rained torrents all night and stopped at dawn. The wind was northeast and cool. Cloudy overhead with a purple horizon all around—a forbidding day. But we decided to go fishing, anyhow. We had new, delicate three-six tackles to try. About seven the wind died away. There was a dead calm, and the sun tried to show. Then another breeze came out of the east.

We went inside after bait and had the luck to find some. Crossing the island, we came out at the old construction camp where we had left the canoe. By this time a stiff breeze was blowing and the tide was rising fast. We had our troubles paddling and poling up to the grove of coconuts. Opposite this we anchored and began to fish.

Conditions were not favorable. The water was choppy and roily, the canoe bobbed a good deal, the anchors dragged, and we did not see any fish. All the same, we persevered. At length I had a bite but pulled too late. We tried again for a while, only to be disappointed. Then we moved.

We had to put the stern anchor down first and let it drag till it held and the canoe drifted around away from the wind, then we dropped the bow anchor. After a time I had a faint feeling at the end of my line—an indescribable feeling. I jerked and hooked a bonefish. He did not feel heavy. He ran off, and the wind bagged my line and the waves also helped to pull out the hook.

Following that we changed places several times, in one of which R.C. had a strike, but failed to hook the fish. Just opposite the old wreck on the shore I had another fish take hold, and, upon hooking him, had precisely the same thing happen as in the first instance. I think the bag of my line, which I could not avoid, allowed the leader to sag down and drag upon the bottom. Of course, when it caught, the bonefish pulled free.

In some places we found water clearer than in others. Flood tide had long come when we anchored opposite the old camp. R.C. cast out upon a brown patch of weeds where we have caught some fine fish, and I cast below. Perhaps in five minutes or less R.C. swept up his rod. I saw it bend forward, down toward the water. The line hissed away toward the right and almost at once picked up a good-sized piece of seaweed.

"It's a big fish!" I exclaimed excitedly. "Look at him go! That seaweed will make you lose him. Let me wade out and pull it off?"

"No! Let's take a chance. Too late anyhow! Gee! He's going! He's got two hundred yards out!"

Two-thirds of the line was off the reel, and the piece of seaweed seemed to be a drag on the fish. He slowed up. The line was tight, the rod bent. Suddenly the tip sprang back. We had seen that often before.

"Gone!" said R.C. dejectedly.

But I was not so sure of that, although I was hopeless. R.C. wound in, finding the line came slowly, as if weighted. I watched closely. We thought that was on account of the seaweed. But suddenly the reel began to screech.

"I've got him yet!" yelled R.C., with joy.

I was overjoyed, too, but I contained myself, for I expected dire results from that run.

Zee! Zee! Zee! . . . went the reel, and the rod nodded in time.

"We must get rid of that seaweed or lose him. Pull up your anchor with one hand. Careful now."

He did so, and quickly I got mine up. What a ticklish business!

"Keep a tight line!" I cautioned, as I backed the canoe hard with all my power. It was not easy to go backward and keep head on to the wind. The waves broke over the end of the canoe, splashing me in the face so I could taste and smell the salt. I made a half a dozen shoves with the paddle. Then, nearing that piece of seaweed, I dropped my anchor.

In a flash I had that dangerous piece of seaweed off R.C.'s line.

"Good work! Say, but that helps. We'd never have gotten him," said R.C. beaming. I saw him look then as he used to in our sunfish, bent-pin days.

"We've not got him yet," I replied, grimly. "Handle him as easily as you can."

Then began a fight. The bonefish changed his swift, long runs and took to slow sweeps to and fro, and whenever he was drawn a few yards closer, he would give a solid jerk and get that much line back. There was much danger from other pieces of floating weed. R.C. maneuvered his line to miss them. All the time the bonefish was pulling doggedly. I had little hope we might capture him. At the end of fifteen minutes he was still a hundred yards from the canoe and neither of us had seen him. Our excitement grew tenser every moment. The fish sheered to and fro and would not come into shallower water. He would not budge. He took nine long runs straight up the shore, in line with us, and then circled out. This alarmed me, but he did not increase his lead. He came slowly around, yard by yard. R.C. reeled carefully, not hard enough to antagonize him, and after what seemed like a long time got him within a hundred feet, and I had a glimpse of green and silver. Then he ran off again. How unbelievably swift! He had been close—then almost the same instant he was far off.

"I saw him! On a wave!" yelled R.C. "That's no bonefish! What can he be, anyhow? I believe I've got a barracuda!"

I looked and looked, but I could not see him.

"No matter what you think you saw, that fish is a bonefish," I declared positively. "The runs he made! I saw silver and green! Careful now. I *know* he's a bonefish. And he must be big."

"Maybe it's only the wind and waves that make him feel so strong," replied R.C.

"No! You can't fool me! Play him for a big one. He's been on twenty-three minutes now. Stand up—I'll steady the canoe—and watch for that sudden rush when he sees the canoe. The finish is in sight."

It was an indication of a tiring fish that he made his first circle of the boat, but too far out for us to see him. This circling a boat is a remarkable feature, and I think it comes from the habit of a bonefish of pulling broadside. I cautioned R.C. to avoid the seaweed and lead him a little more, but to be infinitely careful not to apply too much strain. He circled us again, a few yards closer. The third circle he did not gain a foot. Then he was on his fourth lap around the canoe, drawing closer. On his fifth lap clear round us he came near as fifty feet. I could not resist standing up to see. I got a glimpse of him and he looked long. But I did not say anything to R.C. We had both hooked too many bonefish that got away immediately. This was another affair.

He circled us the sixth time. Six times! Then he came rather close. On this occasion he saw the canoe. He surged and sped out so swiftly that I was simply paralyzed. R.C. yelled something that had a note of admiration of the sheer glory in the spirit of that fish.

"Here's where he leaves us!" I echoed.

But, as luck would have it, he stopped that run short of two hundred yards and turned broadside to circle slowly back, allowing R.C. to get in line. He swam slower this time and did not make the heavy tugs. He came easily, weaving to and fro. R.C. got him to within twenty-five feet of the boat yet still could not see him. It was my job to think quick and sit still with ready hands on the anchor rope. He began to plunge, taking a little line each time. Then suddenly I saw R.C.'s line coming toward us. I knew that would happen.

"Now! Look out! Reel in fast!" I cried, tensely.

As I leaned over to heave up the anchor, I saw the bonefish flashing nearer. At that moment of thrilling excitement and suspense I could not trust my eyesight. There he was, swimming heavily, and he looked three feet long, thick and dark and heavy. I got the anchor up just as he passed under the canoe. Maybe I did not revel in pride of my quickness of thought and action!

"Oh! He's gone under the rope!" gasped R.C.

"No!" I yelled sharply. "Let your line run out! Put your tip down! We'll drift over your line."

R.C. was dominated to do so, and presently the canoe drifted over where the line was stretched. That second ticklish moment passed. It had scared me. But I could not refrain from one sally.

"I got the anchor up. What did you think I'd do?"

R.C. passed by my remark. This was serious business for him. He looked quite earnest and pale.

"Say! Did you see him?" he ejaculated, looking at me.

"Wish I hadn't," I replied.

We were drifting inshore, which was well, provided we did not drift too hard to suit the bonefish. He swam along in plain sight, and he seemed so big that I would not have gazed any longer if I could have helped it.

I kept the canoe headed in, and we were not long in coming to shallow water. Here the bonefish made a final dash for freedom, but it was short and feeble, compared with his first runs. He got about twenty feet away, then sheered, showing his broad, silver side. R.C. wound him in close, and an instant later the bow of the canoe grated on shore.

"Now what?" asked R.C. as I stepped out into the water. "Won't it be risky to lift him into the canoe?"

"Lift nothing! I have this all figured out. Lead him along."

R.C. stepped out upon the beach while I was in the water. The bonefish lay on his side, a blaze of silver. I took hold of the line very gently and led the fish a little closer in. The water was about six inches deep. There were waves beating it—a miniature surf. And I calculated on the receding of a wave. Then with one quick pull I slid our beautiful quarry up on the coral sand. The instant he was out of the water the leader snapped. I was ready for this, too. But at that, it was an awful instant! As the wave came back, almost deep enough to float the bonefish, I scooped him up.

"He's ours!" I said, consulting my watch. "Thirty-three minutes! I give you my word that fight was comparable to ones I've had with Pacific swordfish."

"Look at him!" R.C. burst out. "Look at him! When the leader broke I thought he was lost. I'm sick yet. Didn't you almost bungle that?"

"Not a chance, R.C.," I replied. "Had that all figured. I never put any strain on your line until the wave went back. Then I slid him out, the leader broke, and I scooped him up."

R.C. stood gazing down at the glistening, opal-spotted fish. What a contrast he presented to any other kind of fish! How many beautiful species have we seen lying on sand or moss or ferns, just come out of the water! But I could remember no other so rare as this bonefish. The exceeding difficulty of the capture of this, our first really large bonefish, had a great deal to do with our admiration and pride. For the hard work of any achievement is what makes it worthwhile. But this had nothing to do with the exquisite, indescribable beauty of the bonefish. He was long, thick, heavy and round, with speed and power in every line; a sharp white nose and huge black eyes. The body of him was live, quivering silver, molten silver in the sunlight, crossed and barred with blazing stripes. The opal hues came out upon the anal fin, and the broad tail curled up, showing lavender hints on a background of brilliant blue. He weighed eight pounds. Symbolic of the mysterious life and beauty in the ocean! Wonderful and prolific as nature is on land, she is infinitely more so in the sea. By the sun and the sea we live; and I shall never tire of studying the manifold life of the deep.

from Rivers of the Everglades

For the first time I was powerfully impressed by this strange region. The vast prairie lands and deserts of the West I knew well. This was the Everglades. I could not see the felicitousness of its name, but acknowledged something of charm. Evergrass would have been truer. Far from the low margin of the creek, far as my gaze could grasp, stretched a level plain of saw grass, a sedge resembling cattails, greenish brown in hue. Here and there a lonely palmetto dotted the landscape, and far on, in the dim haze, showed patches of trees, or a group of palmetto. Wildfowl winged wavering flight over that wasteland.

It was summer. Heat veils rose from the prairie. A soft breeze blew hot in my face, bringing the scent of dry grass and distant swamp and far-off fragrance of flowers. No lonely solitude of desert ever equaled that wilderness! Low, level, monotonous, it spread away endlessly to north and east, for what I knew to be over a hundred miles. It was the home of wildfowl and beast and alligator, and the elusive Seminole. Gazing across this waving sea of grass, I had a conception of the Seminole's hatred of all that pertained to the white man. The Everglade Indian must love this inaccessible, inhospitable wilderness that was neither wholly land nor water. He was alone there. No white man could follow him. . . .

Wild places had always haunted me.

* * *

Some ten or twelve miles up the Chatham Bend River we entered a wide bay full of oyster bars; and here we went aground so often that I feared we would never find deep water again. But even shallow water in the Glades had an end. We got through, and eventually, by devious channels, and tunnels under mangroves, and bends that left no doubt as to the felicitousness of part of the name bestowed on this river, we arrived at the creek Captain King averred would be full of tarpon. I ventured to inquire when he had last visited this place.

"Reckon it was aboot nine years ago," he said. "An' it shore was full of tarpon then. Some regular he-rhinoceros busters, too."

King's creek opened into a little bay, an ideal retreat for the great silver fish, snug and smooth in the lee of mangroves. Our diligent survey found only one tarpon. He was big enough to set us keenly to positions, and tackle and bait. While we were getting ready to deprive him of liberty for a while, perhaps his life, he swam to and fro before us, broad tail and dorsal fin above water. No sooner had we got our baits out and a quantity of chum, than the big tarpon got busy. He began to pick up the pieces of fish we had so kindly thrown his way. Every time he stood on his head in the three feet of water his broad forked tail came clear out. Fish fins and fish tails had a compelling power to thrill and excite me. Moreover, our boatmen were expressing most decided ideas as to the inevitable fact that he was already our tarpon. R.C. himself, seldom extravagant, began to calculate the leaps and wanted to bet he would snap so many pictures.

"Shore, he's walkin' to his funeral right now," said King.

"Look at the way he's pickin' that chum," said Thad, "He might just as well swim over here an' give up."

"Hurry and hand him a bait," shouted R.C., impatiently.

Somehow, despite the sanguine remarks of my comrades, I knew that lone tarpon was as safe as if he had been in Lake Okeechobee. He ate up all the chum, swam around and over my bait, and then went to chasing a live mullet. He worked away from our position. Once he broke water, showing himself, and he was big and broad and silvery. My companions were ungracious enough to cast slurs on this beautiful fish.

We abandoned the bay and the creek for others no better and at length turned downstream with the tide. The wind, the glare, the heat made me drowsy, and I fell half asleep. Suddenly I was roused by a yell in my ear.

"Snook! Snook!" R.C. was waving and pointing, as well as yelling. I was in time to see a large school of snook swim away from the boat into deep water. The stream took a sharp turn round a shady point of mangrove. The current was swift.

We anchored the skiffs and went trolling [in the motor launch] with our light tackles, using spinners. We had not gone thirty yards before boils and swirls back of our spinners attested to the rush of snook. R.C. hooked a big one. He came out and shook himself free. Then I hooked another. He made a hard run, under the bank and, fouling on a snag, got away.

"Good chance to snap pictures," I said to R.C. "You fish. We'll take turns."

R.C. caught two snook of several pounds, which we saved to eat. Next he got a fine jump out of a small tarpon. The water was clear and not unlike that of a freshwater stream. In fact, the fishing seemed exactly like that on an inland river where muskellunge and pike abounded. A snook resembles a muskellunge in appearance, strike and fight. We worked up along the bank, keeping close to the overshadowing brush and roots and leaves. R.C. had a strike every ten feet of the way. Some of the snook missed the hook; others hit it and threw it; finally a heavy fellow with a mighty swirl fastened himself tight. He began to jump, and here was where I took advantage of opportunity.

R.C.'s tackle was too light for a snook of this size, and he could not hold him. But luck favored us in this instance. The snook missed snags, and when he jumped to hang himself over brush, the dead branches obligingly gave way. The fish took line, making rushes, sulked in holes, plugged to hang the line on something, and particularly fought on the surface in leaps and long tussling skittering breaks. He had to be handled with skill and extreme delicacy, for the mouth of a snook tears easily. In all he gave an exhibition that thoroughly earned him our admiration, and when R.C. finally subdued him—and I had photographed him—a pale-gold, gleaming, black-lined fish of twelve pounds—we returned him unhurt to the water.

That was the beginning of a most extraordinary lot of fun. We took turns with my rod, after R.C. had broken his. Certain places along the creek we named appropriately. The best was Snook Corner. We never failed to hook one here, and if he freed himself, which two out of three fish accomplished, there was always another ready to rush the spinner.

Together we hooked innumerable of these gamefish, some too heavy to hold; and we caught twenty, the largest of which ranged from eight to twelve pounds. We used up four rolls of film. And when we were thoroughly tired out, after three strenuous hours, we quit fishing and went on our way.

"That was great!" exclaimed R.C.

It did not seem an exaggeration. To fish in a beautiful place, to see the quarry rush and strike and leap, to outwit him by skill and strength, to return him unhurt to the water, sure that there were no sharks to take advantage of his exhaustion, and particularly to have the strikes come thick and fast and heavy—that was indeed all satisfying to my brother, and no doubt even more to me.

On our return we passed a small mangrove island and were attracted by the sight of a huge nest of eagle or osprey, black and ragged, in the top of a tree. When we approached, a large fish hawk left the nest and soared aloft, uttering piercing cries. We soon saw two young hawks, so nearly full fledged that I expected them to fly. But they did not, even

when we went close, even when I climbed an adjoining mangrove to obtain a better picture of nest and birds. At last I was
inspired to climb to the very top of the tree, so that I stood
beside the nest, within reach of the fish hawks. I was more
frightened than they, for I feared the branch would give way
under me or the mother bird would swoop down to scalp me
with those sharp talons.

The hawks were young, but of almost full size, with
breasts of creamy white, and wings, head and tail of mottled
brown. They faced me with what I took for curiosity more
than fear. They certainly did not betray any instinct to fly,
though they backed to the edge of the nest. What sleek,
sharp, small heads, eagle-shaped! The eyes were black and
orange, the orange being the iris; and the light in them was
piercingly wild and beautiful. Wild nature! I did not see
hate of man or fear of death in these eyes, as I have seen in
older birds of prey. Cautiously I laid a hand on the nearer
one, which act excited the bird, though not alarmingly; and
then I backed down the tree and returned to the boat. As
we left I heard the plaintive cries of the young ones and the
piercing reply of the mother. Before we turned a bend she
had swooped down to the nest. I wondered what the re-
united family would say in fish hawk language about the
intruder.

It occurred to me that I had not failed to take note of the
nest. It had been built of dead sticks and was very old, perhaps many years. The under sticks were rotten. The upper
were hard wood, indicating that every year a new layer of
sticks had been added. The top was almost flat and it was
quite solid. I saw no fish bones, and gathered from this fact

that the parents removed these after every meal. There was a good-sized clump of oyster shells in one place, some of the shells being open. Not unlikely, in lieu of fish the parent hawk had fetched a change of diet. But if so, how did she open the oysters?

The next day began with a soft, cool east wind, very delightful. But it dropped early. When we pulled up anchor and headed down the coast, the morning was hot. We ran about two hours and threw anchor at the mouth of another river.

Soon we set out up the creeks to locate tarpon, and before we got well into the mangroves [we] found a round pool where a few fins were showing. We thought to tarry a little while to find out if tarpon were abundant or scarce. Captain Thad baited a rod for me, and while the others watched I fished. Inside of five minutes my line was paying out in a steady strong tarpon strike. I yelled for R.C. to get ready with the camera. But I had scarcely uttered the words when the tarpon leaped, close to the boat. I tried to wind and jerk to set the hook. He leaped again, a long, slim, graceful fish, perhaps of a hundred pounds. R.C. was fumbling with my camera . . . complaining that something was out of 'whack.'

Then with a resounding thump the tarpon slid out and up, almost without splashing, and shot prodigiously high, higher than I had ever seen a tarpon leap, and turning over he came down head first in a beautiful dive, cutting the water like a blade. In that leap he had thrown the hook. His effort had been so magnificent and spectacular that we were all stunned. When we recovered we all exclaimed in unison. R.C. forgot his chagrin over my camera and I regarded the escape of the fish as freedom well earned.

After that we rowed up a narrow creek until we found more fish. R.C. soon hooked a tarpon that would not jump. Nor did it, at first, attempt to go down toward the sea. Space between the mangroves was not more than fifty feet. This tarpon ran off up the creek, making a furrow on the smooth surface. Part of the time he swam under the drooping dead mangroves, breaking off pieces and dragging them along with him. "Good night!" yelled R.C. "We can't hold this bird!"

Captain Thad poled our skiff swiftly up to R.C.'s, jumped into it, and left our engineer, Anderson, to row me. I stood up, camera in hand, but it was hard for me to keep from being lurched overboard, owing to Anderson's heroic efforts to keep up with the other skiff. I had no idea whatever that R.C. would save that fish, but I wanted to see what would happen. He was using a light tackle rod, but fortunately the reel was equipped with a good fifteen-thread [roughly 45-pound test] line.

We chased that queer tarpon a quarter of a mile, and all the time he kept a hundred yards ahead of R.C. The boat-men made powerful efforts with oars and pole to gain on the fish. But only the shallow water and narrow space stopped the tarpon.

When he made a tremendous surge around to head down the creek, he came right at my boat. I shouted for Anderson to row fast, to this side and that. But it seemed we could not get away from R.C.'s line. It was right under us, to one side then the other. It caught on Anderson's oars, and what kept it from snapping I could not guess. Finally we got out of the road and let R.C.'s boat by. Then we followed.

"He's got most of my line out again!" yelled R.C. "Row and pole, you buckoos! We're going to catch this bird."

The tarpon took us back down the creek, beyond the point where R.C. had hooked him. My boat was a hundred feet and more behind. I missed several smashes the tarpon made on the surface. I hoped he would leap, but he never did.

The boys overtook him in the wildest place along that creek. It was where a branch ran off to the left, and on that side the water shoaled to a mud bar. Beyond this point was a constriction of the creek, full of snags. In fact, all along the banks, except on the shoal, there were ugly snags sticking up.

"Hold him here, R.C.!" I yelled. "Lick him in this wide place or lose him."

There the real struggle ensued. The tarpon swam, rolled, lunged, and plunged to go on, in any direction. He towed the skiff. R.C. bent that little rod, and when he got the double line over the reel he shut down with both thumbs. Sometimes we were within thirty feet of him. And more than once I had to hold my camera high to keep it from being wet by the tarpon splashing.

"Light tackle fish, huh!" ejaculated R.C. "Not this bird! I tell you, he's strong."

"You're working too hard on him," I called, warningly. "Ease up. Play him safe. It's a big fish."

But I did not observe that my brother heeded my advice. I could see that he was fighting mad. The heat was intense, the mosquitoes and sand flies ferocious. R.C.'s head net had caught in a mangrove branch and had been pulled awry. I could not see his face, but I did not need that to tell he was most uncomfortable. His shirt showed wet with sweat. I was saturated myself and literally being devoured by mosquitoes.

My sun glasses fogged with the heat and moisture, and I had to remove them. Then the glare hurt my eyes.

After the tarpon thumped far one way, R.C. would succeed in turning him; and they kept repeating this performance. The tarpon would stick up his nose and puff. Then he would roll, showing a broad gleaming side, gold in the amber water. He worked to one shore and went over and under snags. Then he took a notion to plunge under the skiff. R.C. had a bent rod underwater, clear to the reel, for several moments, while the boys turned the boat. Manifestly, this trick appealed to the tarpon, for he essayed it again. R.C. quickly thrust the curving rod down into the water and staggered over seats, around Thad, to clear the stern. Next move of the fish was to make a slow, powerful heave for the west bank. He butted into it, for his nose came out covered with mud. Then, in the center of the widest part of the creek, he resorted to the lunges and plunges that plainly gave R.C. the utmost trouble. He had to hold that tarpon, yet not break him off. I certainly appreciated R.C.'s job.

Suddenly the fish amazed me. He made a swift short run. The reel screeched. In such short space he could not be stopped or turned. "Say good-bye!" called R.C., grimly.

But the tarpon ran up on the mud bar until he was half out of the water. There he began to wallow. . . . He sent sheets of muddy water flying. He churned and threshed until he slid off the mud. But now, after this last expenditure of strength, he appeared to be weakening. R.C. could turn him, hold him, and at last lead him. Soon after that he rolled wearily on his broad side, blazing in the sunlight, and did not right himself. The battle was over. A few minutes later he was roped to the skiff.

R.C.'s rod had a set curve in it, a deep bend that would never come out. And R.C. himself did not look much straighter.

"Queer fight, wasn't it?" I said, as we came alongside. "I never saw you work harder or better. But of course the conditions made this fight. All the same, he was a game fish."

R.C. was panting as he tore off hat, net, gloves, and threw them down. His face was purple in hue and steaming with sweat.

"How—long—was I—on that—bird?" he gasped.

"Nearly an hour," I replied, consulting my watch.

"Gimme the—water jug."

When he had drunk long he drew a deep breath and wiped his face. "Whew!" he exclaimed, finally. "Shades of swordfish! If I'm not—all in—I'll eat your bait."

Captain Thad slaked a thirst only second to R.C.'s. "I'll say it's hot," he said. "No wonder you're all in. I am, too. How about you, Bob?"

"If we hadn't licked him I'd have been dead by now. . . . But ketchin that durned plugger sort of revived me."

This tarpon was short, thick, broad, and heavy, not the leaping kind. We all guessed at his weight. Thad and Bob, as usual, underestimated it. He weighed one hundred and thirty pounds.

Some Rare Fish

It is very strange that the longer a man fishes the more there seems to be to learn. In my case this is one of the secrets of the fascination of the game. Always there will be greater fish in the ocean than I have ever caught.

Five or six years ago I heard the name 'waahoo' mentioned at Long Key. The boatmen were using it in a way to make one see that they did not believe there was such a fish as a waahoo. The old conch fishermen had never heard the name. For that matter, neither had I.

Later I heard the particulars of a hard and spectacular fight Judge Shields had had which the Smithsonian declared to be a waahoo. . . . In February, 1915, I met Judge Shields at Long Key, and, remembering his capture of this strange fish some years previous, I questioned him. He was singularly enthusiastic about the waahoo, and what he said excited my curiosity. Either the genial judge was obsessed or else this waahoo was a great fish. I was inclined to believe both, and then I forgot all about the matter.

This year at Long Key I was trolling for sailfish out in the Gulf Stream, a mile or so south of the Tennessee Buoy. It was a fine day for fishing, there being a slight breeze and a ripple on the water. My boatman, Captain Sam, and I kept a sharp watch on all sides for sailfish. I was using light tackle, and of course trolling, with the reel free running, except for my thumb.

Suddenly I had a bewildering, swift and hard strike. What a wonder that I kept the reel from overrunning! I certainly can testify to the burn on my thumb.

Sam yelled "Sailfish!" and stooped for the lever, awaiting my order to throw out the clutch.

Then I yelled: "Stop the boat, Sam! It's no sailfish!"

That strike took six hundred feet of line faster than any I had ever experienced. I simply did not dare to throw on the drag. But the instant the speed slackened, I did throw it on and jerked to hook the fish. I felt no weight. The line went slack.

"No good!" I called and began to wind in.

At that instant a fish savagely broke water abreast of the boat, about fifty yards out. He looked long, black, sharp nosed. Sam saw him, too. Then I felt a heavy pull on my rod and the line began to slip out. I jerked and jerked and felt that I had a fish hooked. The line appeared strained and slow, which I knew to be caused by a long and wide bag in it.

"Sam," I yelled, "the fish that jumped is on my line."

"No," replied Sam.

It did seem incredible. Sam figured that no fish could run astern for two hundred yards and then quick as a flash break water abreast of us. But I knew it was true. Then the line slackened just as it had before. I began to wind up swiftly.

"He's gone," I said.

Scarcely had I said that when a smashing break in the water on the other side of the boat alarmed and further excited me. I did not see the fish. But I jumped up and bent over the stern to shove my rod deep into the water back of the propeller. I did this despite the certainty that the fish had broken loose. It was a wise move, for the rod was nearly pulled out of my hands. I lifted it, bent double, and began to wind furiously. So intent was I on the job of getting up that slack line that I scarcely looked up from the reel.

"Look at him yump!" yelled Sam.

I looked, but not quickly enough.

"Over here! Look at him yump!" went on Sam.

That fish made me seem like an amateur. I could not do a thing with him. The drag was light, and when I reeled in some line, the fish got most of it back again. Every second I expected him to get free for sure. It was a miracle he did not shake the hook, as he certainly had a loose rein most all the time. The fact was he had such speed that I was unable to keep a strain upon him. I had no idea what kind of fish it was. And Sam likewise was nonplussed.

I was not sure the fish tired quickly, for I was so excited I had no thought of time, but it did not seem very long before I had him within fifty yards, sweeping in wide circles back of the boat. Occasionally I saw a broad, bright green flash. When I was sure he was slowing up, I put on the other drag and drew him closer. Then in the clear water we saw a strange, wild, graceful fish, the like of which we had never beheld. He was long, slender, yet singularly round and muscular. His color appeared to be blue, green, silver crossed by bars. His tail was big, like that of a tuna, and his head sharper, more wolfish than a barracuda. He had a long, low, straight dorsal fin. We watched him swimming slowly to and fro beside the boat, and we speculated upon his species. But all I could decide was that I had a rare specimen for my collection.

Sam was just as averse to the use of the gaff as I was. I played the fish out completely before Sam grasped the leader, pulled him close, lifted him in, and laid him down—a glistening, quivering, wonderful fish nearly six feet long.

He was black opal blue; iridescent, silver underneath; pale blue dorsal and copper-bronze tail, with bright bars down his body.

I took this thirty-six-pound fish to be a sea-roe, a game-fish lately noticed on the Atlantic seaboard. But I was wrong. One old conch fisherman who had been around the Keys forty years had never seen such a fish. Then Mr. Schutt came and congratulated me upon landing a waahoo. . . . Mr. Schutt had observed schools of them on the reef, low down near the coral—fish that would run from forty to one hundred pounds. It made me thrill just to think of hooking a waahoo weighing anywhere near a hundred pounds. . . . It is fascinating to ponder over tackle and bait and cunning calculated to take this rare denizen of the Gulf Stream.

* * *

During half a dozen sojourns at Long Key I had heard of two or three dolphins being caught by lucky anglers who were trolling for anything that would bite. But until 1916 I never saw a dolphin. Certainly I never hoped to take one of these rare and beautiful deep-sea fish. Never would have the luck. But in February I took two, and now I am forbidden the peculiar pleasure of disclaiming my fisherman's luck. . . .

One day, two miles out in the Gulf Stream, I got a peculiar strike, quite unlike any I had ever felt. A fisherman grows to be a specialist in strikes. This one was quick, energetic, jerky, yet strong. And it was a hungry strike. A fish that is hungry can almost always be hooked. I let this one run a little and then hooked him. He felt light, but savage. He took line in short, zigzag rushes. I fancied it was a bonita, but Sam shook his head. With about a hundred yards of line out, the fish leaped. He was golden. He had a huge, blunt, bow-shaped head and a narrow tail. The distance was pretty far, and I had no certainty to go by, yet I yelled:

"Dolphin!"

Sam was not so sure, but he looked mighty hopeful. The fish sounded and ran in on me, then darted here and there, then began to leap and thresh on the surface. He was hard to lead—a very strong fish for his light weight. I never handled a fish more carefully. He came up on a low swell, heading toward us, and he cut the water for fifty feet, with only his dorsal, a gleam of gold, showing in the sunlight.

Next he jumped five times, and I could hear the wrestling sound he made when he shook himself. I had no idea what he might do next, and if he had not been securely hooked would have gotten off. I tried hard to keep the line taut and was not always successful. Like the waahoo, he performed tricks new to me. One was an awkward diving leap that somehow jerked the line in a way to alarm me. When he quit his tumbling and rushing, I led him close to the boat.

This has always been to me one of the rewards of fishing. It quite outweighs for me that doubtful moment when the fish lies in the boat or helpless on the moss. Then I am always sorry, and more often than not let the fish go alive.

My first sight of a dolphin near at hand was one to remember. The fish flashed gold—deep rich gold—with little flecks of blue and white. Then the very next flash there were greens and yellows—changing, colorful, brilliant bars. In that background of dark, clear, blue Gulf Stream water this dolphin was radiant, golden, exquisitely beautiful. It was a shame to lift him out of the water. But—

The appearance of the dolphin when just out of the water beggars description. Very few anglers in the world have ever had this experience. Not many anglers, perhaps, care for the beauty of a fish. But I do. And for the sake of those who feel the same way I wish I could paint him. But that seems impossible. For even while I gazed the fish changed color. He should have been called the chameleon of the ocean. He looked a quivering, shimmering, changeful creature, the color of goldenrod. He was the personification of beautiful color alive. The fact that he was dying made the changing hues. It gave me a pang—to think that I should be the cause of the death of so beautiful a thing. . . .

The beauty of the dolphin resembled the mystery of the Gulf Stream—too illusive for the eye of man.

IV

Nova Scotia

The Nova Scotians keep the Sabbath. They do not fish on the seventh day of the week. I am afraid they made me feel ashamed of my own lack of reverence. . . . When I was a boy I had to go to Sunday school and to church. It made me unhappy. I never could listen to the preacher. I dreamed, mostly of fields, hills and streams, of adventures that have since come true. As I grew older and learned the joys of angling, I used to run away on Sunday afternoons. Many a time have I come home late, wet and weary after a thrilling time along river or stream, to meet with severe punishment from my outraged father. But it never cured me. I always went fishing on Sunday. It seemed the luckiest day. I do not consider it wrong. But I shall respect the custom of the Nova Scotians and stay quietly in the hotel that day.

My father was sure I would come to a bad end because I loved to fish. But he was wrong.

from Giant Nova Scotia Tuna

At Yarmouth we encountered heavy fog, and to me it was like meeting an old friend from across the continent. Long before we ran into this lowering silver bank of fog I could smell it. Probably all fogs are alike. Surely they are all cool, wet, silent, strange, mysterious; and they hide everything from the sight of man. It is a fear inspiring sensation to go driving over the sea through a dense fog. The foghorns, the whistles, the bell buoys all have a thrilling, menacing sound.

Here we disembarked and took a train, without being able to see what the port looked like. Some ten miles on we ran out of the fog into bright sunshine, and I found the province of Nova Scotia to be truly of the northland, green and verdant and wild, dotted with lakes and areas of huge gray rocks, and low black ranges covered with spruce, and rivers of dark clear water.

As we progressed these characteristics enhanced. What welcome relief to eyes seared by sight of barren desert and hot cities! The long grass, the wild flowers, the dense thickets of spruce, the endless miles of green were a soothing balm.

Liverpool proved to be a six-hour journey from Yarmouth, and turned out to be the prettiest little town I ever visited. The houses were quaint and of an architecture unfamiliar to me, very inviting to further attention. Everywhere were huge trees, maples, ash, locusts, and they graced ample yards of luxuriant green. A beautiful river ran through the town, and picturesque fishing smacks lined its shore.

* * *

That evening we went down to the dock to see the native fishermen come in and unload their catch for the market. Docks are always fascinating places for me. This one appeared especially so. The brown river ran between green banks, with farms and cottages on the west side, and low rising piney hills beyond. On the town side a line of weather-beaten storehouses stood back from the plank dock. You did not need to be told that Liverpool was a fisherman's town and very old. The scent of fish, too, was old, almost overpoweringly so. Two small schooners were tied up to the dock, the *Ena C.* and the *Una W.* What beautiful names are given to Englishwomen and flowers and boats! One of these small ships, a two-master, had a crew of six sturdy brown seamen clad in rubber boots. They had been out three days and had a catch of 16,000 pounds, codfish, halibut and two swordfish. I surely had a thrill at the sight of the broadbills. These were small fish compared with most I had seen during June and July on the Pacific. . . .

This schooner, with its weather-and-service-worn appearance, its coils of heavy hand-line, its skiffs dovetailed into one another, its rope and barrels and paraphernalia scattered about on the deck, and the deep hold from which the fishermen were pitchforking cod out on the dock, and the rude pulpit built out over the bowsprit, from which the swordfish were ironed—all these held great interest and curiosity for me, filling me with wonder about the exploits of these brave simple men who lived by the sea, and emphasizing again the noble and elemental nature of this ancient calling.

We inquired to find out if any tuna had been seen lately. Several weeks ago, they told us, tuna had been plentiful in the bays and inlets. They had come with the first run of herring. But none had been seen lately. The first run of herring was earlier than usual. A big season was expected. Sometime around the middle of August the great mass of herring would arrive. These were the species that spawned along this shallow Nova Scotia shore. They were larger than the present fish. The schools of tuna followed them. We were a little early.

* * *

On Sunday afternoon we left Liverpool for East Jordan, and had a different and more entertaining ride through wide country, woods and moose meadows, and thick brush. We emerged from this at Jordan Falls. From that point to the lighthouse on the bay was only a short run.

The sun had shone all afternoon, up until now, and at four o'clock the fog began to roll in. Joe reported seeing numerous tuna around the weir on Saturday, but none on Sunday. After supper I walked along the lonely beach and could not see far through the gloom. The shore was lined with huge gray boulders and fringed with stunted spruce trees. The time and place were not conducive to cheer.

R.C. and I had made our beds in the launch, there being just room for one cot and a bed on the floor. We both slept well. At five o'clock all was mantled in thick gray fog. We could not see the lighthouse from the shore. We had breakfast, and then there seemed only waiting. But at seven-thirty I decided to go in the launch after herring. We towed the skiff and crossed the bay in the fog. Finally we saw shore and soon encountered several fishermen from whom we bought a barrel of bait. One of them said there ought to be tuna at his nets, and I hired him to go with us. One of his companions went also, which made us eight in the launch. Too many! As we ran down the bay the fog began to whiten and thin. Soon we saw net-buoys, then Gull Rock, and at last Blue Island. The sun shone pale through the fog. I began to reproach myself for complaints that the fog would never lift.

We found the fisherman's nets full of herring, Romer and Joe began picking herring from the meshes. They were still alive, caught behind the gills. Presently another fisherman came along in his boat and told us he had just been feeding herring to a big albacore [tuna] round his net. I hired him to take us over there and stand by.

The distance was short. Soon we were tied to the net-buoy and chumming. I put a bait over, rather with a feeling that there was not much chance of a tuna coming along. But in less than five minutes I had a terrific strike, and I jerked with all my might, yelling: "*Strike! Strike!*"

Excitement reigned on that boat. The tuna lunged, dragging my tip into the water, and he ran off away from that net toward another. Sid had the engines going and we were after him with wonderful quickness. I could not believe that I was hooked to a tuna. My legs shook as they used to shake years ago when I had my first swordfish experiences. But gradually I recovered, and as we went after the fish, I pumped and wound in line, there was hilarity added to the excitement on board. The tuna ran around the net-buoy and fouled the line. I loosened the drag, then while the boys frantically endeavored to free my line, the tuna went off on his first terrific rush. He took two hundred yards off the reel. Suddenly I felt my line free of the buoy. Bob had cut the rope on the buoy. We were free, and away we sped after him! The fisherman followed in his launch.

There was sunshine all around us, and the shore glimmered through fog. I fought this fish pretty hard while he was taking us up the bay. Sometimes he towed us. The little launch handled perfectly. We were a wildly excited crowd. I endeavored to calm myself and to face the fact that the tuna would probably get away.

Meanwhile the sun came out and we could see everywhere. It was beautiful along the shore. The fish had taken us four miles up the bay. In an hour he appeared to be slowing down and getting tired.

Then he made for shore. Ugly rocks stuck up all around us. The fisherman was of the opinion the tuna had gone in there to cut the line on the rocks. But I did not take this seriously.

R.C. stood up on the bow, and presently he yelled: "I see him! A whale! He'll go five hundred!"

This at once terrified and elated me. I worked as hard as I could. The tuna kept ahead of us, and he turned every way. The leader got tangled around his tail. At first we welcomed that, as we thought it would soon exhaust him. But it did not. He swam near the surface and kept among the rocks. Once Captain Mitchell said: "We'd better lead him out of here." But he would not [be] led, and we followed him around. When he swam quickly to one side, dragging the line under the boat, I jumped up, threw off my drag, and poked my rod down in the water to clear my reel. I had not yet realized the hazardous position into which the fish had dragged us. I was not worried. In fact I had begun to feel he was weakening and that I would get him.

It began to dawn on me presently that there was something most unusual and sinister in the action of this fish, turning and wheeling for the rocks. I could not see those rocks deep under the surface, but I heard the boys yell: "Look out! Slack off! Rocks! Starboard!" and various other alarms. When, however, the fish ran straight for a black-nosed reef that was wreathed in foamy breakers, then I gave way to panic. We turned and tacked this way and that. Time after time the big tuna ran under the boat, and I had to leap up, throw off my drag, and plunge the rod into the water. Seven times I did this successfully. But it was risky business. We followed him in and out, round the black rock, through channels, over shoals, and toward the beach. Then he swept out a couple of hundred yards. I began to breathe easier. But my relief was short-lived. Again he made for the rocks.

"Say, we're following him too much!" shouted R.C.

That warning fell on deaf ears, for I still had no consistent fear he would cut off on the rocks. We got in a bad position, nearly sliding upon a flat rock we had not seen. The tuna went round it and we had to navigate between the rock and the breakers in order to free the line.

"Go to it!" I yelled, above the roar. "We can swim if we have to!"

Romer, whose face I happened to see, was white and rapt, perfectly wild with excitement and joy. He kept shouting advice to me. R.C. looked stern and grim as he stood up on the bow and waved Sid to steer to port or starboard. Once he called to me, "Good night!" and pointed to a green curling breaker with its white crest. How it boomed! Fifty feet in shore! With the tuna going strong! Still something happened to save us, and we ran around the bad rock away from the heave of the swell that raced toward the ledge. I had a few moments of comparative relaxation.

But when the stubborn tuna deliberately swerved back for the rocks, I realized that he was not lunging for shoal water by accident. He had tried every means in deep water to dislodge the infernal thing that held him, and, failing, he had headed for the rocks. How strange I had not believed this before! But it was hard to fight the fish and think deliberately at the same time. I had called these giant tuna stupid, an accusation made without careful consideration, and I was now compelled to retract it. At least this tuna was keen, cunning, resourceful, and probably unbeatable. It was instinct that guided him.

Suddenly he made a quick surge on the surface. I saw him—huge, blue-moving mass! It shook my heart, that sight. He swept round, and again the line went under the bow. I leaped up, and threw off my drag. Too quick! As I plunged my rod down into the water I saw some loops of slack line drift back toward the tip. I was frightened. I feared they would catch on the guides. They did catch. I felt a powerful pull—then the rod shot up. My line had caught on the tip and cut off on a guide!

Perhaps I had suffered more at the loss of a great fish—years ago. But not lately. I was stunned. Poor Romer looked sick. R.C. swore roundly and said we had bungled by letting the fish stay in shallow water. For my part I did not see how we could have helped that. Bob thought we might have dragged him, turned him. So did Captain Mitchell. We saw him twice after he was free, a blur of blue, moving ponderously away. I felt weak and had a nausea.

"Two hours and ten minutes!" reckoned R.C. "And you had him coming! Rotten luck!"

"Well, it was my fault," I replied, finally. "There's nothing to do but swallow it—and try again."

* * *

Next morning I was up at four-thirty. There were gray clouds in the east and patches of sky, colorless, like the hue of a moonstone, very soft and misty. The air was cool, sweet, damp, laden with mingled scent of sea and forest. How strange to have my view unobstructed by fog. Far down the bay I could see the points of the headlands, and two islands, one large and one small, that I at once recognized, though I had not seen them at this distance. We had breakfast at five o'clock. When we came out again the east was a wonderful delicate gold, too exquisite to attempt to describe.

Soon we were off down the bay, the launch leading the way to pick up the native fisherman who had piloted us to his nets. The water was as level as a mirror and as reflective. The delicate gold suffused all the soft misty clouds, growing stronger as I watched, until at length the sun burst forth gloriously, a golden fire, bathing forest, bay, and meadow slopes in a wondrous luster. Fire at sunset and gold at sunrise! After all the gloomy, foggy weather, I had been rewarded. It gave me such a different feeling toward this rugged land of seashore and rock-ridged forest.

In less than half an hour we had reached the first of the nets, and soon after that arrived at a point between Gull Rock and Blue Island where the morning before I had hooked my first tuna. How different a scene now! Gentle heaving sea, sparkle of water, bobbing boats of fishermen lifting their nets, the tang of salt, fresh from the vast open space beyond, the clear outline of Gull Rock, a desolate, forbidding gray stone, the swelling rise of Blue Island, green and dark, and bathed in a sunrise gold, and then out over the promontories a low belt of land fog—these met my roving glances and gave me the delight that makes so much of the worthiness of fishing and the good fortune that befalls the early angler.

We procured a basketful of herring from the fisherman who had accompanied us down the bay. Then we ran on to the next fisherman, who had seen one tuna about his net, but not for some time. Nevertheless we tied on to his buoy and began to grind chum and throw out herring. I put a bait over and waited with my heart in my throat. One tuna strike had prepared me for a second.

"Look down there!" exclaimed Captain Mitchell. "By Jove! That fisherman is punching at a tuna near his boat."

It did seem so. I saw the man strike with an oar, saw the splash, and then when he poised, as if waiting for another chance to hit something, I yelled out:

"Let's get there pronto."

And in less time, almost, than it takes to tell it we were on our way. . . .

We ran straight down on the fisherman we had watched and hauled in close.

I made an eager query: "Didn't we see you hit a fish?"

"Yes. There are two [tuna] round; one of them's a big one. He was stealing herring almost out of my hands."

We explained our intentions and asked if we could tie to his buoy. He nodded, and grinned when he said he hoped we would hook on to the big one.

No doubt of our excitement! The certainty of a strike made it impossible to be calm. In less than two minutes I was holding tenaciously to my rod and watching the shiny slick float down along the net.

"Bad place to hook one, if he runs up the bay," warned Captain Mitchell, pointing to the net-buoys. Indeed the lane between them was torturous and narrow. My feeling was one of dismay at that prospect; my hope was that if I hooked one, he would run out to sea.

"*Oh-h!*" yelled Sid, hoarsely, in most intense excitement. At the same instant I heard a tremendous splash. Wheeling, I saw white and green water settling down near the net, not fifty yards from us.

"That was a tuna!" exclaimed Captain Mitchell. "Did you hear the smash? He was after a herring."

Sid jabbered like a wild man, until finally I made something of his speech: " . . . big, blue tuna! He had a back like a horse! He came half out!"

Bob's eyes flashed like keen blue fire. "I saw him. Some he-scoundrel, that fish!"

"You'll get a strike in no time," added Captain Mitchell. "If only he doesn't run up the bay!"

My state was one of supreme rapture, dread, and doubt combined. I really was not a rational being. There I sat, left hand holding about four feet of loose line of my reel, my right clutching the rod, my eyes everywhere. I saw the net, the slick, the drifting particles of chum Bob was grinding, the shiny floating herring Captain Mitchell threw in, the bright green water, the buoys and boats and fishermen. R.C. and Romer sat perched upon the deck of their boat, perhaps a quarter of a mile distant. Romer was watching us through glasses. How long would I have to wait? Five minutes seemed an age.

Suddenly the loose line whipped out of my hand and ran through the guides on the rod.

"There!" I whispered, hoarsely.

My line swept away, hissing through the water. Gripping rod with both hands I jerked with all my might. What tremendous live weight! Again—two—three—four times I struck, while my line whizzed off the reel. Hard as I jerked I never got the curved rod upright.

"You've hooked him!" yelled Captain Mitchell, with great elation. Both the boys yelled, but I could not tell what. The rush of the tuna wheeled me in the revolving chair, dragged me out of it, with knees hard on the gunwale. My rod made rapid nods. But despite the terrific strain I got the drag off. Right there began a demonstration of the efficiency of the great Coxe reel.

The tuna had run round the net, on the ocean side, and had headed for Blue Island. I had heard the scream of a reel, the rush of a flying line, but that run beat any other I ever saw. An ordinary reel or line would have failed. Of course I had wet my line. I felt the fine spray hit my face stingingly. I could judge yards only by the space on the reel, and this fish took off two hundred or more in what seemed like a single flash. If he had kept on! But he ended that rush. And in two more seconds the engines were roaring and the launch was wheeling. We were after him with half my five hundred yards still on the reel.

"How about it?" shouted Sid, red-faced and fierce, bending over the open engine box.

"Slow down! Plenty of line!" I called back.

Then we got settled. The surprise of the attack had not upset us, but it had surely been electrifying. Many times on the *Gladiator,* while roaming the sea for swordfish, had R.C. and Sid and Bob and I talked over the way to meet just such a strike and rush as this.

I sat facing the bow, rod high, line taut for several hundred feet out of the water. The tuna headed for Blue Island, about a mile away. We were leaving the dangerous labyrinth of nets. All was serene on board then.

"Some run, I'll tell the world!" rejoiced Bob. "Makes a tarpon look slow!"

I had, of course, put my drag on when the fish had slowed and we had started after him. We were running seven or eight miles an hour, and the tuna was taking line slowly off the reel. This chase extended in a straight course for some distance and it was singularly exhilarating. We all complimented the work of the little launch. The quick start was what had saved us. "I had both engines going before you got through hooking him," boasted Sid.

When half the line had slipped off my reel I said: "Run up on him. Let me get back the line."

Sid speeded up, and I worked to recover line and not allow any slack. When I got back all that was possible at the time, I was sweating and panting. Then we slowed down again.

My tuna headed up the bay and ran a mile or more before he turned. We did not want him to go up the bay and welcomed his swerving. But when he pointed us toward the nets I was suddenly filled with dread.

"Port, Sid," I called, sharply. "Sheer off a little. We'll quarter with him and head him out to sea . . . Or lose him right here!"

"That's the idea," replied Captain Mitchell. "Fight him now. We've got two miles before he reaches the nets."

So we ran with him yet a little to his left while I pulled with all my might and used all the drag I dared. He took line—one hundred yards—two hundred yards—three hundred yards. Still he did not turn. But he slowed down. Dragging three hundred yards of thirty-nine line, and the launch besides, told perceptibly on his speed.

Meanwhile, our other boat, with R.C. and Romer wildly waving, joined the chase, and falling in behind us kept close as possible. It was a grim ticklish time. I hated to risk so much. But that was the game—to keep him out of the nets or lose him.

"Shore he's headin' out!" yelled Bob.

That was good news, but I could not see it. Bob, however, knew more about lines in the water than I, and presently I saw it proved. My tuna was slowly turning away from the dreaded nets.

"Close in, Sid. Help me get back some line," I said.

Still keeping that strain on him, we narrowed the distance between us until I had all the line back except a hundred yards or so, and with this we were well content. When we had him headed straight for the open sea, we gradually moved over to a point behind him. Then I eased the drag, let him set a pace, which we adopted; and he led us out to sea. It was a great situation. The sun had come out, not bright, but enough to make the water glimmer and the distant headlands show distinctly. The lighthouse on the southwest point gradually faded; only Gull Rock and Blue Island remained in sight. We passed a bell buoy some five miles outside the bay. A foghorn bayed in faint hoarse notes its warning to mariners.

"What time did we hook up with this fellow?" I inquired.

Seven-ten," replied Sid, consulting his watch. "It's now eight-thirty."

"Wal, I reckon it's aboot time to settle down to a fight," drawled Bob. "He's shore well hooked."

"All right. Get my coat off and put the harness on," I said.

I had never gotten much satisfaction or help out of any harness we had ever bought or made, but I expected much from the one Coxe had constructed for me. . . . It was made of leather, and like a vest with the front cut out. Straps hooked on to my rod below my reel. It felt good. I could pull with my shoulders. Thus equipped . . . I settled down to the grim job.

With slow steady sweeps and swift winds of reel I went through the usual procedure of fighting a heavy fish. But I could gain line only when Sid ran the boat faster than the tuna swam. Nevertheless I slowed him down in his headlong flight toward the open sea. Otherwise I could not see that I had made the slightest impression upon him. Time flies while one is fighting a fish. I was amazed when Sid sang out: "Ten-thirty—and all's well!"

There was no wind. The sea resembled a dimpled mirror. The sun shone through pale gray clouds and it was warm. The land fog began to encroach upon the sea, hiding the headlands under a silver belt. Only the dark shoreline of Blue Island showed us the direction of the bay.

We were eight miles off before I stopped the tuna and turned him. I was not in the best of condition for a hard, grueling battle, as I had fought only one fish during the summer—a 413-pound broadbill swordfish. I had tried to keep fit, but there is nothing like actual work with a rod on a fish to keep an angler hard and strong.

At the end of three hours I was wet and hot. All this time, even when I had pulled my hardest, the tuna had continued to tow the launch. Sometimes more slowly than at others, but always he towed it, bow first! Most of this strain had fallen upon my back and shoulders, where the harness fitted so snugly. And about this time I made the discovery that, if I held high on the rod and let all the strain come on it instead of the harness, I could stand the mighty pull for only about two minutes at a stretch. Then I would have to transfer the strain back to the harness. Which of course meant to my shoulders! I felt chafed under the arms and I ached a little, but otherwise did not appear to be suffering any great discomfort from this unusual demand on my muscles. It struck me forcibly, however, that the tuna was towing the launch absolutely by pulling against my back. What amazed me was the great value of the Coxe harness. During all this time, which seemed short, the fight itself and the remarks of my comrades, especially the droll speech of my Florida boatman Bob, kept me in a state of excitement. Probably I could not have felt even an injury at that stage.

All fights with big fish have stages, and this one was no exception. The great tuna came to the surface, and abandoning a straight course out to sea he began to swim in circles. He was still fast, still strong. But he had shown his first indication of weakening. He had lost sense of direction. He was bewildered. He pushed a wave ahead of him and left a wide wake behind.

"Bob, get up on the bow and watch him," I ordered. "Never take your eye off him."

An experienced fisherman such as Bob, if he could see a fish, could tell exactly what he was going to do. It turned out that I had chosen wisely to give this scout duty to Bob. The tuna was in front a couple of hundred feet and half as far to starboard. He was deep under the surface, so that I could only see the waves he started in motion. But to Bob he was visible. Suddenly he shouted, piercingly: "Look out!"

I saw a surge in the water and a pale gleam, incredibly swift, right at the boat. Leaping up, I threw off the drag and plunged my rod deep in the water. Not a second too soon! All I saw was the bag of line shoot under the boat. Then I felt a lunge on my rod, and the whir of the reel. Sid had been as swift with the levers and wheel. Bob and Captain Mitchell were leaning over the gunwale.

"All clear!" sang out Sid.

"Son of a gun!" ejaculated Bob. "Talk about puttin' it in high!"

"Splendid work!" declared Captain Mitchell, rising. "By Jove! But he made a dash!"

I lifted the dripping rod and reel, fell back in the seat, jammed the butt into the socket, and tightening the drag, faced about to look for the tuna. What a cunning, wonderful rush that had been! If Bob had not been standing on the bow,

I would never have perceived that action in time to avert disaster. A bagged line floating on the surface and dragged under a boat oftener than not will cut off on the propeller. It had been a narrow shave.

"Boys, we've got to get mad or he'll fool us, same as that one did yesterday," I said.

We all grew silent and watchful then. I began to conserve strength, to leave more to my reel, to study every move of the tuna, to make absolutely sure he never had an inch of slack line. As he circled here and there at random, sometimes in wide curves, at others in short turns, he always towed the launch. I kept on a good stiff drag, but not strong enough to break the line, should he suddenly rush. And the line paid off the reel slowly as he dragged the launch. Sid said he towed us four miles an hour, but I thought that a little too much. But he kept us moving. Gradually he drew us back toward the bell buoy, and around this he hung, near or far, as it happened. During this strenuous hour he never sounded once. Always that bulge on the smooth surface and the swelling wake behind! These were new and fascinating tactics in a gamefish.

About at this period of the battle the physical man began to rebel. There is a limit to the time emotion and imagination can make a man oblivious to pain and fatigue. Long had I been tired, but it was a tired feeling I rather reveled in. It had not made any difference. But suddenly I was made to realize that something was wrong. My hands, wrists and arms were still strong, and I felt I had a reserve in them for what we call the finish of a fight, sometimes the most strenuous part. My shoulders likewise seemed as good as ever. But my back, low down where the harness fit so like a glove, had begun to hurt.

I thought about this carefully. We never mind pangs. It would not be any achievement to catch a great fish without toil and sweat, endurance and pain. Anybody can catch some kind of fish without these. But no one will ever catch a great tuna without them. Accidents happen, and the lucky fluke captures of giant gamefish are on record. But I never had one and I do not take any account of them. So up to that point I had not paid any particular attention to my growing discomforts. I decided the pain in my back was due to a different kind of pull. In fact, my whole body was pulled. It was harnessed to that tuna. But I could stand the strain, and so entered upon the second half of the struggle.

The weather grew even better, if that were possible. The sea appeared flat without heave or swell. Not a breath of wind stirred. The transparent film of cloud let sunlight through, but little heat. It seemed a wonderfully lucky day.

R.C. and Romer in the large boat followed us, plying cameras and motion picture machines with great assiduity. Sometimes they came within a hundred feet behind us or off to one side. I could hear the boy's shrill voice: "Some fish! Hang on, Dad! You can lick him! Don't work too hard! Let him pull the boat!" Occasionally R.C. yelled a word of encouragement. I waved to them once in a while until the time came when I forgot everything but the tuna.

While I went through the labored motions with rod and reel I waited and hoped for some expression from Bob that we had a chance to whip this fish. Bob knew fish nature as well as Sid knew the workings of an engine. And I knew I could absolutely rely on what Bob said. But what a long time I waited! He stood balanced on the bow, his keen profile against the sky, his eyes glued to the shadowy blue shape of the tuna.

"Wal," he said finally, "if the hook doesn't tear out, we'll lick him."

That gave me renewed life and energy.

"If he ever heads this way yell to me, so I can release the strain," I said. "We just won't pull the hook out."

Captain Mitchell sat or stood at my side all the while, sometimes silent, often giving a quiet word of praise or encouragement. He was always optimistic. "You're going to kill this tuna," he averred. "I'm a lucky man to have in the boat." He was particularly keen to observe our handling of the launch and manipulation of tackle; and it was plain that he was deeply and favorably impressed.

"We always have a long double line above the leader," he said. "Then when we get the end of that over the reel we hold hard and let the tuna tow the skiff around. When it's safe to do so we have the boatman row against the fish."

"But, Captain, wouldn't a tuna like this one tow a skiff all day and all night?" I queried.

"I'm afraid so. He's a mighty game fish and a big one. Some tuna give up quicker than others. One now and then is a terrific and unbeatable fighter. This fellow amazes me. He's a stubborn devil."

I had an eighteen-foot leader and double line about the same length. It was an occasion for cheers when I got the end of that double line up to the tip of my rod for the first time. But I could not get it over the reel. After several more attempts and aided by Sid slipping in closer on the fish, I did get the double line over my reel. Also we saw the end of the leader. These things marked another stage in the fight—hopeful ones for me. I had the most trouble in going slow, in holding back, in maintaining patience. It must necessarily be a very long contest. But to know this and to practice it were vastly different things. The sweat from my forehead ran down in my eyes and over my nose.

To and fro over the unruffled ocean we glided, seldom under our own power. Now and then Sid would throw in the clutch of one engine to help me get back some line. Bob stuck to his post and had nothing to say. Captain Mitchell did not let me grow discouraged.

"He's shoving a bigger wave all the time," he said. "That means he's swimming higher. Soon his fins and tail will show."

Sure enough they did. His ragged dorsal, and the long curved yellow spike behind it, and then his blue-black tail, at last cut the calm surface of the water. Yells from the other boat attested to the close attention and pursuit our comrades were giving us. During the next half hour we sighted his fins many times, always within a hundred feet. I could have held him at that distance just as long as my strength would stand it, but when we got him close so he saw the boat, he would move ahead. A hundred times or more we ran him down and I dragged him within thirty feet of where Bob stood. Gradually he got used to the boat and always he tired almost imperceptibly. All I could see was the last third of his body, the huge taper of his blue bulk, decorated with the little yellow rudder-like fins, and his wagging tail. But of course Bob could see every inch of him. At length I had to yell:

"Say, Bob, how big is he?"

"Huh! I'm shore afraid to say," replied Bob.

"Tell me!"

"Wal, it'll do you more good not to know."

"Where's he—hooked?" I panted.

"Deep I reckon. I see the leader comin' out of his mouth this side."

"Is he wearing out?"

"He can't put it in high any more, that's shore. Just hang on and save yourself for the finish."

Time and again the tuna got the leader round his tail. This made the rod wag up and down in a kind of weaving motion, and it lifted me to and fro in my chair. So far as we could see, it did not inconvenience the tuna in the least. When a marlin or broadbill gets tangled in the leader, he cannot fight until he is free again. But not so with this tuna!

"Sid, ease in behind him," I called. "I'm going to pull the leader up to Bob. Captain, you go forward and get ready for a possible chance to gaff him."

"Not yet! It's too soon," replied Captain Mitchell.

"It may not come soon. But I want you there . . . Bob, grab the leader and hold it—not stiff—but just enough to let it slip. We'll see. Now, all do as I say—and if we lose him, I'll be to blame."

I shut down on the drag and began to haul and wind with everything I had left. Of course, without Sid's help I never could have pumped the leader out of the water, not at that time. No man unaided could have pulled that tuna toward him. In a few moments Bob's eager sinewy hands closed on the end of the leader just below the ring. He never uttered a word, but I saw his tense expression change. The others whooped. That relieved me of the terrific strain. It was such a change that for an instant my head swam.

The tuna did not like it. He lashed the water white. He towed us faster. Then he pulled the leader away from Bob.

"Boys, we'll try that," I said, doggedly. "We'll keep at him. Be quick, careful. Do the right thing at the right time."

"Reckon it's our chance," replied Bob. "I'll shore handle that leader easy. It'll work if the hook doesn't tear out."

Then I had the task of hauling that leader back to Bob. It took moments of strenuous work. Bob stood far out on the bow, reaching for it. The double line passed him. It would have been risky at that stage to have trusted the double line. When he got hold of the leader I had another little rest. What welcome relief! I was burning, throbbing, aching. Still, both hands and arms were strong. I felt that I could last it out. The tuna lashed the water and sheered to starboard. Sid had one engine in reverse, the other full speed ahead, and he was working the wheel. Quick as we turned, however, we could not keep the leader from being torn out of Bob's hands. The tuna made a roar on the surface and then sounded. He went to the bottom. I had the pleasant job of lifting him. As a matter of fact I did not budge him an inch. But I pulled as mightily as I could and persuaded him to come up again. Then we went after him. I got the leader to Bob, and once more was free of that awful drag at my vitals. Bob held the fish longer this time, and Sid threw out the clutches.

We warmed to these tactics, for in them we saw sure capture of the tuna, if the tackle held. My task seemed tremendous. When the tuna sheered away, tearing the leader from

Bob, I had to haul it back. I could turn the fish now and move him a very little. But, oh, what a ponderous weight! When he shook his head I thought he would crack my back. Many times we tried this, so many that after fifteen I quit counting them. But they worked. The tuna was weakening. If I did not give out first, we might get him. Every time I could see him, and the sight seemed to inspire me momentarily with the strength of Hercules. It was that sight of him, marvelous blue massive body and tail, and the short rest following my getting the leader to Bob, which kept me up.

After what seemed like a long while, Bob was able to hold to the leader while the tuna towed us round and round. Then began another stage, that of hauling him closer. At first it would not work. When Bob hauled away hand over hand, very cautiously and slowly for a few feet, then the tuna would lunge and break away. By degrees, however, this method worked as had the mere holding of the leader. The awful thing for me was that now when the fish tore the leader out of Bob's hands, he would sound and I had to pump him up. There was nothing else to do. I had to do it. Both my excitement and my agony augmented, yet somehow I was able to carry on and keep a cool head.

When Bob finally turned to us with his keen blue eyes flashing, I knew something was up.

"I can hold the leader and drag him. If we all work right now he's marchin' to his funeral."

How cool he was! I knew he lent us all confidence. Sid had surely had his hands full at the wheel and clutches. I was worn to a frazzle. But Bob's patience and endurance seemed to grow. He looked at me.

"A few more times and he's a lost fawn-skin," he said. "Don't let him rest. Haul him up."

"Bob—your—words—sound—like—music," I panted. "Sure—I'll—haul—him—right up."

My tuna was down deep. He had become almost a dead weight. Yet every wag of head or tail had irresistible power. Fortunately his wags had become few. I had now to favor my lame back. I pulled with my arms, lifted with my knees. Only such tackle as this could ever have lifted this fish. I was afraid something would break. But reel, rod, line, all held. At last I heaved him out of the depths. When Bob got the leader again I gasped.

"Hang on—till I come to!"

Then Bob began what turned out to be the greatest performance I had ever seen. He held the tuna. Sometimes he would let a yard or two of the leader slip through his hands, to relieve the strain of a roll or lunge, but he never let go of it. He was pulled from side to side as the fish wagged across the bow; sometimes on his knees; again straddling the leader; often bent forward almost ready to let go. His face was sharp and stern and full of tense cords of pain. It must have hurt to hold that wire. Sid's motions were no less active and tense. According to Bob's signs, which came mostly through nods of his head, Sid had to throw the clutches in or out, reverse one and full speed ahead on the other, all the time working the wheel. The launch spun like a top; it never went straight any more. How the two of them kept that tuna from running under the boat was astounding to see. But they accomplished it. I was on edge, however, ready at a second's notice to act my part and plunge the rod overboard to save the line from fouling on the propellers. I also had to keep the line from catching on the bow or the gaff in Mitchell's hands, and as much as possible out of Bob's way. This strain was almost as hard to bear as had been the one of weight.

Thus the fight narrowed down to the climax. Many times the huge tuna rolled within reach of the long gaff. But I wanted a sure chance. Bob knew when far better than I, and he never said a word. Captain Mitchell leaned over one gunwale, then the other. Sid had begun to wear nervous under the strain. He talked a good deal, mostly to himself. He had many things to operate all at once, and to do so without mistake required tremendous concentration. Back and forth he swiftly bent from wheel to clutches.

The tuna heaved on the surface, he rolled and gasped, lunged out his huge head with jaws wide and black eyes staring—a paralyzing sight for me. Then he wagged toward the bow, his wide back round and large as a barrel, out of the water.

"Gaff him!" I yelled hoarsely.

Captain Mitchell reached over him and hauled on the big gaff. It did not even stick in the fish for a second. I could not speak. I expected the tuna to smash our boat and break away. But he only rolled wearily, and Bob dragged him closer. Captain Mitchell tried again, with like result. I feared he did not know how to use a detachable gaff such as we had built for swordfish. I yelled for Sid to try. He leaped over the engine box, attached the gaff to the pole and extended it out. The tuna was rolling alarmingly. My heart stopped beating.

"Take time. He's all in," shouted Bob, cool and hard.

Sid dropped the wide hook over the broad back and lunged back with all his might. He pulled the tuna against the launch. Bang! Slap! The big tail jarred me almost off my feet.

"Shiver our timbers!" yelled Bob. "That gaff won't go in his body. It's too big."

Sid hauled the gaff in, and plunging over the gunwale he caught the fish on the side of the head. It did not go deep, but it held. Still, if the tuna had been capable of violent action, he would have torn it away. Captain Mitchell as quickly put the other gaff in the mouth of the fish and jerked it through his jaw. Then Bob followed that action with a rope, slipping it through the ring on the gaff. When I saw the great fish had finally and surely been captured, I flopped back in my chair, dizzy, reeling, scarcely aware of the acclaim about my ears. . . . Captain Mitchell radiated delight and congratulations.

"Gamest tuna I ever saw or heard of," was his praise of the fish.

He measured 8 feet 4 inches in length, 6 feet 2 inches in girth and weighed 684 pounds.

V

Pacific Northwest

If there had been anyone to observe me closely during those trying and thrilling days he would have had something to tell. Perhaps his point of view as to what was funny would have differed materially from mine. Tragedy and comedy in fishing are practically synonymous. It depends on who is looking and who is doing. To the former most incidents are funny, though to the latter they may be supremely tragical.

The happiest lot of any angler would be to live somewhere along the banks of the Rogue River, most beautiful stream of Oregon. Then, if he kept close watch on conditions, he could be ready on the spot when the run of steelhead began.

After breakfast R.C. and I donned waders and rubber boots and sallied forth valorously to meet certain defeat. We had been there before.

At the Mouth of the Klamath

Upon arriving in Seattle from Vancouver Island we sent our Tuna Club light tackles home by express, reserving only the fly rods and casting rods we expected to use on steelhead trout in Oregon. And this circumstance seems wholly accountable for the most extraordinary fishing adventure I ever had, up to that time. It happened on our way home, after the beautiful Rogue River, with its incomparable steelhead, had captivated us and utterly defeated us, and when we had given up for this trip.

Leaving Grant's Pass, Oregon, we visited the remarkable caves west of there, and then journeyed on over the Cascades to Crescent City, on the coast. I have no space to tell here of that beautiful ride and of the magnificent forests of redwoods still intact in northern California.

Some miles below Crescent City we came to a quaint little village called Requa. All we knew was that it was the place where we had to ferry across the Klamath River. The town, perched on a bluff, high over the wide river, appeared to have one street. A long low white tavern, old and weather-beaten, faced the sea, and the few stores and houses were characteristic of a fishing village. Indeed, the place smelled fishy. I saw Indians lolling around on the board walks, and as we drove down under the bluff toward the ferryboat I espied numerous Indian canoes and long net boats, sharp fore and aft.

We had to wait for the ferryboat to come across. While watching the wide expanse of river, more like a bay, I saw fish breaking water, some of them good heavy ones. Next I heard two young men, who were behind us in a Ford, talking about fish. Whereupon I got out and questioned them. Fish! Why, Requa was the greatest place to fish on the coast! In justification of their claim they showed me three Chinook salmon, averaging thirty pounds, and several large steelhead, all caught that morning in less than an hour.

"What'd you catch them with?" I inquired.

"Hand lines and spoons," was the reply.

Then I went back to our car and said to the driver who was about to start for the ferryboat:

"Back out of here somehow. We're going to stay."

R.C. and Lone Angler Wiborn [ZG's friend from college] eyed me with slow dawning comprehension. They were tired. The trip had been long and hard. The drive over that dangerous road of a thousand sharp curves had not been conducive to comfort or happiness. And on the whole they had been very much disappointed in our fishing. The end of September was close at hand, and we were due to arrive in Flagstaff, Arizona, on the 29th for our hunt in the wilds of Tonto. I appreciated their feelings and felt sorry, and rather annoyed with myself. But obviously the thing to do was to take a chance on Requa.

"Only one day, boys," I added, apologetically.

"What for?" queried R.C.

"Why, to fish, of course," I replied.

"Ahuh!" he exclaimed, with a note of grim acquiescence.

Lone Angler's face was perfectly expressionless, calm as a mask. He looked at R.C.

"Sure we're going to stop. I knew that all the time. I was just waiting until the Chief smelled fish."

"But we haven't any tackle," protested R.C.

I had forgotten that. Assuredly our trout tackles were not fitted for Chinook salmon.

"Maybe we can buy some tackle," I said. "Anyway, we're going to wet some lines."

Whereupon we went back to the inn, engaged rooms, got our baggage and tackle out of the car, and after lunch proceeded to investigate Requa in reference to things piscatorial.

Verily it turned out to be a fishing village, and the most picturesque and interesting one I ever visited. But all the tackle we could discover in the several stores were the large spoons and hand lines which were used there. We purchased some of the spoons, but the hand lines we passed by. Next we got one of the storekeepers to engage a launch and two skiffs and men to operate them for us, and somewhere around three o'clock we were out on the water.

I drew a long flat-bottom net boat, which was a great deal easier to handle than one would suppose from looking at it; the young man who rowed it was employed in the canning factory. He did not appear to be communicative, but he did say that the tide was going out and that the morning incoming tide was best.

The day was not propitious. With the sky overcast, dark, and gloomy, and little fine gusts of rain flying, the air cold, and the wind keen, it did not appear a favorable or opportune enterprise. I regretted submitting R.C. and Lone Angler to more privation, discomfort and work. Not that they were not cheerful! Two gamer comrades never pulled on wet boots in the dark of dawn! As for myself, I did not really care—the thing to do was to try—no one ever could tell what might happen. So we made ready to troll around that bay.

Lone Angler had found a steel rod, which he equipped with a trout reel full of light line, and he waved that at me with these enigmatical words: "Now fish, you Indian! We got here first!"

R.C. and I had found two green Leonard bait rods that had been made for me some years before and had never been used. They were about nine feet long, slender and light, but remarkably stiff, and really unknown quantities. I had ordered them to try on bonefish but had never used them. For bass they would have been ideal. I had a good sized reel half full of No. 6 linen line, and to this I tied the end of two hundred yards of braided silk bass line. For a leader I used one purchased at Campbell River for tyee salmon, and selected a moderate-sized spoon with two hooks. Thus equipped, and with misgivings and almost contempt at my incomprehensible assurance, I began to fish. I did not look to see what R.C. put on his rod. I knew he was doomed to catastrophe, so it did not matter.

There were several other boats out with fishermen, dragging hand lines behind them. Here and there on the yellow, rather muddy surface, fish were breaking. I trolled up and down and around that bay until I was thoroughly cold and tired and discouraged, without a strike. R.C. and Wiborn had no better luck. We went back to the inn, where a warm fire and a good supper were most welcome.

After supper I went over to talk with the storekeeper. He struck me as being part Indian, and I had confidence in him. I have Indian blood in me. I told him of our luck. He advised me to stay on and try the incoming tide, early in the morning. He said the outgoing tide was no good for fishing. So after considerable argument with myself I decided to stay.

"Boys, go to bed early," I said. "Tomorrow we'll try again."

Next morning was clear. I saw the sun rise. What a difference it made! The air was crisp and clear, invigorating, and the day promised to be one of Indian summer. We got to the boats early, before anyone else was down. The man with the launch had not arrived. Lone Angler said he would wait for him, while R.C. and I took out one of the long skiffs. I found it very easy to row.

Requa and the mouth of the Klamath did not seem the same place as yesterday. All the way down the bay I marveled at the difference. Could it have been wholly one of spirit? The sun was bright on the dancing waves. Fish were breaking everywhere. Pelicans were soaring and swooping and smashing the water. Myriad sea gulls were flying and screaming over the long sand bar. Low and clear came the sound of the surf.

I rowed straight for the mouth of the river to get into that narrow channel where my advisor had earnestly solicited me to be. Before we got down to it I was struck by the singular beauty of the place. Huge cliffs, all broken and ragged and colored, loomed over the west shore of the channel, and on the eastern side the long bar ran down to a point where I could see the surf breaking white.

"Say, some place!" exclaimed R.C., as he turned to look ahead. His eyes lightened with enthusiasm. "Fish, too . . . Gee! Look at that splash!"

When we got to the channel we found it to be several hundred yards long and perhaps a hundred wide at the narrowest part. It was not straight, having a decided curve. A swift current of dark green sea water was running in, to be checked by the pale yellowish muddy water of the river. There was a distinct irregular line extending across the channel, the line of demarcation where the fresh water contended against the incoming tide of salt water. There was indeed a contest, and the sea was slowly conquering, driving the river back. In this boiling, seething maelstrom salmon and steelhead and cohoes were breaking water. On the point of sand a flock of seagulls were gathered, very active and noisy. They were flying, wading, standing around, some of them fighting, and all of them screaming. Black cormorants were diving for small fish, and every time one came up with his prey in his bill several of the gulls would charge him and fight for his prize.

I took everything in with quick appreciative glances. How glad I was I had elected to try this morning! The charm of the place suddenly dawned on me. Looking out toward the sea I saw the breakers curl green and sunlit and fall with a heavy boom. Along the rocky point of the channel there was a line of white water, turbulent and changing, the restless chaffing of the waves. And that river of dark ocean water, rushing in, swelling in the center, swirling around the rocks and running over the sandy bar assuredly looked as dangerous as it was beautiful.

"New sort of place for us, hey?" inquired R.C. gazing around. "Never saw the like. What do you make of it?"

"Great!" I exclaimed. "I'll bet we break some tackle here."

I rowed to and fro along the edge of the incoming tide several times without R.C. getting a strike. Then I said: "I'm going to get out into that tide. You let your spoon down to where the salt and fresh water meet."

R.C. looked dubiously at the swelling green current, as if he thought it would be hard to row against, and perhaps not safe. I had found that the big skiff moved easily, and I had no trouble getting out fifty yards or more right into the middle of the channel.

Almost immediately R.C. yelled: "Strike! Missed!" Inside of a minute he had another and hooked the fish. It began to leap.

"Steelhead, by Jove!" he shouted. I rowed out of the current, back into the river water, and watched as pretty an exhibition of leaping fish as one would want to see. This steelhead cleared the water eight times and fought savagely. R.C. handled him rather severely. After he had landed the steelhead I rowed back into the channel and R.C. let his spoon down into that frothy melee of waters.

"This won't be much fun for you," asserted my brother.

"Fish!" I yelled. It was not easy to hold the boat in one place. Only by rowing hard could I keep even with a certain point. R.C. had two strikes, one of which was very heavy, but both fish missed the hook. Then he connected with one, a fish that kept low down and pulled hard. I rowed with all my might, holding the boat in the current while R.C. fought his fish. But I gave out and had to drift back into the dammed-up river water, where my brother soon landed a cohoe.

"Let's try anchoring out there," suggested R.C. "Maybe we won't stick. But we can't drift out to sea, that's certain."

This was a good idea. Promptly rowing back to the same position, and then twenty yards farther, I dropped the oars and, scrambling to the bow, threw over the anchor. It caught and held in perhaps twenty feet of water. The boat swung down current and, straightening, rode there as easily as a cork. We were amazed and delighted. R.C. let out his spoon, down into that eddying, fluttering riptide, while I took up my own tackle to get it ready. This was a moment of full contentment. No hurry to fish! I gazed around me, at every aspect of this fascinating place, as if to absorb it with all senses. I saw that the attractive features were all increasing. The sun was higher and brighter. The sky had grown deeply blue. Thousands of sea fowl were now congregated on the sand bar, and their piercing cries sounded incessantly. There the sea could not be forgotten for a moment. How the green billows rose higher and higher to turn white and spread on the strand. The surf was beating harder, the tide coming in stronger. Foot by foot the yellow water receded before the onslaught of the green. How strange that was! These waters did not mix. Music and movement and color and life! Every time a rosy, shining steelhead leaped near the boat I had a thrill. I felt grateful to him for showing the joy of life, the need of a fish to play and have a moment out of his natural element. Yet I also wanted to catch him! This was not right, and I knew it, but the boy in me still survived and was stronger than all the ethical acquisitions.

"Wow!" yelled R.C., jumping up with his green rod wagging. I heard his reel whiz. "Did you see that son of a gun? Goodbye to your green rod!"

The fish broke water on the surface, but he did not come clear out. I saw the pink color of him and part of his back.

"Big steelhead. Pull him to the boat," I said.

"Aw!" That protest was all R.C. made. Perhaps he wanted to save his breath. For he certainly had all he could handle in that swift water. The steelhead did not jump or run; he just stayed down at the end of that millrace and defied R.C.

Fifteen minutes had passed when I inquired of my brother whether he intended to land that fish so that I could put my line overboard. No reply, but he risked my rod a little more! Meanwhile I saw the queer flat launch with Wiborn coming down the bay, and after it a half a dozen skiffs. R.C. paid no attention to them. He was intent on landing his steelhead. I did not think he would ever do so. What a terrific strain he put on that slender green rod. It bent double and more. Gradually R.C. worked that stubborn fish close to the boat, and there we had our trouble, for when, by dint of effort, he got the steelhead nearly within reach of my gaff, the swift current swept it away. Naturally I grew excited and absorbed in our fight with him and did not look up again until we finally captured him— not a steelhead, after all, but a ten pound cohoe.

When we had him in the boat we looked up to see the launch close at hand and a fleet of eight or ten skiffs anchoring or about to anchor right in front of us. For all we could see, there was only one rod in that formidable crowd, and that was a long flimsy buggy whip sort of pole in the hands of a girl. Her boatman was a young fellow who could not row, that was certain. They looked like tourists, bride and groom, perhaps. I hoped they would hook a good-sized salmon, but I knew if they did they would never catch it. Several of the skiffs kept coming on, and actually got in front of us, ready to let their anchors down where R.C.'s spoon was twirling. This was terrible. R.C. and I were trained in a school where an angler respects the rights of others. Besides, to use Lone Angler's favorite expression, "We got here first!"

R.C. yelled at them, and finally they reluctantly rowed out of direct line with us and let their anchors down somewhat to our right. Next my driver and his man, who had brought us down from Seattle, came splashing along in another skiff, and they anchored even with our position, not twenty feet distant. Lone Angler, coming in the launch on the other side, laughed at us. "Ha! Ha! You'll have a fine time—if you hook a salmon."

R.C. looked at me and I looked at him with the same thoughts in our minds—that here was a perfectly wonderful morning spoiled almost at its very beginning. Only a matter of twenty yards of the channel lay open, and that was to our left under the cliffs. All the space to the right was covered by skiffs with anchors and heavy hand lines down. What chance now had we to catch a fish? There were Indians in these boats and white natives of Requa, all probably fishing for their livelihood. We could see that they regarded us with friendly amusement, as if they would soon have some fun at our expense. Soon see the delicate little rods smashed!

"Reckon we're up against it," said R.C. soberly. "Hard luck, though. What a grand place to fish if those ginks weren't here."

"If we hooked a heavy fish now we'd not have one chance in a thousand, would we?" I queried, hopelessly.

"I should say not," replied my brother. Then suddenly he called out. "Look! Lone Angler has snagged on to something. Gee!"

Thus directed I saw Wiborn frantically hanging on to his little black rod. The launch was below us to our left. The fish he had hooked—most manifestly a big one—was running fast across the channel straight for the anchored skiffs. Plain it was to us how our comrade was suffering. Usually a skillful and graceful angler, here he was bent out of position, hanging on to his rod with both hands, obviously thumbing the reel with all his might, in an effort to turn that fish. In vain! The rod nodded, bent down, straightened—then the line broke, and Lone Angler fell backward into the cockpit of the launch. R.C. and I had to laugh. We could not help it. Humor is mostly founded on the mishaps of others! Lone Angler rose from his undignified position and seemed divided between anger and sheepishness. What a disgrace! When he saw us waving our arms he waved back at us.

"He was a whale!"

R.C. and I were next attracted by the commotion in the skiff nearest to us. My driver was a Greek named Pappas, and fishing was new to him. His companion must have known still less. From the yelling and rocking of the skiff and wild action, I gathered both of them had hooked fish at the same time. At any rate they were frantically hauling on their hand lines. The lines became tangled, but the boys kept on pulling. They got in each other's way. Something broke or loosened. Pappas nearly fell overboard and his friend, stupidly holding his limp hand line, made no offer of assistance. Finally scrambling back to safety, Pappas entered into a hot argument with his companion, and they almost came to blows.

Next, one of the natives in a skiff hauled in a good sized salmon, and others had strikes. Then suddenly the girl angler with the buggy whip rod had a strike that nearly jerked her overboard. She screamed. The rod went down, and evidently under and around the boat. The fair angler did not seem to want to catch the fish but to get rid of the rod. Her escort took it, holding an oar at the same time, and when he managed to stand up the fish was gone.

"What do you know about that?" queried R.C., ruefully. Manifestly it was no unusual occurrence to hook big fish at the mouth of the Klamath.

For answer I let my spoon drift down into the place where the salt tide was more and more damming back the fresh water. No sooner had it reached the spot when a heavy fish hit and began to run off with my line.

"Pull up anchor and grab the oars," I yelled. "We'll follow this bird."

R.C. lost no time, and before the fish had half my line off the reel, we were following him. He swam straight through the narrow opening between the cliffs and the anchored boats, out into the wide waters of the bay. There, by careful handling of the light tackle, I brought this fish to gaff in twenty minutes. It proved to be a Chinook salmon weighing twenty two pounds, the first of that species I had even caught and certainly large enough to inspire and lure me back to try again.

As we rowed back past the skiffs some of the natives called to ask us to show our fish. R.C. lifted it up. They were outspoken and fine-spirited in their tribute to the little tackle. We anchored again in the same place. Conditions were perceptibly changed. The current ran swifter, fuller, with more of a bulge in the center. It lifted our skiff, and I knew that soon the anchor would drag. The sea was booming heavier behind us, and the swell of the waves now rolled into the channel. All the lower end of the sand bar was covered with water. Yet still the black cormorants and the white gulls contended for the little fish. Their screams now were almost drowned by the crash and wash and splash of threshing waters. Still farther back had the dark-green tide forced the yellow river. There was a mist in the air.

R.C. and I let out our spoons together. This time they drifted and sank, down to the margin of the tide. Something hit my spoon but missed the hooks. I was about to tell R.C. when an irresistibly powerful fish ponderously attached himself to my spoon and made straight for the skiffs with their network of anchors and hand lines.

"Oh, look at him!" I wailed, as I tried to thumb my reel. It burned too severely.

"Good night! I knew it was coming. But stay with him till your hair falls out!" cried my brother, as he swiftly reeled in and then jumped to heave the anchor and get to the oars.

When he had done so and was backing the skiff down the channel all the two hundred yards of silk line were gone off the reel, and the green linen line was going. My fish ran straight for the boats, and then apparently began to zigzag. Not the slightest hope had I of saving either fish or line. It was fun, excitement, even if no hope offered. R.C. had risen to the occasion. If my line had been around a hundred anchors, he would not have quit. Lone Angler appeared beyond the skiffs, and he was watching.

"Whatever you do must be quick," was R.C.'s advice.

The whizzing of my reel began to lessen. I calculated that was because the line had become fouled on some of the anchor ropes. We cleared the first skiff. My line stretched between the anchor rope of the second skiff and the skiff itself. I had to pass my rod between skiff and rope. It went under. I heard my reel handle splashing round. Both natives and Indians were helpful, both in advice and with their efforts. They pulled in all their hand lines, the nearest of which was wound round my line. What a marvel it seemed that my fish apparently stopped pulling while we untangled my line from the big lead sinker and spoon on that hand line! But so it actually was! The next skiff had out a long slack anchor rope. It appeared that my line had fouled this deep under the water. I put my tip down, tried to feel the line, then dipped my rod under the rope and lifted it out on the other side. Wrong! I had only made a loop around the rope. I had to laugh. How futile! Yet I did keep on—did not surrender. I dipped the rod back again, and then a second time. The line came free. It began to run off my reel, faster and faster. There was only an inch of thickness left on the spool.

"I'm a son-of-a-gun if I don't believe we'll get clear," said R.C., giving in to excitement.

I had not yet awakened to any new sensation. It had been a foregone conclusion that I would lose this fish.

But I stood up and looked ahead. To my amazement my line was out of the water for a long distance ahead of my rod. Then I saw a man in the last skiff, standing up, holding my line high. It was slipping through his fingers.

"I got you free of my line. You're all clear now. He's on— and he's a whopper," called this fellow.

Impossible to believe my eyes and ears! I saw this fisherman, a big brawny man, bronzed by exposure. His face bore an expression of good will and pleasure and admiration that I will never forget. Somehow in a flash it electrified me with the idea that I might catch this fish.

"Look out, you'll fall overboard!" shouted R.C. "Brace your knees on the seat. I'll catch up with that son-of-a-gun!"

R.C. began to row fast, and fortunate indeed was it that he had grasped the situation. For as he got into action, I glanced at my reel to see only a very few laps of the green line round the spindle. I turned cold. For an instant my right hand seemed paralyzed. Then I began to reel in readily. With sinking heart I watched it, sure, painfully and dreadfully sure, that my fish had gotten away. Why had I given credence to a futile hope? Why had I been so foolish as to surrender to a wild dream? He was gone. Then the line suddenly came so taut that the reel handle slipped out of my fingers and knocked on my knuckles.

"He's on yet. Row fast. If I can only get back to the silk line!" I called.

R.C. saved me there, and very soon I had all the green line on my reel. With the stronger silk line to rely upon now I had more and more irresistible hopes. I could not help them. To hook that tremendous fish, whatever it was, to get safely through that maze of skiffs, anchors and hand lines, to feel the silk slipping on my reel—it was unbelievable, too good to be true.

R.C. rowed perhaps three hundred yards beyond the last skiff before I could get enough line in to feel safe. Then we took it more easily, and gradually I got so much line in that I knew the fish was close. In fact it soon transpired that he was directly under us, swimming slowly. This was good, and I could not have asked for more. But when he turned and swam back toward the skiffs—that was another matter. It made me sick. It began to worry R.C.

More and more I thumbed the reel. The rod bent in a curve so that I had great difficulty in keeping the tip up. I did not dare look often at the rod, because when I did I would release the strain, and the fish would take line. At times it would be nip and tuck. Then when I held him a little too hard he would make off toward the skiffs and the channel. In time he led us back to within fifty yards of the danger zone.

"Hold him here or lose him," said R.C. sharply. "No use to follow him farther . . . Be awfully careful, but hold him. That rod's a wonder or it would have broken long ago."

I stepped up on the stern seat and desperately strained every nerve . . . . To hold that fish, to check him, turn him and lead him without breaking rod or line, seemed an impossible achievement.

I elevated the rod and shut down on the reel. Slowly the arch of the rod descended, the line twanged like a banjo string, and just as something was about to break I released the pressure of my thumb and let the fish have a few feet of line. Then I repeated the action. Again!

"Row just as slowly as possible," I admonished R.C. "Not back, but across, quartering the current. Maybe that will turn him."

R.C. had no answer for me then. He rowed with great caution. And the fish gradually worked down toward the other skiffs at the same time that our boat was moving across the current. I could see all the other fishermen watching intently. We were close enough for them to see clearly our every move. From somewhere came Lone Angler's call of encouragement.

For me those moments were long, acute, fraught with strained suspense. How many times I closed down on that reel I never counted, but they were many. My efforts to continue this method could not have lasted long. My arms ached and my right hand became almost numb. I grew breathless, hot, and wet with sweat, and when my eyes began to dim from the strain of nerve and muscle, I knew the issue was short.

My fish had just about reached the zone of the anchored skiffs when almost imperceptibly he began to sheer to the right. Not a minute too soon! R.C. let out a pent-up whoop.

"We're leading him," he said. "Careful now. Only a little more and we'll be out of danger."

I had stood about all I could stand of that strain, so that even if the fish did come with us a little, it was not easy for me. Gradually we worked him across the outlet of the river, behind the rocky bluff into wide placid waters. There I let him swim around while I rested my aching arms and cramped hands. Soon I felt equal to the task again and began to work on him. In the deep still water I soon began to tire him, and in a half an hour more he came to the surface and wearily leaped out, a huge Chinook salmon. Eventually he gave up and we lifted him aboard.

Then I was indeed a proud and tired angler.

"Good Lord! Look at that fish—to catch on bass tackle!" exclaimed R.C.

Broad and long and heavy, silvery and white, with faint spots and specks, and a delicate shimmering luster, with the great sweep of tail and the cruel wide beaked jaws, he was indeed a wonderful fish.

We rowed back to the point to exhibit him to the interested spectators, and then we went ashore on the sand bar to take pictures. It was all I could do to lift him high enough. Fifty seven pounds! That was not an excessive weight to lift with one hand, but I was exhausted.

R.C. and Lone Angler refused to compete with me any more that day. I heard R.C. speak in an undertone to Lone Angler, and what he said sounded something like, "Hope he's got enough this trip!"

This I pretended not to hear, and I told my companions to take a last look at the most fascinating and thrilling place to fish I had ever seen. The world is wide and there must be innumerable wild beautiful places yet unexplored that await the hunter and fisherman. Of these I am always dreaming and creating mental pictures. Yet the waters a fisherman learns to love always call him back.

Requa, the fishing hamlet, quaint and old-fashioned, picturesque and isolated, stood out on a bluff above the Klamath and faced the sea apprehensively. By the sea it lived. And its weather-beaten features seemed to question the vast heaving blue.

Down under the bluff the river was damming against the encroachment of the sea, and now the green water was slowly receding before the yellow. Ebb tide! The salmon and the steelhead had ceased playing on the surface. But the glancing ripples were still there, the swooping pelicans and the screaming gulls, and the haunting sound of the surf.

from Rocky Riffle

That old adage "the third time is the charm" worked truthfully for me on my 1924 trip to Oregon. It was a wonderful fishing experience, beginning disastrously for me, wearing on through the miserable and inexplicable bad luck, and winding up gloriously.

* * *

For days I had used a five-ounce rod and a lighter reel, a cheap one that had given me trouble. It was necessary to have a reel which would hold a hundred yards of line besides the forty yards of casting line. I had given my Hardy reel to R.C. The eight-ounce rod and heavy reel and line I had started out with had been abandoned through Burnham's [ZG's guide] advice. "You'll wear your arm out," he protested. And indeed I did.

From my collection of rods he selected a five-ounce Leonard. This I equipped with the only reel I had left, and a medium weight line. To me that tackle appeared far too light, yet I certainly appreciated the less amount of effort required in casting. And after two weeks of constant endeavor—practice—practice—I had learned to cast very well up to sixty feet. But what had not happened to me, in the way of tantalizing opportunity and miserable misfortune, never happened to any angler on this earth.

Every angler has bad days, except those few called lucky-stab anglers, for whom the fish seem to crawl out on the bank. . . . Some anglers have a bad season now and then. But I have never met an angler who had the same brand of misfortune that haunts me. In a way these spells resemble those batting slumps I used to get in college and professional baseball days. I would be hitting at a high clip around .400 average. But then one day I would hit the ball just as hard, but right at some fielder. The same would happen next day. That would focus my mind on the accident of bad luck. It would irritate and then worry me. I would fall off in batting until I ended in a regular slump and could not hit a ball tied on a string. Baseball slumps are common to every ball player. They are real and one of the peculiar weaknesses or misfortunes of the game.

My angling bad luck always seemed so singularly exasperating. At the outset of a trip I would utterly have forgotten it. Suddenly it would rise up like a hydra-headed monster. And there I was with my old giant beside me, like a shadow. The familiar old mood would return, and following it, the ridiculous certainty that I must labor ten times as hard and ten times as long as any other fisherman, to catch the illusive fish which so willingly attached itself to his line.

Maybe this tormenting mental aberration visits all anglers. What a relieving thought! But I can never believe that.

These Rogue River steelhead must have had a council before my arrival to decide upon the infinitely various and endless tricks they would play upon me. To be sure, they played a few upon my comrades, but the great majority, and the hopeless ones and the terrible ones, fell to my lot.

During those unforgettable ten days I kept secret and accurate account of what happened to R.C. and the boys. Some of this I saw, myself; part of it I learned at the general campfire narratives of the day's experience; and the rest I acquired by a casual and apparently innocent curiosity.

To some wag of a writer are credited the lines anent the universal fisherman: "he returneth in the evening smelling of strong drink, and the truth is not in him." I regard this as an injustice to many anglers. The best and finest anglers I have known did not return in the evening redolent of drink. And outside of a little exaggeration, natural to the exciting hour and the desire to excel, the tales of these fishermen could be accepted as truth.

As to R.C. and the boys, the weakness in my argument may be that they did not tell everything, or that they did not observe keenly or remember correctly. At any rate, the monstrous fact seemed to be that, during these ten days, I had as many strikes from steelhead as all of them put together.

But how vastly different the conditions of my strikes! Here was where the fiendish tricks of the steelhead began. For me the river was empty of fish at first; then suddenly they began to rise. They bewildered me. They flustered me. They baffled me.

If I made a poor cast, with a bag in my line, then a steelhead would rush the fly. Another would suck the fly in when it floated deep, and spit it out before I was aware I had a strike. Whenever I cast from an awkward or precarious position I was sure to feel a nip at my fly. And once—crowning piece of incredible bad luck of that whole trip!—when I was wading far out in the river, I had a strike on my back cast. My fly hit the water behind me and a rascally steelhead took it. I thought I was fast to the familiar willow or rock. When I turned to free myself a big broad steelhead leaped and savagely shook out my hook. I was stunned, then insulted, then furious. Could anything worse happen?

Many a rosy silvery steelhead loomed up out of the dark depths and put his game snub-nose against my fly, as if he meant to gulp it. But he did not. Many a steelhead, always choosing the inevitable and unaccountable instant when I was not ready, would strike my fly hard and jerk the slack line out of my hand. Faithfully I would cast for a whole hour, on the *qui vive* every instant, then just as I relaxed or looked away from my leader, or lifted my foot to step—smash!

Along with all these dreadful happenings occasionally I would hook a steelhead or he would obligingly do it for me. Then he would proceed to show me how quickly he could get off. The time came, however, when I held one for a long hour. I did not see this one rise. But I felt him hook himself. He was heavy. He swam upstream and stayed in the current. R.C. yelled encouragement. I replied with Takihashi's classic expression, "He stick right there!" Indeed he did. He never leaped, never made a fast run, never frightened me by a sudden move. He plugged deep. He got behind this stone and that one, and under the ledge across the river, and he stayed by each place a long time, tugging at my line. My rod nodded with his jerks. At last, after a half an hour or more, he came toward me and got behind another stone, in a deep eddy. Here he plugged slower and slower. Several attempts to lead him forth proved futile. But at least he gave up plugging and allowed himself to be led out of deep water. R.C. had decided it was a salmon. So had I. But when I led him into the shoal water I saw the beautiful opalescent glow of a steelhead. When he came clearly into view and I had actual sight of his great length and depth my heart swelled in my throat. Still, no angler could have handled him more gently. He rolled and twisted—rolled and twisted, and finally he twisted the slight hold loose. I saw him drift on his side, gleaming rosily, then right himself and swim off the bar into deep water. . . .

On October 15th we were due in southeastern Oregon, to take a hunt in a new country. I had still several days to fish before we started, and I could prolong the stay a couple of days longer, if desirable. R.C. now had eighteen steelhead to his credit, taken on a fly. The boys had added several to their string. And I still cherished unconquerable hopes. Next day I actually caught a steelhead on a fly, so quickly and surprisingly that I scarcely realized it.

I went down to the river later than usual, and found Ken and Ed casting from the dry rocks at the head of Rocky Riffle. R.C. was about in midstream. When I rigged up my tackle I put on an English salmon fly. It was unlike any fly the steelhead had been rising to, and I meant to try it just for contrariness. Wading in fifty feet above Ken, I made a preliminary cast and let the fly float down. Tug! Splash! A steelhead hooked himself and leaped, and ran right into the water Ken was fishing. I waded out, ran below, and fought the fish in an eddy, and soon landed it, a fine plump steelhead weighing about four pounds.

"Bingo! Out goes a fly—in comes a fish!" exclaimed Ed. "Say, you're a fast worker!"

Ken cupped his hand and yelled up to R.C., "Hey, Rome, he's busted his streak of bad luck!"

R.C. waved and called back: "Good night! Lock the gate."

I took R.C.'s good-natured slang—an intimation that they would now have to look out for me—as a happy augury for the remaining days. Next I caught three, a small one, another around four pounds, and a third over five and a half.

"Too late, old boy!" quoth R.C. "I have you trimmed. Nineteen to date, and the biggest seven and three-quarters."

"Heavens!" I replied. "Can't you recognize a grateful and innocent angler? I don't dream of equaling your splendid record. Too late, indeed!"

"Well, I reckon I'd better cinch this fishing trip," he said drily. "There's no telling how you'll finish. I'll stick on the job."

The day before our last day found me with a total of twelve steelhead, the largest weighing six pounds. I was seven behind R.C. Yet still no ambition or even dream of catching up with him crossed my mind. I was fishing desperately hard to prove something to myself, as well as for the thrill and joy of it.

The day happened to be Sunday, a still, cloudy day, threatening rain. I reached Rocky Riffle ahead of everybody, even the native fishermen that usually flocked there on this day. It was a fishy day if there ever was one. I had before me the pleasure of fishing that quarter mile of best water all to myself. I seemed to be a different angler from the one who had first waded in there nearly three weeks before. Trial, struggle, defeat, persistence—how they change and remake a man! Defeats are stepping stones to victory.

The water was dark, mirroring the shade of the green mountain slope opposite. It had amber shadows and gleams. Autumn leaves floated on the swift current. From upstream came the shallow music of the riffle; from below the melodious roar of the channel sliding over the rocks into the deep pool.

Wading in to my hips, I began the day with a cast far from perfect and short of record distance, but I placed it where I wanted to and softly, at the end of a straight leader. Thus I worked downstream.

Suddenly, as the current swept my line down even with me, I saw a wave, then a dim pale shape, seemingly enormous in length. Lazily this steelhead took my fly. When I struck I felt the fly rip through his hard mouth. He made an angry swirl as he disappeared. "Oh! Why can't I hook one of these big fellows!" I muttered, groaning inwardly. And I went on with a grim certainty that I soon would do so. After making a few casts I waded down several yards. From the instant my fly touched the water until I withdrew it to cast again I was strung keen as a whipcord. I had paid dearly for my lesson.

My line straightened out with fly sunk. Then came a vicious tug. Quick as a flash I struck and hooked what felt like a log. Down river he raced and my reel sang. He did not leap. With wagging rod held high—no easy task—I began to wade out and down. But I could not make fast enough time. I wallowed, plunged. Then I forgot to hold the loose click on my reel. It slipped off, releasing the drag, and the spool whizzed. I felt a hard jerk—then a slack line.

"That *was* a ten-pounder," I muttered, and then I gave vent to one of those emotion-releasing cuss words. As I pulled out the loops of the tangled line my fingers trembled. At last I got my line in, to find the leader minus a fly. Wading out, I sat down to put on another of the Golden Grouse flies. A glance up and down stream failed to add other fishermen to the scene.

Below the place where I had hooked that big one there was a flat submerged rock in midstream. The water swirled around it, with little eddies below. On the second cast my fly floated beyond and round it. I caught a gleam of light as if from a mirror under the surface. I sharply elevated my rod even as the steelhead struck the fly. Solidly came the weight. I knew he was hooked well. He ran upstream fifty feet, leaped prodigiously, showing himself to be a long, slim male fish. He had bagged the line against the current, and when he leaped again he got some slack. But the hook held. Downstream he turned, and I was hard put to hold the click on my reel. Twice it slipped, but I got it pushed back before the spool overran. Meanwhile the steelhead was running and I was following as fast as possible. Far down the channel he leaped again; then he went into the rapids. When I got to shore all my line was out. I ran splashing, scattering the gravel. But I saved the line, and in the pool below I bested this steelhead. He did not weigh much short of seven pounds.

I tied him on a string. Far upstream I made out Ken whipping his favorite hole, and in the riffle above I saw R.C.'s white hat. Rocky Riffle, wonderful to see, was still untenanted by any fisherman save myself. Too good to be true! Where were the native fishermen, all out on Sundays? It occurred to me that fishing must be too good up the river. The clouds did not break, though in places there was light. Ideal conditions improved. My day seemed to have dawned.

Beyond the flat submerged stone was a deep channel with a ragged break in the ledge. Here the water swirled smoothly. To reach it meant a long cast for me, fully sixty feet, even to the outer edge of that likely spot. Wading deeper, I performed as strenuously as possible, and missed the spot by a couple of yards. My fly alighted below. But the water exploded and the straightened rod jerked almost out of my hand.

My whoop antedated the leap of that Rogue River beauty. After I saw him high in the air, long, broad, heavy, pink as a rose, mouth gaping wide, I was too paralyzed to whoop. I had established contact with another big steelhead. Like lightning he left that place. He ran up the river, making four jumps, one of them a greyhound leap, long, high, curved. I had to turn so my back was downstream, something new in even that ever-varying sport. When he felt the taut line again he made such a tremendous lunge that I lost control of the click and could not prevent him from jerking my rod partly under water. I was up to my waist, and that depth and the current augmented my difficulties. The fish changed his course, swerving back between me and the shore, and he leaped abreast of me, so close that the flying drops of water wet my face. As I saw him then I will never forget him.

The slack line did not seem to aid him in any way, for he could not shake the hook. I anticipated his downstream rush, and was wading out, all ready, when he made it. Otherwise— *good night*, as R.C. was wont to say. He leaped once more, a heavy, limber fish, tiring from the furious speed. I followed him so well that he never got more than half the line. He took me down the channel, along the gravel far below, down the narrow green curve into the rough water below, where I could neither follow nor hold him.

That fight gave me more of an understanding of these gamefish and the marvelous sport they afford. As I wearily plodded back, nearly a half a mile, I felt sick, and yet I had to rejoice at that unconquerable fish. My tackle was too light, but I would not have exchanged it for my heavy one, with that magnificent fish again fast to my line.

from Down River

Next morning I took the trail for Winkle Bar. It led round the mountainside, through a thick forest of moss covered oaks and under wide spreading pines, cool, dark, and odorous of damp woods. And it came out on a bluff high above the river, from which point the wilderness scene would have been hard to rival.

Directly below, the river flowed dark and still between lofty cliffs that faced out of the dense forest. Ducks with white barred wings floated on the light mirroring water, and salmon breaking on the surface spread ever-widening circles. Across the river a magnificent fir forest rose out of a five-sloped canyon, rising bearded and mossy and black to the far, ragged summits.

Winkle Bar appeared to be a level flat of sand and gravel, dotted with clumps of small trees and sloping to a lengthy curve, along which the current glided.

I descended from my lofty perch and clambered over the boulder down to the sand. And then, up and down Winkle Bar, I fished all of one of the briefest and happiest days I ever had. I cast and rested and watched the river and listened to the murmur of the running water. Then I cast again. Where the hours sped I never knew. Not a sign of a strike or sign of a fish did I have. But that did not matter. There was something in the lonely solitude of the great hills, something in the comradeship of the river that sufficed for me.

Toward sunset heavy clouds rolled up out of the west and billowed over the mountains. A gray mist like a veil drifted toward me, and presently I was enveloped in a fine, blowing, soft rain, sweet and wet and cold to the face. The valley filled with a gray pall. I heard the roar of a shower come toward me, pass over, and on up the river. Then I watched and listened to another storm. I grew uncomfortably cold, and after nine hours of Winkle Bar I surrendered to fatigue and failing day.

Wearily I climbed to the high trail. The falling oak leaves, and the thick carpet underfoot, reminded me that autumn was at hand, the melancholy prelude to winter. The leaves rustled; the trail was lonely. No sign of living creature, nothing to suggest the presence of man. The twilight filled the side canyon where the tinkling little streams fell to the river. And at last the flicker of a campfire through the trees.

* * *

I heard the boys talking about the caddis flies falling upon the water to be devoured by small trout. I had observed the same phenomenon during the last several days at The Meadows. The next time I went fishing, I took particular pains to watch for these flies, and I discovered the larvae from which they had hatched sticking on rocks at the riverside. Presently I found a caddis fly three-quarters out of his shell, so to speak; or for that matter, more than half born. His tail still adhered to the inside of the mysterious little shell, and when I helped him out he flew a few feet over the water and then fell. Vainly he fluttered his dark wings to rise. I fancied there was terror in his efforts. But though he struggled desperately and fluttered over the surface, he did not have the strength to get up. Suddenly a little trout snapped him in voraciously. Gone! He had vanished like a flash.

I was at once confounded by this incident. And I gave up precious moments when I might have been fishing to think about the little caddis fly, the wonder of his origin and the tragedy of his end. My aberration reminded me of a remark made by an Eastern angler, criticizing my stories about fish. He said that I never caught any fish, and that all I wrote about were pretty little birds and flowers. That, naturally, was meant to be a derogatory statement, but somehow it pleased me. And here I was at my old tricks. There is such a thing as love of nature. The fate of the caddis fly had struck me deeply.

For half a second it had enjoyed freedom from its cell-like home, and then it had fallen into the merciless current to be espied by the sharp eyes of a trout. Perhaps nature meant that fly to take its part in the furthering of the species before completing its existence by becoming food for fish. But only a very small percent of nature's newly born creatures live long enough to propagate their kind. The life of this caddis fly, as a flying insect, was indeed brief. The facts connected with its presence there on that particular rock, however, were to my mind singularly wonderful and thought-provoking. The eggs had to be deposited in or near the river; the larvae had to go through a long period, perhaps months, of incubation; they had to crawl out on the rocks in the heat of the sun, where the caddis flies were born. What was the instinct behind this living organism? Who propelled it? Why were the caddis flies born just when the steelhead were coming up the river to spawn? Where did this great moving spirit of living organism originate?

Well, I never arrived any nearer the truth, for all my thinking. But I question the supposition of its being a waste of time. The next two hours of patient fly casting did not gain me as much.

from Rocky Riffle

Presently I arrived at a swift break in this riffle, where shallow water ran into deep, and the river narrowed, with gravelly bar on my side and rocky shelf on the other. As I rigged up my rod I had a vague sensation of sweetness, peace and beauty of time and place. Something haunting and far away attended my mental state. I waded in and began to cast, as best I could. It was not that I was conscientious or determined. Mind and eye merely answered to a dreamy instinct. I was fishing. All was well with the world and forgotten. I did not expect to catch a fish and did not care whether I did or not. I waded down my quarter-mile stretch, cast my fly a thousand times, more or less, went back to repeat the performance, and then again. The sun rose high and warm; the river murmured and flowed on; the enchantment of the day strengthened rather than lost its hold on me. For all I knew there might not have been a fish in that part of Oregon.

more from Rocky Riffle

When we reached a point opposite R.C.'s favorite water we stopped, and I sat down on a rock and laid my rod across my knees. He was looking down upon me.

"Take a crack at that place, won't you?" he asked.

"No. I'll enjoy more seeing you raise one," I replied.

"I haven't fished it for two days. And I've never failed to get a strike here. Let's see. I've caught five there, hooked three that got away, and raised some I missed. It's the greatest place on this river."

And finally we fell to arguing as to who should fish it this last evening. Finally I had to refuse positively and remind him of the passing time. At that he waded in.

The river was wide here, swift and smooth, quickening its current for the incline below. The water was flecked by spots of sunlight. The sharp-toothed ledge of rock gleamed like bronze under the water, and the deep dark channels opened alluring mouths to the current. R.C. waded out until he was up to his waist, and perhaps fifty feet above the tempting break in the level surface. He made several casts before he got his fly in line with the desired channel. Then he let it float down. I could see his leader shine.

He was elevating his rod preparatory to making another cast, when it was bent double and pulled down straight. His reel screeched. Then a big steelhead came out so fast and so high that we both yelled. I got up and ran into the water. Where was my camera? He leaped again, prodigiously, shooting up out of the first broken water, this time into the sunlight. He shone black and white. I had seen bigger steelhead, but not one such a jumper.

"Pile out and chase him," I yelled to R.C. "He's going through."

"I'll say he is," shouted my brother, surging toward shore. "Oh, look at him jump!"

Indeed I was looking. In fact, I was spellbound. My delight at his marvelous exhibition was embittered by the thought of my neglect in not bringing my camera. Four times more the steelhead sprang convulsively into the air, the last two leaps being out of the white water of the rapids. He had taken a hundred yards of line while executing those pyrotechnics. But R.C. had a large reel and a long line. He ran along the shore and I kept pace with him. The steelhead went over both the falls before R.C. could wind back a yard of line. Below the rapids the river swept to the right and presently opened out wide, with a deep cover running into a gravel bar. Here R.C. had it out with the fish. He made five more leaps before he yielded to the rod. Then R.C. drew him into the shallow water where the bottom was clean sand. The steelhead began that peculiar twisting, gyrating work which nine times out of ten tore out the hook. R.C. seemed divided by anxiety and caution. I was afraid to make a suggestion, for I saw that the fish was far larger than any R.C. had landed.

"Wade in behind him," called R.C., sharply, to me. "I'll try to beach him. If he breaks off, pitch him out."

That looked to me a very wise move, and I quickly waded to a point outside the fish. Not until R.C. had dragged him on his side in a few inches of water did I appreciate the size of the steelhead. He was so big that R.C. could scarcely budge him. Suddenly the hook tore out. I sprang to scoop the fish up on the bar. But it was not necessary. He only gaped with wide jaws and curled up his broad tail.

"Ten pounds!" I yelled, with wild enthusiasm, and picking up the steelhead I carried him a safe distance up the bank. There R.C. weighed him on the little scales. An ounce or so over nine pounds! R.C. was too elated to talk. Not for long years had I seen his face alight like it was then. Not even when he had landed his four-hundred-pound broadbill swordfish had he looked so happy.

The steelhead lay flat on the gravel. I stared, longing for the art of the painter, so as to perpetuate the exquisite hues and contours of that fish. All trout are beautiful. But this one of sea species seemed more than beautiful. He gaped, he quivered. What a long broad shape! He was all muscle. He looked exactly what he was, a fish-spirit incarnate, fresh run from the sea, with opal and pearl hues of such delicate loveliness that no pen or brush could portray them. He brought the sea with him and had taken on the beauty of the river.

Three Years Later, Again on the Rogue

I did not start in fishing very soon. I wanted to rest and watch the green hills and listen to the river. . . . After several days I got out my tackle and—after my Tongariro [New Zealand] experience in 1927, when I caught eighty-seven trout—I expected to catch all the steelhead in the Rogue. Well, in four days I never raised a single trout. The first day I laughed and joked; the second day, I wondered, and I worked harder; the third day I swore; and at the end of the fourth day I began to feel badly. A fisherman cannot help this. It is in him.

VI

New Zealand

There is always something so wonderful about a new fishing adventure trip. For a single day, or for a week, or for months! The enchantment never palls. Years on end I have been trying to tell why, but that has been futile. Fishing is like Jason's quest for the Golden Fleece.

*   *   *

Soon all the annoying sensations returned, and I began to feel a little seasickish from the infernal toss and pitch of the boat. The rain poured down in a torrent. Still, I fished on, a most miserable wretch. As many and many a time before, I wondered what made me do this. What fettered me to this unhappy state? How utterly absurd and perfectly asinine this fishing game in such weather! I would certainly start back to camp presently, to a warm fire, clothes and supper; still, I kept on fishing. I did not envy, nor would I emulate, the myriad anglers who had recourse to strong hot whisky, but I at least understood them. . . . The boy in me existed as always. It was this then that nailed me to my martyrdom; this enchantment of mind, this illusion.

Black Marlin

That night the strong wind beat the flaps of my tent, the *ti* trees moaned, and the flags rustled. The tide surged into the bank, low, sullen, full of strange melody. And it seemed to me that an old comrade, familiar, but absent for a long time, had returned to abide with me. His name was Resignation.

Daylight next morning disclosed gray scudding clouds and rough darkened water. We remained in camp and tried our hands at the many odd jobs needful to do but neglected. After a while the sun came out, and at noon the wind appeared to lag or lull. The thing to do was to go fish. I knew it, and I said so.

Out at Bird Rock we found conditions vastly better than we had expected. The schools of bait, white and frothy, were working everywhere, with the sea gulls screaming over them. High swells were rolling in, but without a break or a crest. Four boats besides ours were riding them. The clouds had broken and scattered, letting in a warm sunshine.

We trolled around the rock, to and fro past the churning foamy schools of *kahawai*, and out farther, long after the captain had taken to drifting. At last we raised a large striped marlin. He was so quick that he got hold of a teaser. That made him wary, and though he at last swam off with my bait, he soon let it go. After such treatment we took to drifting. Pretty soon Frank called:

"They're waving on the captain's boat."

"Sure enough," I said. "Guess he must have a strike or have seen a fish."

But when Bill appeared waving the red flag most energetically, I knew something was up. It took us only a moment or two to race over to the other boat, another one for me to leap aboard her, and another to run aft to the captain.

His face was beaming. He held his rod low. The line ran slowly and freely off his reel.

"Got a black marlin strike for you," he said with a smile. "He hit the bait, then went off easy . . . Take the rod!"

I was almost paralyzed for the moment, in the grip of amaze[ment] at his incredible generosity and the irresistible temptation. How could I resist? "Good heavens!" was all I could mumble as I took his rod and plumped into his seat. What a splendid, wonderful act of sportsmanship—of friendliness! I think he realized that I would be just as happy over the opportunity to fight and capture a great black marlin as if I had had the strike myself.

"Has he showed?" I asked breathlessly.

"Bill saw him," replied the captain.

"Hell of a buster!" ejaculated Bill.

Whereupon, with chills and thrills up my spine, I took a turn at the drag wheel and shut down with both gloved hands on the line. It grew tight. The rod curved. The strain lifted me. Out there a crash of water preceded a whirling splash. Then a short blunt beak, like the small end of a baseball bat, stuck up, followed by the black and silver head of an enormous black marlin. Ponderously he heaved. The water fell away in waves. His head, his stubby dorsal fin, angrily spread, his great broad deep shoulders climbed out in slow wags. Then he soused back sullenly and disappeared.

"Doc, he's a monster," exclaimed the captain. "I sure am glad. I said you'd get fast to your black marlin."

After the tremendous feel of him, and then the sight, almost appallingly beautiful, my uncertainty eased. He was there, solid and heavy. Whereupon amid the flurry of excitement on board I settled down to work, to get the hang of the captain's tackle, the strange chair and boat. None of these fitted me, and my harness did not fit the rod. But I had to make the best of it.

The swordfish headed out to sea, straight as an arrow, and though I pumped and reeled with fresh and powerful energy, he gained line all the time. We had to run up on him so that I could get the line back. My procedure then was to use all the drag of reel and hands I dared apply. This checked him. He did not like it. Slowly the line rose, so slowly that we all knew when and where he would show on the surface, scarcely a hundred feet away. Frank and Peter, in my boat, were opposite, running along with us; and they were ready with the cameras. Mitchell and Morton also had cameras in hand. What a long time that break was in coming. A black blunt bill first came out. Then with a tremendous roar of water the fish seemed to slip up full length, a staggering shape of black opal, scintillating in the sunlight, so wide and deep and ponderous, so huge in every way, so suggestive of immeasurable strength that I quaked within, and trembled outwardly with a cumulation of all the thrills such moments had ever given me.

As he thumped back, sheets of green and white spread, and as he went under he made a curling swirl that left a hole in the water. Then he sounded, but he did not stay down long. That is one of the fine things about marlin swordfishing. As he came up again at the end of that run, I had to have the help of the boat to recover two hundred yards of line.

The sun had come out hot. The seas were flattening. I began to sweat and burn, but never did an angler enjoy such results of labor. This swordfish was slow. I could tell what his moves would be. Still, remembering the others that had fooled me, I did not trust him. With hawk eyes I watched the tight singing line. If it curved the least at the surface I saw and gauged accordingly.

When we ran close again it was evident that the black marlin meant to rise and come out. How wonderful to see the line rise! To expect the leap and know for sure! We were all ready, with time to spare. Yells of various kinds greeted his glistening bulk, his great wagging head. He veritably crashed the water. And he rose so high that he lifted my line clear of the water, straight and tight from fish to rod, ten feet above the surface. That was a remarkable thing; and I did not remember having it happen to me before.

He led us out to sea, and in two miles he flung his immense gleaming body into the air ten times. Naturally this spectacular performance worked havoc with my emotions. Every time I saw him I grew a little more demented. No child ever desired anything more than I that beautiful black marlin. It was an obsession. I wanted him, yet I gloried in his size, his beauty, his spirit, his power. I wanted him to be free, yet I wanted more to capture him. There was something so inexpressibly wild and grand in his leaps. He was full of grace, austere, as rhythmic as music, and every line of him seemed to express unquenchable spirit. He would die fighting for his freedom.

Whenever he showed himself that way I squared my shoulders and felt the muscles of Hercules. How little I suspected pride goes before a fall!

Again I maneuvered to work close to him, and this time saw the double line slip out of the water. That was an event we all hailed with a shout.

"How much double line?" I asked the Captain.

"Only fifteen feet," he replied dubiously. "You see that line is short anyway. I couldn't spare more."

This was the beginning of the other side of the battle, the fearful, worrying, doubtful time that was to grow into misery. A great fight with a great fish runs all the gamut of feelings.

Grimly I essayed to pump and reel that double line to my clutching thumbs. I got it almost to the tip of the rod. As the leader was only twenty feet long my black marlin was close. I risked more, straining the rod, which bent like a willow.

"I see him," yelled somebody out forward. Captain Mitchell and Morton ran with their cameras.

Suddenly the double line swept down and my reel whirred. A quick wave heralded the rise of the swordfish.

"Look sharp!" I called warningly, as I released my drag.

As he had been slow, now he was swift. Out of a boiling hissing smash he climbed, scarce a hundred feet from the boat, and rose gloriously in the light, a black opal indeed, catching the fire of the sun. But he could not clear the water. He was too heavy. I saw his great short club bill, his huge gaping jaw, his large staring black eye, terrible to behold. My own voice dinned in my ears, but I never knew what words I used, if any. His descent was a plunge into a gulf, out of which he thundered again in spouting green and white, higher this time, wilder, with catapultic force—a sight too staggering for me ever to see clearly enough to describe adequately. But he left me weak. My legs, especially the right one, took on the queer wabbling, as if I had lost muscular control. If the sight of him was indescribable, then much more so were my sensations.

Tense we all were, waiting for another burst on the waters. But it did not come. My swordfish quickened his pace out to sea. The sight of him, so close, had acted as a powerful, even an intoxicating stimulant. Like a fiend I worked. Half an hour of this sobered and steadied me, while it certainly told upon my endurance. I had labored too violently. As many and many a time before, I had not kept back a reserve of strength.

Suddenly with a crack the reel came off the rod. My grasp of it kept it from going overboard. "Quick!" I yelled frantically. "The reel's come off. Help!"

The situation looked desperate. I released the drag, letting the swordfish free of strain. Fortunately he did not rush off. While Captain Mitchell bound the reel seat on the rod, I performed the extremely difficult task of carrying on without a bungle.

Naturally, though, I lost confidence in the tackle. I could not trust it. I did not know how much I could pull; and that with a new trouble, a slow rolling swell which made it almost impossible for me to keep my seat in the chair, operated to help the fish and wear me out. It took time to conquer this, to get back what I had lost.

Then the reel broke off again. As I was holding it, more than the rod, I lost my balance and half fell into the cockpit. All seemed lost. Yet, like the fool I was, I would not give up, but stung my companions to quick and inspired tasks, and then got the reel fastened on again. And in a short time I had gained all the line lost. My spirits did not revive to any degree, but at least grim disaster left me for the moment.

In the next half hour, strange to relate, encouragement did rise out of the gloom; and I worked so well and so hard that I began to imagine I might whip this great fish yet. To that end I called for my boat to come round behind us, so Peter could board us with my big gaff, and Morton could go on board my boat with his motion picture camera. This change was made easily enough, and with Peter beside me I felt still more hopeful. I knew from the feel of my back, however, that I had overdone it, and should ease up on the rod and patiently save myself. But this was impossible.

Then the reel broke off the third time. I almost pitched both rod and reel overboard; but Peter's calmness and his dexterous swift hands had a cooling influence on me.

"You could fight him better from our boat," said Peter.

Why had I not thought of that before? This boat was new to me; and the location of the chair, the distance to the gunwale, the fact that at some turns of the chair I had no support for my feet, made all my extreme exertion of no compelling avail. After a little more of it, I again called for my boat to run close.

I released the drag, and holding the rod up, with Peter holding me, I made the change in to the *Alma G.* without mishap. And then in my own chair I fell to fighting that

147

swordfish as hard as I had fought him two hours before. He felt it, too. Slowly his quick, free, tremendous moves lost something; what, it was hard to say. Eight times I got the double line over the reel, only to have it pulled away from me. Each time, of course, the leader came out of the water. Bill, who had come on board my boat with the captain, leaned over at least and grabbed the leader.

"Careful," I warned. "One hand only. Don't break him off."

Twice Bill held momentarily to the leader, long enough to raise my fluctuating hopes.

Peter stood back of me, holding my chair. The tremendous weight of the swordfish, thrown against the rod socket, pushed the chair round farther and farther.

"Mr. Grey," said Peter. "What you want on that fish is your big tackle. If you pull the leader up again, I can slip your line through the swivel."

"By George," I panted. "Peter—you're—the kind of boatman—I want around."

Fired by this sagacious idea I strained rod, reel and line and eventually drew the leader up a foot out of the water— two feet—three, when Bill grasped it, and Peter with swift careful fingers slipped my line through the swivel, knotted it, and then with a flash of knife cut the captain's line.

"By gad! That's great!" ejaculated the captain. "You'll lick him now."

Everybody whooped, except me, as I hauled away with the big rod that had killed so many fish. I seemed to have renewed strength—certainly I saw red for the moment and swore I would pull his head off. In short order I had the leader out of the water again, closer and closer, until Bill once more grasped it.

This time he held on. Frank kept the boat moving ahead. We gained on the fish. Slowly he rose, a huge shining monster, rolling, plunging. My heart leaped to my throat. Bill yelled for help. Peter, with gaff in right hand, leaned over to take the leader in his left. I could see how both men strained every nerve and muscle. That frightened me. How many great fish had I seen lost at the boat! The swordfish pounded the water white just out of reach. I ordered the men to let go; and with a thumping splash he disappeared and took line rapidly.

He seemed a changed swordfish. He ran off much line, which was hard to get back. He grew wild and swift. He had got his head again. Perhaps the stronger tackle, the narrow escape at the boat, had alarmed him. Anyway, he was different. He kept us going. But I felt master now. I knew I could whip him. My aching arms and paining back were nothing. His long runs did not worry me. Let him drag three hundred yards of line! But when he got too much line we shot ahead so that I could recover it.

So that stage of the fight went on and neared the end. I felt that it would mean victory. There are signs a fisherman can detect, movements and sensations which betray a weakening fish. I kept my knowledge to myself. How many mistakes fishermen make!

This period was somewhat after the third hour. It had not afforded me much relief, although a restored equilibrium certainly helped. The next action of significance on the part of Mr. Black Marlin was to sound. He had not attempted this before to any extent, but now he went down. I made no effort to check him. Indeed, that would have been useless. I watched the line slide off, in jerks, yard by yard; and through my mind went many thoughts, all optimistic. When a great fish sounds after a long fight, it is favorable to the angler. At the depth of five hundred feet the pressure of the water is tremendous, and farther down then the greater proportionately. Broadbill swordfish often sound with their last flurry of departing strength.

My black marlin continued to go down. I asked Captain Mitchell if his record nine hundred and seventy-six-pound marlin sounded like that.

"Yes, only not so deep; and earlier in the fight," responded the captain. "I don't like the idea of this fellow. He's getting too deep. Suppose he should die down there?"

"Well, I reckon the old tackle will lift him," I replied confidently.

Nevertheless Captain Mitchell's concern was transferred to me. It was too late to attempt more strain; indeed I had to ease off the drag. Slowly and more slowly sounded the swordfish, until he was taking inches instead of feet. Then, at last, he stopped taking line altogether. One thousand feet down! There he seemed anchored.

Hopefully I waited for some sign of his working back. Then I braced my shoulders, heaved on my harness, and stretched my arms in a long hard lift. The old rod described a curve, till it bent double and the tip pointed straight down at the water. I waited for the spring of the rod, for the slow rise of the tip that always helped so materially to bring up a fish. The spring came, but so slowly that I had more concern added to my trouble. By dropping the rod quickly and swiftly winding the reel I gained a few inches of line. This action I repeated again and again, until sweat broke out hot upon me. All the same a cold chill waved over my back. I realized my gigantic task. The great swordfish had fought to the last gasp and had died down at that tremendous depth. Now he was a dead weight, almost impossible to move more than a few inches at each lift. But still I had perfect confidence in the tackle, and that by pushing myself to extremes I could bring this black marlin up.

So I toiled as never before; and as I toiled all the conditions grew worse. It took both Captain Mitchell and Peter to hold my chair straight. The roll of the boat as it went down on a swell, added to the weight of the rod, pulled me from one side to the other, aggravating in the extreme.

Inch by inch! That old familiar amaze[ment] at myself and disgust at such Herculean drudgery took possession of my mind. What emotions were possible that I had not already felt? I could not name any, but I was sure there were some, and presently I must suffer them.

When I timed a heave on the rod with the rise of the swell I managed to gain half a foot perhaps. If I missed the proper second then I failed to gain line. And as I lost strength the roll of the boat grew harder to bear. I was swung from one side to the other, often striking my knees hard. Then the chair whirled around so that I had no brace for my feet, in which case only the support of Captain Mitchell kept me in my seat at all. It grew to be torture that recalled my early fights with broadbills. Still I sweated and heaved and toiled on.

The moment arrived when I became aware that my rod was dead. It bent down to the water and did not spring up a fraction of an inch. The life of the rod had departed on this giant black marlin. If despair had not seized me, followed by a premonition of stark tragic loss, I would have been happy that this wonderful Murphy hickory rod—which had caught the world's record tuna, seven hundred and fifty-eight pounds . . . nine broadbill swordfish and many marlin—had bent its last on such a wonderful fish. But all I thought of was now I could never lift him!

Yet so intense was my purpose and longing that I found both spirit and endurance to lift him, inch by inch, more and more, until I knew that if I did not die myself, as dead as both rod and swordfish, I would get him.

All of a sudden Bill yelled out hoarsely and wildly: "My Gawd! Look at that mako fin!"

We gazed in the direction indicated. As I was sitting down and hunched over my rod, I was the last to see. The others, however, yelled, shouted and otherwise exclaimed in a way calculated to make one thrill.

"He's fooling around that box of bait Peter chucked overboard," cried Frank.

"By gad!" ejaculated the captain, breathing hard.

Then I saw at quite some distance the yellow box, and close to it a dark fin glistening in the sun, cutting the water swiftly, and so huge that I could not believe my eyes.

"Boys, that's no fin," I said. "That's the sail of a boat."

"Oh, he's a monster," added Frank.

"Mr. Grey, that's the biggest mako fin I ever saw," said Peter, who was the only calm one of the lot.

"Captain, there's your chance. Go after him," I suggested forcibly.

"No. You need me here, Doc. We can't catch all the fish. A fish on the line is better than two in the water, you know."

"I don't need you," I protested. "I've got this black marlin killed, and I can lift him. Take my other big tackle and go hand a bait to that mako. . . . Say, but isn't that some fin? Never saw one to compare with it."

Captain Mitchell still refused; I actually had to drive him away from my chair. I yelled for the other boat to run close, and I saw Peter put my other big tackle in the captain's hands.

"Good luck!" I shouted as the boat sped away.

I could not forget my own fish, for the tremendous weight bore down upon my shoulders, but I just held on while I watched the captain circle that mako. The big dark green fin disappeared and then showed again. I had a feeling something tremendous was about to happen.

The intervening distance was close to a quarter of a mile. I saw the boat circle the fin, get ahead of it, slow down. Captain Mitchell leaned far forward with his rod.

Suddenly the fin vanished.

"Somethin' doin'" yelled Frank, "and there'll be more in a minute."

It appeared to me that the captain was jerked forward and lifted. I saw a low wide swift splash back of the boat. Next, the rod wagged most violently.

"Boys, he's hung that mako!" I shouted, with wild delight. Captain Mitchell's ambition to capture a great mako was second only to mine regarding the black marlin.

"*There he is!*" shrieked Frank.

A huge, long, round gold-white fish pierced the sky. Up, up! He had not raised the slightest splash. Up he shot, then over in the air—a magnificent somersault, and down, slick as a trick diver.

The enormous size of the mako, even at that distance, could not be mistaken.

"Oh, Peter, he's big, or am I seeing something?" I implored.

"Big? He sure is big. That mako will go over twelve hundred pounds."

As Peter ended, a cream-white torrent of water burst nearer to us, and out of it whirled the mako going up sidewise, then rolling, so his whole underside, white as snow, with the immense pectoral fins black against the horizon, shone clearly in my distended eyes. His terrific vigor, his astounding ability, were absolutely new in my experience with fish. Down he smashed into a green swell. We all heard the crash.

With bated breath we waited for his next leap; but it did not come. When we turned our fearful gaze back to the boat, we saw the captain reeling in a limp line. The mako had shaken free or broken off. I sustained a shock then that I could liken only to several of my greatest tragic fishing moments.

The comments of my comrades were significant of their feeling.

"Well, Mr. Grey," continued the practical Peter, "you've got a fish here that'll take some landing."

That nailed me again to my martyrdom; and somewhat rested, or freshened by the intense excitement, I worked prodigiously and to some purpose. Presently, when the pressure became overpowering, and I felt something in me would burst, I asked Frank to throw the clutch and start the boat very gently to see if we could not break the swordfish from his anchorage. We were successful, but I did not want to risk it again. The next time that ponderous weight became fixed, immovable, I asked Peter to reach down with one hand and carefully pull on my line, so as to start the fish again. This, too, was successful, without too great a risk. Once started, the fish came, inch by inch, until I gave out momentarily and he felt like an anchor.

The captain's return to my boat was an event. He looked pretty agitated. Among other things he said: "Great heavens! What a fish! I was terrified. It seemed that mako filled the whole sky. He was the most savage and powerful brute I ever saw, let alone had on a line!"

"Too bad! It makes me sick, Captain," I replied. "I never wanted anything so badly as to see you land that mako."

Then I went back to my galley-slave task again; and in a half an hour I had the great black marlin up. Never shall I forget the bulk of him, the wonderful color, the grand lines. We had to tow him in.

Sunset was at hand when we passed Bird Rock, where the black marlin had struck. The sea was smooth, rolling in slow swells, opalescent and gold. Gulls were sailing, floating, all around the rock, like snowflakes. Their plaintive sweet notes filled the air. Schools of *kahawai* were moving in dark patches across the shining waters. Cape Brett stood up bold and black against the rosy sky. Flocks of gannets were swooping in from the sea. In the west the purple clouds were gold rimmed above, silver below; and through the rifts burned the red-gold sun. I watched it sink behind the low cloud bank; and at the instant of setting, a glamour, an exquisite light, shaded and died. It was the end of day, of another of my ever-growing number of wonderful fishing days!

My black marlin might have been the brother of either of Captain Mitchell's. He had great symmetry, though carrying his weight well back to his tail. His length was eleven feet, eight inches; his girth five feet, six inches; and the spread of his tail three inches short of four feet. Seven hundred and four pounds!

The Tongariro River and The Dreadnaught Pool

I suppose many New Zealand anglers will inquire, as I am an advocate of the heaviest of specially made tackle for the great tiger fish of the sea, why I put such stress on the use of delicate and light tackle for the wonderful rainbows of the Tongariro. I suppose, at least I hope, the answer can be found in the perusal of my story, material for which and the writing of which cost me so much labor and pains.

Hoka, our genial Maori guide, whom I had begun to like very much indeed, averred one morning that the trout had begun to run up the river, for he saw them. Both Captain Mitchell and I could verify this. To our delight and exasperation, we saw them, too; but to make these rainbows rise to an ordinary fly was something which would tax the patience of a saint, not to mention a good deal of skill. The captain did it, and so did I, but at the expense of infinite labor. We resorted to large Rogue River flies, mostly number four, and then to salmon flies number two, and finally we got to dressing our own flies. This was fun for me. Some of the outlandish lures I dressed up should have scared a rainbow trout out of his wits. Nevertheless they answered the purpose, and one of them, a fly so extraordinary that I could not make another like it, turned out to be a "killer." The only difficulty about large flies was that they were hard to cast. By diligent practice and strenuous effort, however, I at length achieved considerable distance, making an average of sixty feet, often seventy, and rarely even eighty feet. And when I saw that gaudy fly shoot out to such extreme distance, I certainly felt exultant and vain.

We had word of another record catch of eleven fish at the mouth of the Tongariro. This was given us by Mr. Gilles, the mail driver, who stopped at our camp on an errand. He saw the fish and vouched for their weight; a fourteen-pound average, with the largest weighing sixteen and one-half pounds. All caught on a fly at night. But no other information had been vouchsafed. I asked Mr. Gilles many questions about this remarkable catch, very few of which he could answer. He was himself a fisherman of long experience, a native of Tokaanu, and it was his opinion that the trout were caught by fishermen letting out a large fly or spinner a hundred or two hundred feet from the boat and then drawing it back by hand until he had a strike. I shared this opinion.

By climbing to the bluff above the river, when the sun was high, we could see the big trout lying in the pale-green crystal water; ten, twelve, fifteen pound rainbows and an occasional brown trout, huge and dark, upward of twenty pounds. This was a terrible, though glad experience for Captain Mitchell and me. To sight such wonderful fish and not get a rise from them! Alma Baker took it more philosophically and considered the privilege of seeing them quite enough. Cap and I, however, wanted to feel one of those warriors on the end of a line. In the pool below camp we tried at sunrise, through the day, at sunset and then after dark. Fly fishing at night was an awful experience for me. I got snarled in the line. I continually hit my rod with my fly, and half the time it spun around the rod, entailing most patient labor. Moreover, I was standing through the night in ice-cold water. Finally I whipped the big hook in the back of my coat. That gave me sufficient excuse to go back to camp. What a joy the campfire! Captain Mitchell returned presently, wet and shivering. He did not complain of the cold water, but he lamented a great deal over the loss of his best fly. He had snagged it on a rock and nearly drowned himself trying to rescue it.

Next morning, while the rest of the party were at breakfast, I stole down to the bank and made a cast into the swirling waters. I made another, and when I strove to retrieve the line, lo!, I was fast to something that moved. I struck, and I hooked a trout. For fear he might rush out into the swift current, I held him harder than I would otherwise, and thus tired him out before he could take advantage of me. When I was sure of him, a fine seven-pounder rolling in the clear water, I yelled loudly. The whole breakfast contingent rushed pellmell to the bank, and to say they were amazed would be putting it mildly.

"By Jove," ejaculated Baker. "You lucky devil! That's a fine fish."

"I wondered where you were," added Mitchell, with an experienced eye on my fish.

"You fellows have to have your tea, you know," I responded cheerfully.

That was the prelude to a strenuous day for all of us. Baker elected to fish the pools below the camp, where he did not have to wade. Hoka took Captain Mitchell and me, accompanied by Morton, up the river.

"Only a little way, about a mile," said Hoka, with the smile that always robbed me of a retort. It was a long, long mile before we even got off the road; and even a short mile in heavy waders, three pairs of woolen socks, and iron-studded clumsy wading boots was always quite sufficient. I can pack a gun and walk light-footed far up and down canyons, but the wading paraphernalia burdens me down.

Hoka led us into a fern trail, one of those exasperating trails where the ferns hook your fishing line and leader and will not let go. Then he arrived at a precipitous bluff under which an unseen river roared musically. It was not the Tongariro. The captain naturally wanted to know how we got down.

"We go right over," replied Hoka, and with the remark he disappeared. We heard crashing in the ferns. Next I went "right over." I held my rods high above my head and trusted my seven-league, eight-ton boots to the depths. Then I went right over, but also down, my only concern being my rods. When at last I arrived at a comparative level, I awaited to see what would happen to my comrades. I knew there would be a fall all right. Soon I heard what might have been a rhinoceros plowing down the ferny cliff; but it was only Captain Mitchell who arrived beside me, hot, furious, forgetful of all save his precious pipe, which a tenacious fern still clung to.

The real fun, however, came with Morton. Our genial cine-matographer was burdened with cameras, also a pair of iron-hoofed boots that I had insisted he must wear. I have no idea how Morton got down, unless he fell all the way. We heard him talking vociferously to the obstructing ferns. At last he arrived, red of face, and grimly hanging on to his load. . . .

Hoka was waiting for us with his disarming smile.

"You came down easy," he said. "But this panel over the river will be hard."

"Huh! What's a panel?" I asked. "Hoka, I've begun to have suspicions about you."

He soon showed us the panel. It was no less than a rickety old pole bridge, swung on wires attached to branches of trees, and spanning a dark rushing little river that must have been beautiful at some other time. Just now it seemed a treacher-ous one. How the current swept on, down, down, rushing, swirling, gurgling under the dark over-reaching trees.

Hoka went first. He weighed seventeen stone, which in our language is over two hundred pounds; and I felt that if the panel could hold him it would certainly hold me. He crossed safely and quite quickly for so large a man. I went next. Such places rouse a combative spirit in me, and that made the cross-ing something different. Nevertheless, when I was right in the middle, where the thin crooked poles bent under my heavy boots, I gazed down into the murky water with grim assurance of what might happen if the poles broke. I got across, proving how unnecessary the stirring of my imagination often is.

Once safe on the bank I was tempted to yell something facetious to Morton and Mitchell. But I desisted, for this was hardly the place for humor. They reached our side without mishap, and then again we beat into the jungle of ferns and *ti* trees. It was hard going, but soon I heard the mellow roar of the Tongariro, and with that growing louder and louder I found less concern about difficulties. We came at length into an open thicket of *ti* brush, bisected by shallow waterways and dry sandy spaces, through which we emerged to the wide boulder-strewn river bank.

"This pool here is called Dreadnaught," said Hoka, pointing to a huge steep bluff strikingly like the shape of a dismantled man-of-war. It stood up all alone. The surrounding banks were low and green. After one glance, I gave my attention to picking my steps among the boulders, while Hoka kept on talking. "My people once fought battles here. They had a *pa* [fort] on top of this bluff. I'll show you graves that are wearing away. The skulls roll down into the river. Yes, my people, the Maoris, were great fighters. They stood up, face to face, and gave blow for blow, like men."

At last I found a seat on a log, laid aside my rods, camera and coat, and looked up. I was interested in the Dreadnaught Pool, of course, but as I did not expect to catch a trout I did not feel my usual eagerness and thrills. The captain probably would land one, but the few preceding days and the condition of the river had dashed my hopes. So I seemed a sort of contented, idle comrade, agreeably aware of the music of the river, of the westering sun, of the sweet open space all about me, and the dark mountain range beyond.

I espied Captain Mitchell, pipe in mouth, rod in hand, tramping over the boulders to the head of the pool.

"Hey, Cap, what're you going to do?" I shouted.

"Fuinish!" replied the Captain, whom you could never understand when he had that black pipe in his mouth.

Thus I was brought back to the motive of this climb, slide and plow back up to Dreadnaught Pool.

The Tongariro ran sweeping down in an S shape, between soft green banks; a white swift river, with ample green water showing, and rapids enough to thrill one at the idea of shooting them in a Rogue River boat. Not a canoe, thank you! The end of the last rapids piled against the hull of the Dreadnaught bluff. A little rippling channel ran around to the right, out of sight, but it must soon have stopped, for the high embankment was certainly not an island.

I began to grow more interested. The bluff had a bold, bare face, composed of three strata; the lowest a dark lava studded thickly with boulders, the next and the middle one a deep band of almost golden sand, and the topmost a gray layer of pumice in the top of which I saw the empty graves of the bygone Maoris.

The current deflected from the base of the bluff, sheered away and swept down through the pool, farther and farther out, until it divided into three currents running into three channels.

The lower and larger end of that pool grew fascinating to me. Under the opposite bank the water looked deep and dark. A few amber colored rocks showed at the closer end of the current. It shoaled toward the wide part, with here and there a golden boulder gleaming far under the water. What a wonderful pool! It dawned on me suddenly. The right channel, or the one farthest over, ran glidingly under the curving bank, and disappeared. I could not see the level below.

Points of rock and bars of boulders jutted out from a luxuriantly foliaged island. The middle channel was a slow wide shallow ripple, running far down. A low bare gravel bar rose to the left, and stretched to where the third channel roared and thundered in a deep curving rapid. Here most of the river rushed on, a deep narrow chute, dropping one foot in every three, for over a hundred yards.

I had to walk to the head of the rapid to see where the water ran, heaping up waves higher and higher, down the narrow channel that curved away under another high wooded bluff. This indeed was a green-white thundering Athabaska. Most of the water of the pool glided into the channel, growing swift as it entered. Green crystal water! I could see the bottom as plainly as if the depth had been ten inches instead of ten feet. How marvelously clear and beautiful! Round rocks of amber and gold and mossy green lay imbedded closely, like colorful tiling.

My gaze then wandered back over the head of the pool, where the captain stood hip deep, casting far across into the current. And it wandered on down to the center, and then to the lower and wide part of the pool. What a magnificent place to fish! I made up swiftly for my laggard appreciation. I could see now how such a pool might reward a skillful far-casting angler, when the rainbows were running. After a long climb up rapids, what a pool to rest in! There might even be a trout resting there then. So I picked up my rod and strode down to the river.

A clean sand bar ran out thirty yards or more, shelving into deep green water. Here a gliding swirling current moved off to the center of the pool, and turned toward the glancing incline at the head of a narrow rapid. The second and heavier current worked farther across. By wading to the limit I imagined I might cast to the edge of that bad water. I meant to go leisurely and try the closer current first. It was my kind of a place. It kept growing upon me. I waded into my knees and cast half across this nearer current. My big fly sank and glided on. I followed it with my eye and then gave it a slight jerky movement. Darker it became and passed out of my sight, where the light on the water made it impossible for me to see. I had scarcely forty feet of line out. It straightened out below me, and then I whipped it back and cast again, taking a step or two farther on the sand bar.

Then I had a look at Captain Mitchell. He was standing with that pose of incomparable expectancy and patience. No use for me to try to imitate him! The tilt of his old black pipe demonstrated his utter contentment. Well, I thought, I did not have any pipe, because I never smoked, but I felt I was just as contented as he. Indeed I was not conscious of any other emotion. The fact that we were ahead of the running season for trout had operated to inhibit my usual thrill and excitement. It was the game to fish, to keep on trying, but I had not the slightest idea of raising a trout. If it had been otherwise I would have told Morton to be ready with the camera.

My line curved and straightened. Mechanically I pulled a yard or so off my reel, then drew perhaps twice as much back, holding it in loops in my left hand. Then I cast again, letting all the loose line go. It swept out, unrolled and alighted straight, with the fly striking gently. Was that not a fine cast? I felt gratified. "Pretty poor, I don't think," I soliloquized, and stole a glance upriver to see if the captain had observed my beautiful cast. Apparently he did not know I was on the river. Then I looked quickly back at my fly.

It sank just at the edge of the light place on the water. I lost sight of it, but I knew where it floated. Suddenly, right where I was looking on this glancing sunlit pool, came a deep angry swirl. Simultaneously with this came a swift, powerful pull, which ripped the line out of my left hand and then jerked my rod down straight.

"Zee-eee!" shrieked my reel.

Then the water burst white, and a huge trout leaped in spasmodic action. He shot up, curved and black, his great jaws wide and sharp. I saw his spread tail quivering. Down he thumped, making splash and spray.

Then I seemed to do many things at once. I drew my rod up, despite the strain on it; I backed toward the shore; I reeled frantically, for the trout ran upstream; I yelled for Morton and then for Captain Mitchell.

"Doc, he's a walloper!" yelled the captain.

"Oh, biggest trout I ever saw!" I returned wildly.

Once out of the water I ran up the beach toward Captain Mitchell, who was wading to meet me. I got even with my fish and regained all but part of the bag in my line. What a weight! I could scarcely hold the six-ounce rod erect. The tip bent far over and wagged like a buggy whip.

"Look out when he turns!" called Mitchell.

When the fish struck the swift current, he leaped right before me. I saw him with vivid distinctness—the largest trout I ever saw on a line of mine—a dark, bronze-backed and rose-sided male . . . black-spotted, big-finned, hook-nosed. I heard the heavy shuffle as he shook himself. Then he tumbled back.

"Now!" yelled Captain Mitchell, right behind me.

I knew. I was ready. The rainbow turned. Off like an arrow!

"Zee. Zee! Zee!" He took a hundred yards of line.

"Oh, Morton! Morton! . . . Camera!" I shouted hoarsely, with every nerve in my body at supreme strain. What would his next jump be? After that run! I was all aquiver. He was as big as my big black marlin. My tight line swept up to the surface as I had seen it sweep with so many fish. "He's coming out!" I yelled for Morton's benefit.

Then he came out magnificently. Straight up six feet, eight feet, and over, a regular salmon leap he made, gleaming beautifully in the sun. What a picture! If only Morton got him with the camera I would not mind losing him, as surely as I must lose him. Down he splashed. "Zee!" whizzed my line.

I heard Morton running over the boulders and turned to see him making toward his camera. He had not been ready. What an incomparable opportunity lost! I always missed my greatest pictures. My impatience and disappointment vented themselves upon poor Morton, who looked as if he felt as badly as I. Then a hard jerk on my rod turned my gaze frantically back to the pool, just in time to see the great rainbow go down from another grand leap. With that he sheered round to the left, into the center of the wide swirl. I strode rapidly down the beach and into the water, winding my reel as fast as possible. How hard to hold that tip up and yet to recover line! My left arm ached, my right hand shook; for that matter my legs shook also. I was hot and cold by turns. My throat seemed as tight as my line. Dry-mouthed, clogged in my lungs, with breast heaving, I strained every faculty to do what was right. Who ever said a trout could not stir an angler as greatly as a whale?

One sweep he made put my heart in my throat. It was toward the incline into the rapids. If he started down! But he ended with a leap, head upstream, and when he soused back he took another run, closer inshore toward me. Here I had to reel like a human windlass.

He was too fast; he got slack line, and to my dismay and panic he jumped on that slack line. My mind whirled, and the climax of my emotions hung upon that moment. Suddenly, tight jerked my line again. The hook had held. He was fairly close at hand, in good position, head upriver, and tiring. I waded out on the beach; and though he chugged and tugged and bored, he never again got the line out over fifty feet. Sooner or later—it seemed both only a few moments and a long while—I worked him in over the sand bar, where in the crystal water I saw every move of his rose-red body. How I reveled in his beauty! Many times he stuck out his open jaws, cruel beaks, and gaped and snapped and gasped.

At length I slipped him out upon the sand, and that moment my vaunted championship of the Oregon steelhead suffered an eclipse. The great Oregon rainbow, transplanted to the snow waters of the Tongariro, was superior in every way to his Oregon cousin, the silver pink steelhead that had access to the sea. I never looked down upon such a magnificent gamefish. No artists could have caught with his brush the shining flecked bronze, the deep red flush from jaw to tail, the amber and pearl. Perforce he would have been content to catch the grand graceful contour of body, the wolf-jawed head, the lines of fin and tail.

He weighed eleven and one half pounds. I tied him on a string, as I was wont to do with little fish when a boy, and watched him recover and swim about in the clear water.

Meanwhile Morton stood there using language because he had failed to photograph those first leaps, and Captain Mitchell went back to his fishing. Presently a shout from him drew my attention. He had broken his rod on the cast.

"Well, what do you know about that?" I burst out. "If that isn't tough luck!"

The Captain waded out and approached us, holding two pieces of rod out for my inspection. The middle ferrule had broken squarely. While I tried to sympathize with Captain Mitchell, he anathematized the rod in several languages.

"But, Cap, you've had it for years. Even the best of rods can't last forever," I protested. "We'll take turns using mine."

He would not hear of this, so I returned to fishing, with my three companions all on the *qui vive.* I thought to try the same water, and to save that wonderful space out there between the currents for the last.

* * *

As if by magic the Dreadnaught Pool had been transformed. The something that was evermore about to happen to me in my fishing had happened there. There! The beautiful pool glimmered, shone, ran swiftly on, magnified in my sight. The sun was westering. It had lost its heat and glare. A shadow lay under the bluff. Only at the lower end did the sunlight make a light on the water, and it had changed. No longer hard to look upon!

I waded in up to my knees and began to cast with short
line, gradually lengthening it, but now not leisurely, content-
edly, dreamingly! My nerves were as keen as the edge of a
blade. Alert, quick, restrained, with all latent powers ready
for instant demand, I watched my line sweep out and unroll,
my leader straighten and the big dark fly alight. What singularly pleasant sensations attended the whole procedure!

I knew I would raise another rainbow trout. That was
the urge, wherefore the pool held more thrill and delight
and stir for me. On the fifth cast, when the line in its sweep
downstream had reached its limit, I had a strong vibrating
strike. Like the first trout, this one hooked himself; and on
his run he showed in a fine jump—a fish scarcely half as
large as my first one. He ran out of the best fishing water
and eventually came over to the sand bar, where I soon
landed him, a white-and-rose fish, plump and solid, in the
very best condition.

"Fresh-run trout," said Hoka. "They've just come up
from the lake."

"By gad! Then the run is on," returned Captain Mitchell
with satisfaction.

This second fish weighed five and three-quarter pounds.
He surely had all the strength of an eight-pound steelhead in
his compact, colorful body. I was beginning to understand
what the ice water of the Tongariro meant to the health and
spirit of a rainbow.

"Cap, make a few casts with my rod while I rest and hug
the fire," I said. "That water has ice beaten a mile."

"Not on your life," replied the captain warmly. "I've a
hunch it's your day. Wade in; every moment now is precious."

So I found myself out again on the sand bar, casting and recasting, gradually wading until I was over my hips and could go no farther. At that I drew my breath sharply when I looked down. How deceiving that water! Another step would have carried me over my head. If the bottom had not been sandy, I would not have dared trust myself there, for the edge of the current just caught me and tried to move me off my balance; but I was not to be caught unawares.

Sunlight still lay on the pool, yet cool and dark now, and waning. I fished the part of the pool where I had raised the two trout. It brought no rise. Then I essayed to reach across the gentle current, across the narrow dark aisle beyond, to the edge of the strong current, sweeping out from the bluff. It was a long cast for me, with a heavy fly, eighty feet or more. How the amber water, the pale green shadowy depths, the changing lights under the surface seemed to call to me, to assure me, to haunt with magical portent!

Apparently without effort, I cast my fly exactly where I wanted to. The current hungrily seized it, and as it floated out of my sight I gave my rod a gentle motion. Halfway between the cast and where the line would have straightened out below me a rainbow gave a heavy and irresistible lunge. It was a strike that outdid my first. It almost unbalanced me. It dragged hard on the line I clutched with my left hand. I was as quick as the fish and let go just as he hooked himself. Then followed a run the like of which I did not deem possible for any fish short of a salmon or a marlin. He took all my line except a quarter of an inch left on the spool. That brought him to the shallow water way across where the right-hand channel went down. He did not want that. Luckily for me, he turned to the left and rounded the lower edge of the pool. Here I got line back. Next he rushed across toward the head of the rapid. I could do nothing but hold on and pray.

Twenty yards above the smoothing glancing incline he sprang aloft in so prodigious a leap that my usual ready shout of delight froze in my throat. Like a deer, in long bounds, he covered the water, how far I dared not believe. The last rays of the setting sun flashed on this fish, showing it to be heavy and round and deep, of a wonderful pearly white tinted with pink. It had a small head which resembled that of a salmon. I had hooked a big female rainbow, fresh run from old [Lake] Taupo, and if I had not known before that I had a battle on my hands, I knew it on sight of the fish. Singularly indeed the females of these great rainbow trout are the hardest and fiercest fighters.

Fearing the swift water at the head of the rapid, I turned and plunged pellmell out to the beach and along it, holding my rod up as high as I could. I did not save any line, but I did not lose any, either. I ran clear to the edge of the sandy beach where it verged on the boulders. A few paces farther on roared the river.

Then with a throbbing heart and indescribable feelings, I faced the pool. There were one hundred and twenty-five yards of line out. The trout hung just above the rapid and there bored deep, to come up and thump on the surface. Inch by inch I lost line. She had her head upstream, but the current was drawing her toward the incline. I became desperate. Once over that fall she would escape. The old situation presented itself—break the fish off or hold it. Inch by inch she tugged the line off my reel. With all that line off and most of it out of the water and in plain sight, tight as a banjo string, I appeared to be at an overwhelming disadvantage. So I grasped the line in my left hand and held it. My six-ounce rod bowed and bent, then straightened and pointed. I felt its quivering vibration and I heard the slight singing of the tight line.

So there I held this stubborn female rainbow. Any part of my tackle or all of it might break, but not my spirit. How terribly hard it was not to weaken! Not to trust to luck! Not to release that tremendous strain.

The first few seconds were unendurable. They seemed an age. When would the line or leader give way or the hook tear out? But nothing broke. I could hold that wonderful trout. Then as the moments passed I lost that tense agony of apprehension. I gained confidence. Unless the fished wheeled to race for the fall I would win. The chances were against such a move. Her head was up current, held by that rigid line. Soon the tremendous strain told. The rainbow came up, swirled and pounded and threshed on the surface. There was a time then when the old fears returned and augmented; but just as I was about to despair, the tension on the rod and line relaxed. The trout swirled under and made upstream. This move I signaled with a shout, which was certainly echoed by my comrades, all lined up behind me, excited and gay and admonishing.

I walked down the beach, winding my reel fast, yet keeping the line taut. Thus I advanced fully a hundred yards. When I felt the enameled silk come to my fingers, to slip on the reel, I gave another shout. Then again I backed up the beach, pulling the trout, though not too hard. At last she got into the slack shallow water over the wide sand bar.

This dreamy, Victorian-style portrait shows Dolly fishing
near Lackawaxen around 1905.

For Grey, fishing was an art, a sport, a sublime recreation.

Years later, when he came to Florida, he was able to net his catch,
a rare permit, on the coral shoals off Long Key.

When word got back that the author had tied into a mammoth broadbill, a crowd gathered at the dock for a glimpse of the catch. This shot was taken in 1926.

The *Gladiator* was a seaworthy yacht with a specially rigged crow's nest and fishing chair.

Zane Grey with world record broadbill caught off Catalina Island in
1926. The one he landed weighed in at 582 pounds.

On his Nova Scotia adventure, ZG brought in this world record
bluefin tuna, scaled at 758 pounds.

Zane Grey with a 19-pound Atlantic salmon caught on an
expedition to Nova Scotia.

ZG once wrote, "My childhood dream was to have a great white yacht with sails like wings and sail into lonely tropic seas." When he sailed *Fisherman I* to New Zealand in 1927, he made that dream come true.

The writer was duly proud of his world record 318-pound yellow fin tuna
caught off Cabo San Lucas, Mexico in 1925.

The writer's first broadbill brought smiles to the faces of New Zealanders Peter Williams, standing, right, and Frances Arledge.

The New Zealand fishing camp was equal to his best Hollywood sets.
Here he compares notes on tackle with J.A. "Doc" Wiborn, whom he
called the "Lone Angler."

ZG fishing in the "Dreadnaught Pool," one of the most famous
fishing holes on the Tongariro River in New Zealand.
This shot was taken on the 1926 expedition.

Romer's 15-pound, 8-ounce Tongariro trout was the largest ever caught on ZG's expeditions. ZG took the picture.

He was equally proud of his own fine catch of rainbows.

Grey never neglected his writing. He would always find a time and a place to work at the craft which made all of his adventures possible. This picture was taken at his fishing camp in New Zealand in 1927.

ZG found that he needed extra heavy duty gear to fish the South
Pacific and had this reel, the largest ever made, built for him
by Arthur Kovalovsky. Today the reel is in the Zane Grey
Museum at Zanesville, Ohio.

Even after hours of battle, ZG's record 1,040-pound marlin continued to struggle until the end. After the creature was hauled in and weighed, the chief of the district of Vairao, Tahiti came out with his entourage to congratulate Grey. Note the tail mauled by sharks.

Though it could pass for a tranquil brook along the Thames, this photograph actually captures ZG as he attempts to land one of the famed *nato*, native to Vairao, Tahiti.

ZG with a pair of bonefish caught near Tetiaroa. There is reason to believe that this catch, in 1934, may be the first recorded catch of bonefish in the South Pacific.

The writer's 1,036-pound tiger shark, caught off Sydney Head,
Australia was a world record in 1936.

ZG with 460-pound Australian record black marlin caught off
Bermagui in 1936.

Inspecting the razor-sharp teeth of the 800-pound shark caught off the Australian coast.

There was an air of peace when ZG returned in search of steelhead
trout on the North Umpqua River, Oregon, in 1936.

The author's study, around 1937, contained relics of his great
fishing adventures around the world.

The writer appears in a still photograph from the movie, *White Death*, fighting the great white shark.

ZG often shared his knowledge of using sophisticated gear with local fishermen. In return, the size of their catches was unprecedented.

Loren's 11-pound steelhead caught on the North Umpqua River, around 1955, was a sample of the treasures ZG and his crew had gone after on the famed Northwestern river.

Here began another phase of the fight, surely an anxious and a grim one for me, with every move of that gorgeous fish as plain as if she had been in the air. What a dogged, stubborn, almost unbeatable fish on such tackle! Yet that light tackle was just the splendid thing for such a fight. Fair to the fish and calling to all I possessed of skill and judgment! It required endurance, too, for I had begun to tire. My left arm had a cramp, and my winding hand was numb.

The fish made short hard runs out into the deeper water, yet each run I stopped eventually. Then they gave place to the thumping on the surface, the swirling breaks, the churning rolls, and the bulldog tug, tug, tug. The fight surpassed any I had ever had with a small fish. Even that of the ten-pound steelhead I hooked once in wild Deer Creek, Washington! So strong and unconquerable was this rainbow that I was fully a quarter of an hour working her into the shallower part of the bar. Every time the silvery side flashed, I almost had heart failure. This fish would go heavier than the eleven and a half-pound male. I had long felt that in the line, in the rod; and now I saw it. There was remarkable zest in this part of the contest.

"Work that plugger in close where the water is shallower," advised Captain Mitchell.

Indeed I had wanted and tried to do that, for the twisting, rolling fish might any instant tear out the hook. I held harder now, pulled harder. Many times I led or drew the trout close to shore, and each time saw the gleaming silver-and-pink shape plunge back into the deeper water.

The little rod wore tenaciously on the rainbow, growing stronger, bending less, drawing easier.

After what seemed an interminable period there in this foot-deep water the battle ended abruptly with the bend of the rod drawing the fish head-on to the wet sand. Captain Mitchell had waded in back of my quarry, suddenly to lean down and slide her farther up the beach.

"What a bally fine trout!" burst out Morton. "Look at it! Deep, fat, thick. It'll weigh fourteen."

"Oh, no," I gasped, working over my numb and aching arms and hands.

"By gad! That's a wonderful trout!" added Captain Mitchell, most enthusiastically. "Why, it's like a salmon!"

Certainly I had never seen anything so beautiful in color, so magnificent in contour. It was mother-of-pearl tinged with exquisite pink. The dots were scarcely discernible, and the fullness of swelling graceful curve seemed to outdo nature itself. How the small thoroughbred salmon-like head contrasted with the huge iron-jawed fierce-eyed head of the male I had caught first! It was strange to see the broader tail of the female, the thicker mass of muscled body, the larger fins. Nature had endowed this progenitor of the species, at least for the spawning season, with greater strength, speed, endurance, spirit and life.

"Eleven pounds, three-quarters!" presently sang out the captain. "I missed it by a couple of pounds . . . Some rainbow, old man. Get in there and grab another."

"Won't you have a try with my rod?" I replied. "I'm darn near froze to death. Besides, I want to put this one on the string with the others and watch them."

He was obdurate, so I went back into the water; and before I knew what was happening, almost, I had fastened on to another trout. It did not have the great dragging weight of the other two, but it gave me a deep boring fight and deceived me utterly as to its size. When landed, this, my fourth trout, weighed six and three-quarters, another female, fresh run from the lake, and a fine rainbow in hue.

"Make it five, Doc. This is your day. Anything can happen now. Get out your line," declared Mitchell, glowing of face.

The sun had set as I waded in again. A shimmering, ethereal light moved over the pool. The reflection of the huge bluff resembled a battleship more than the bluff itself. Clear and black-purple rose the mountain range, and golden clouds grew more deeply gold. The river roared above and below, deep-toned and full of melody. A cool breeze drifted down from upstream.

I cast over all the water I had previously covered without raising a fish. Farther out and down I saw a trout rising, curling dark tails out of the gold gleam on the water. I waded a foot farther than ever and made a cast, another, recovered line, and then spent all the strength I had left in a cast that covered the current leading to the rising trout. I achieved it. The fly disappeared, my line glided on and on, suddenly to stretch like a whipcord and go zipping out of my left hand. Fast and hard! What a wonderful thrill ran up and down my back, all over me!

"Ho! Ho! . . . Boys, I've hung another!" I bawled out, in stentorian voice. "Say, but he's taking line! Oh, look at him jump! . . . , Oh, two! . . . Oh, three! . . . Four, by gosh! . . . Oh, Morton, if we only had some sunlight! What a flying leapfrog this trout is! . . . Five!"

The last jump was splendid, with a high parabolic curve, and a slick cutting back into the water. This rainbow, too, was big, fast, strong and fierce. But the fish did everything that should not have been done, and I did everything right. Fisherman's luck! Beached and weighed before my cheering companions; nine and one-half pounds; another silvery rosy female rainbow, thick and deep and wide.

Then I forced Captain Mitchell to take my rod, which he would not do until I pleaded I was frozen. But what did I care for cold? I made the day a perfect one by relinquishing my rod when I ached to wade in and try again.

The day, however, had begun badly for Captain Mitchell and so it ended. He could not raise a trout. Then we left the rousing fire and strode off over the boulders into the cool gathering twilight. Hoka carried two of my trout, Captain two and Morton one. We threaded the *ti*-tree thicket and jungle of ferns and crossed the perilous panel in the dark, as if it had been a broad, safe bridge.

My comrades talked volubly on the way back to camp, but I was silent. I did not feel my heavy wet waders or my leaden boots. The afterglow of sunset lingered in the west, faint gold and red over the bold black range. I heard a late bird sing. The roar of the river floated up at intervals. Tongariro! What a strange, beautiful, high-sounding name! It suited the noble river and the mountain from which it sprang. It was calling me. It would call me across the vast lanes and leagues of the Pacific. It would draw me back again. Beautiful green-white thundering Tongariro!

VII
Tahiti

Four miles out and somewhat to the eastward of our an-
chorage I had my first view of the most beautiful part of
Tahiti.... The eastern end ... was cut into sharp peaks
and deep gorges, all mantled in exquisite soft green. There
was not one bare spot of rock. Some of the high peaks held the
oncoming trade wind clouds that resembled grand wreaths of
white. For the most part, however, the peaks were bare, clean-
cut against the sky. It was a big country, and I knew I could
not grasp its true range. But some of the mountains were
high, fully five thousand feet, and all spear pointed. Green
shafts towered into the sky; cone-shaped peaks pierced the
clouds, knife-edged foothills raised sharp edges to the domi-
nating heights. Some of the clouds were letting down misty
veils of gray rain; some of the canyons were full of golden
light. I gazed until my eyes ached, and I forgot I was fishing.

* * *

Fishing keeps men boys longer than any other pursuit.

* * *

Here was a stretch of eighty-three days without catching a
fish. I know quite well it cannot be beaten. There is a re-
cord that will stand.

Nato Fishing

Most all of the rivers of Tahiti are swift, cold streams fed from mountain springs. Some, however, are subject to daily rain storms and go dry with a week of dry weather. The little rivulet that runs through my camp belongs to this last class. One evening it will be dry and the next morning a roaring brook.

The nato does not run up any but the spring-fed streams, and the nato, I should explain, is a most beautiful and interesting little fish. He lives in the sea and runs up the rivers, and he will take a fly just like a trout.

Tautari River, across the mountain from Vairao, and emptying into the sea on the north shore, is one of the largest streams on Tahiti, and perhaps the best for nato.

The natives catch the fish in nets. We were indebted to Mr. Allister Macdonald, an English artist residing in Papeete, for knowledge about nato and that it affords capital sport on very light tackle. I went fishing one evening with Romer and Mr. Macdonald and liked it so well that I spent the next day on the Tautari.

I had a two and a half-ounce Leonard rod and some fine line, very light leaders and tiny flies—a delicate rig aptly suited to a delicate but game little fish. I raised several before I hooked my first one. Then I was treated to a surprise. For a fish only a few inches long this nato certainly did put up a battle. But finding I could not tire him out, I most unconcernedly jerked him out. That was the first I ever saw. He had the shape of a bass, in fact he was a bass, a brilliant mother-of-pearl, dotted with black spots. I caught two more, and then fastened on to a good one, which took an extraordinary amount of skill and hard work to land. Six inches long and as wide as my hand!

Next day we went again, and I had time to see the wonderful scenery, as well as enjoy the fishing. Tautari comes down out of a magnificent canyon, and is a wide swift stream of crystal water with a slight greenish tinge. Palms and breadfruit trees, hibiscus and water hyacinth, lined the green banks. Just below the long riffle where I fished the whole day, the sea broke with boom and roar on the sandy beach.

It rained on and off. Soon we were soaking wet. But you do not mind the rain at Tahiti. The dark sky and fine mist brought the nato up in schools. I could see them turn and shine like silver. I think they fed mostly on the bottom, though occasionally one rose to something on the surface. They would bite greedily at times and at others could not be tempted. I was several hours, really, in learning how to fish for them. Eventually I got the hang of it, and had such sport as I had not had for many a day. It brought back Dillon's Falls and Joe's Run—where as a boy I learned to fish. We used to fish with long, slim, light, stiff reed poles, very fine silk thread, and tiny hook and a bit of helgrammite tail for bait. The method was to cast into swift, shallow riffles and work the bait with the current, to entice shiners and chubs. I became a past master at this art. And here on the Tautari it came back to me—absolutely the first time since I was a boy. The fishing was identical, except the nato were larger, and of course very much gamer than shiners or chubs.

I fished with a short line and trolled my fly with success, and then I cast a long line quartering down stream in deep water, with like result. After some heavy rains the water grew dark in color, and then the nato shone gold instead of silver. If anything, they bit better in the roily water than in the clear. In all, I caught about forty nato, the largest being about six inches. But I had hold of a couple of whales. The little rod wagged like a buggy whip. Both these nato pulled loose, when I imagined I was handling them very deftly. They were amazingly strong and quick. As always for me, the big ones got away!

What a far cry of difference between nato and the great *espadon* of the Pacific. The one a dainty little bit of silver, big eyed and speckled, the other a grand purple monster with a sword. But there is no telling the fascination of fishing. I loved it as a boy, and now no less as a man. And to tell what I owe to fishing would take a better book than I have written.

The Tautari, sliding down from the mighty cliffs, where the waterfalls gleamed like white lace, and the luxuriant flowered jungle grew to the peaks, was another beautiful river to add to the treasure store of an angler. Along its banks I waded knee-deep in green moss and amber lilies and lilac hyacinths, and gazed up at tropic slopes. And always and ever in my ears sounded the trumpet call of the sea, the thundering surge, the boom and hollow roar, and the scream of the pebbles in the undertow.

* * *

The trout fishing in the high Sierras and the grayling fishing in Colorado came nearer to this game than any I had known. But nato fishing surpassed them. The nato had the advantage and influence of being from the sea; he was cunning and wary, as beautiful and strong, as delicate a biter as either of the two mentioned; and lastly he lived in rivers bewildering for the beauty and glory of their environment. . . .

All anglers are lovers of nature and artists in their hearts. . . . Music of running water, of wild birds, the wind in the trees, the sense of utter solitude—these things are dear to every fisherman.

Marlin!

On the 15th of May—which was the seventh day of clear, hot, sunny weather—I stayed in camp to do some neglected writing, and let Cappy run out alone off the east end, where we had not scouted for several weeks. He returned to report a rather choppy sea, but he had raised two marlin, one of which was a good-sized fish that came for his bait three times to refuse it, no doubt because it was stale. Tuna, a small species, were numerous, and there were some bonito showing.

"Same old story," averred the Captain. "If I had a fresh bait I'd have hooked that bird. A lunker, too. All of 500 pounds."

Just what transpired in my mind I was not conscious of then. It all came to me afterward, and it was that this game was long, and some day one of us *might* capture a giant Tahitian marlin. We would go on trying.

That night the dry spell broke. The rain roared on the pandanus roof, most welcome and dreamy of sounds. Morning disclosed dark, massed, broken clouds, red-edged and purple-centered, with curtains of rain falling over the mountains. This weather was something like March come back again for a day!

I took down a couple of new feather jigs—silver-headed with blue eyes—just for good luck. They worked. We caught five fine bonito in the lagoon, right off the point where my cottage stands. Jimmy held up five fingers: "Five bonito. Good!" he ejaculated, which voiced all our sentiments.

Cappy had gone up the lagoon toward the second pass, and we tried to catch him, to give him a fresh bait. As usual, however, Cappy's natives were running the wheels off his launch, and we could not catch him. The second pass looked sort of white and rough to me. Cappy went out, however, through a smooth channel. Presently we saw a swell gather and rise, to close the channel and mount to a great, curling white crested wave which broke all the way across. Charley, who had the wheel, grinned up at me: "No good!" We turned inshore and made for the third pass, some miles on, and got through that wide one without risk. Afterward Cappy told me Areirea [his boatman] knew exactly when to run through the second pass.

We headed out. A few black noddies skimmed the dark sea, and a few scattered bonito broke the surface. As usual— when we had them—we put out a big bonito on my big tackle and an ordinary one on the other. As my medium tackle holds one thousand yards of thirty-nine thread [roughly 117-pound test] it will seem interesting to anglers to speak of it as medium. The big outfit held fifteen hundred yards of line— one thousand of thirty-nine thread and five hundred of forty-two for backing; and this story will prove I needed it.

Off the east end there was a brightness of white and blue, where the clouds broke, and in the west there were trade wind clouds of gold and pearl, but for the most part a gray canopy overspread mountain and sea. All along the saw-toothed front of this range inshore the peaks were obscured and the canyons filled with down-drooping veils of rain.

What a relief from late days of sun and wind and wave! This was the kind of sea I loved to fish. The boat ran easily over a dark, low, lumpy swell. The air was cool, and as I did not have on any shirt, the fine mist felt pleasant to my skin. John was at the wheel, Bob sat up on top with Jimmy and Charley, learning to talk Tahitian. The teasers and heavy baits made a splashing, swishy sound that could be heard above the boil and gurgle of water from the propellers. We followed some low-skimming boobies for a while, and then headed for Captain M's boat, several miles further out. A rain squall was obscuring the white tumbling reef and slowly moving toward us. Peter sat at my right, holding the line which had the larger bonito. He had both feet up on the gunwale. I noticed that the line on this reel was white and dry. I sat in the left chair, precisely as Peter, except that I had on two pairs of gloves with thumb-stalls in them. I have cut, burned, and skinned my hands too often on a hard strike to go without gloves. They are a nuisance to wear all day, when the rest of you, almost, is getting pleasantly caressed by sun and wind, but they are absolutely necessary to an angler who knows what he is doing.

Peter and I were discussing plans for our New Zealand trip next winter—boats, camp equipment and whatnot. And although our gaze seldom strayed from the baits, the idea of raising a fish was the farthest from our minds. We were just fishing, putting in the few remaining hours of this Tahitian trip, and already given over to the hopes and anticipations of the New Zealand one. That is the comfortable way to make a trip endurable—to pass from the hard reality of the present to the ideal romance of the future.

Suddenly I heard a sounding, vicious thump of water. Peter's feet went up in the air.

"Ge-zus!" he bawled.

His reel screeched. Quick as thought I leaned over to press my gloved hand on the whizzing spool of line. Just in time to save the reel from overrunning!

Out where Peter's bait had been showed a whirling, closing hole in the boiling white-green water. I saw a wide purple mass shooting away so close under the surface as to make the water look shallow. Peter fell out of the chair at the same instant I leaped up to straddle his rod. I had the situation in hand. My mind worked swiftly. It was an incredibly wonderful strike. The other boys piled back to the cockpit to help Peter get my other bait and the teasers in.

Before this was even started the fish ran out two hundred yards of line, then turning to the right he tore off another hundred. All in a very few seconds! Then a white splash, high as a tree, shot up, out of which leaped the most magnificent of all leaping fish I had ever seen.

"GIANT MARLIN!" screamed Peter. What had happened to me I did not know, but I was cold, keen, hard, tingling, motivated to think and do the right thing. This glorious fish made a leap of thirty feet at least, low and swift, which gave me the time to gauge his enormous size and his species.

Here at last on the end of my line was the great Tahitian swordfish! He looked monstrous. He was pale, shiny gray in color, with broad stripes of purple. When he hit the water he sent up a splash like the flying surf on the reef.

By the time he was down I had the drag on and was winding the reel. Out he blazed again, faster, higher, longer, whirling the bonito round his head.

"Hook didn't catch!" yelled Peter, wildly. "It's on his side. He'll throw it."

I had instinctively come up mightily on the rod, winding with all speed, and I had felt the tremendous solid pull. The hook had caught before that, however, and the big bag in the line, coupled with his momentum, had set it.

"No, Peter! He's fast," I replied. Still I kept working like a windmill in a cyclone to get up the slack. The monster had circled in these two leaps. Again he burst out, a plunging leap which took him under a wall of rippling white spray. Next instant such a terrific jerk as I had never sustained nearly unseated me. He was away on his run.

"Take the wheel, Peter," I ordered, and released the drag. "Water! Somebody pour water on this reel! . . . *Quick!*"

The white line melted, smoked, burned off the reel. I smelled the scorching. It burned through my gloves. John was quick to plunge a bucket overboard and douse reel, rod and me with water. That, too, saved us.

"After him, Pete!" I called, piercingly. The engines roared and the launch danced around to leap the direction of the tight line. "Full speed!" I added.

"Aye, sir," yelled Peter, who had been a sailor before he became a whaler and a fisherman.

Then we had our race. It was thrilling in the extreme, and though brief it was far too long for me. Five hundred yards from us . . . he came up to pound and beat the water into a maelstrom.

"Slow up!" I sang out. We were bagging the line. Then I turned the wheel-drag and began to pump and reel as never before in all my life. How precious that big spool—that big reel handle. They fairly ate up the line. We got back two hundred yards of the 500 before he was off again. This time, quick as I was, it took all my strength to release the drag, for when a weight is pulling hard it releases with extreme difficulty. No more risk like that!

He beat us in another race, shorter, at the end of which, when he showed like a plunging elephant, he had out four hundred and fifty yards of line.

"Too much—Peter!" I panted. "We must—get him closer—Go to it!"

So we ran down upon him. I worked as before, desperately, holding on my nerve, and when I got three hundred yards back again on the reel, I was completely winded, and the hot sweat poured off my naked arms and breast.

"He's sounding . . . Get my shirt . . . Harness!"

Warily I let go with one hand and then the other, as John and Jimmy helped me on with the shirt and then with the leather harness. With that hooked on to my reel and the great strain transferred to my shoulders, I felt that I might not be torn asunder.

"All right. Let's go," I said, grimly. But he had gone down, which gave me a chance to get back my breath. Not long, however, did he remain down. I felt and saw the line rising.

"Keep him on the starboard quarter, Peter. Run up on him now. Bob, your chance for pictures!"

I was quick to grasp that the swordfish kept coming to our left, and repeatedly on that run I had Peter swerve in the same direction, in order to keep the line out on the quarter. Once we were almost in danger. But I saw it. I got back all but one hundred yards of line. Close enough! He kept edging in ahead of us, and once we had to turn halfway to keep the stern toward him. But he quickly shot ahead again. He was fast, angry, heavy. How his tail pounded the leader! The short powerful strokes vibrated all over me.

"Port—port, Peter!" I yelled, and even then, so quick was the swordfish, I missed seeing two leaps directly in front of the boat as he curved ahead of us. But the uproar from Bob and the others was enough for me. As the launch sheered around, however, I saw the third of that series of leaps—and if anything could have loosed my chained emotion on the instant that unbelievably swift and savage plunge would have done so. But I was clamped. No more dreaming! No more bliss! I was there to act and think. And I did not even thrill.

By the same tactics the swordfish sped off a hundred yards of line and by the same we recovered them and drew close to see him leap again, only two hundred feet off our starboard, a little ahead, and of all the magnificent fish I have ever seen, he excelled. His power to leap was beyond credence. . . . this swordfish was so huge that when he came out in dazzling swift flight, my crew went simply mad. This was the first time my natives had been flabbergasted. They were as excited, as carried away, as Bob and John. Peter, however, stuck to the wheel as if he was after a wounded whale which might at any minute turn on him. I did not need to warn Peter not to let that fish hit us. If he had he would have made splinters of that launch. Many an anxious glance did I cast toward Cappy's boat, two or three miles distant. Why did he not come? The peril was too great for us to be alone at the mercy of that beautiful brute, if he charged us either by accident or design. But Cappy could not locate us, owing to the misty atmosphere, and missed seeing this grand fish in action.

How sensitive I was to the strain on the line! A slight slackening directed all my faculties to ascertain the cause. The light on the moment was bad, and I had to peer closely to see the line. He had not slowed up, but he was curving back and to the left again—the cunning strategist!

"Port, Peter, port!" I commanded.

We sheered, but not enough. With the wheel hard over, one engine full speed ahead, the other in reverse, we wheeled like a top. But not swift enough for that Tahitian swordfish.

The line went under the bow.

"Reverse!" I called, sharply.

We pounded on the waves, slowly caught hold, slowed, started back. Then I ordered the clutches thrown out. It was a terrible moment and took all my will not to yield to sudden blank panic.

When my line ceased to pay out I felt that it had been caught on the keel. And as I was only human, I surrendered for an instant to agony. But no! That line was new, strong. The swordfish was slowing. I could yet avert catastrophe.

"Quick, Pete! Feels as if the line is caught," I cried, unhooking the harness from the reel.

Peter complied with my order. "Yes, by cripes. It's caught. Overboard, Jimmy. Jump in! Loose the line!"

The big Tahitian in a flash was out of his shirt and bending to dive.

"No!—Hold on, Jimmy!" I yelled. Only a moment before I had seen some sharks milling about. "Grab him, John!"

They held Jimmy back, and a second later I plunged my rod over the side into the water, so suddenly that the weight of it and the reel nearly carried me overboard.

"Hold me—or it's all—day!" I panted, and I thought that if my swordfish had fouled on keel or propellers, I did not care if I did fall in. "Let go my line, Peter," I said, making ready to extend my rod to the limit of my arms.

"I can feel him moving, sir," shouted Peter, excitedly. "By jingo! He's coming! It's free! It wasn't caught!"

That was such intense relief I could not recover my balance. They had to haul me back in to the boat. I shook all over as one with palsy, so violently that Peter had to help me get the rod in the rod socket of the chair. An instant later came the strong electrifying pull on the line, the scream of the reel. Never such sweet music! He was away from the boat—on a tight line. The revulsion of feeling was so great that it propelled me instantaneously back to my former state of hard, cold, calculating and critical judgment, and iron determination.

"Close shave, sir," said Peter, cheerily. "It was like when a whale turns on me, after I've struck him. We're all clear, sir, and after him again."

The gray pall of rain bore down on us. I was hot and wet with sweat and asked for a raincoat to keep me from being chilled. Enveloped in this, I went on with my absorbing toil. Blisters began to smart on my hands, especially one on the inside of the third finger of my right hand, certainly a queer place to raise one. But it bothered me, hampered me. Bob put on his rubber coat and, protecting his camera more than himself, sat out on the bow, waiting.

My swordfish, with short, swift runs took us five miles farther out, and then welcome to see, brought us back, all this while without leaping, though he broke water on the surface a number of times. He never sounded after that first dive. The bane of an angler is a sounding fish, and here in Tahitian waters, where there is no bottom, it spells catastrophe. The marlin slowed up and took to milling, a sure sign of a rattled fish. Then he rose again, and it happened to be when the rain had ceased. He made one high, frantic jump about two hundred yards ahead of us, and then threshed on the surface, sending the bloody spray high. All on board were quick to see that sign of weakening, of tragedy—blood.

Peter turned to say, coolly, "He's our meat, sir."

I did not allow any such idea to catch my consciousness. Peter's words, like those of Bob and John, and the happy jargon of the Tahitians, had no effect on me whatever.

It rained half an hour longer, during which we repeated several phases of the fight, except slower on the part of the marlin. In all he leaped fifteen times clear of the water. I did not attempt to keep track of his threshings.

After the rain passed I had them remove the rubber coat, which hampered me, and settled in to a slower fight. About this time the natives again sighted sharks coming around the boat. I did not like this. Uncanny devils! They were the worst of these marvelous fishing waters. But Peter said: "They don't know what it's all about. They'll go away."

They did go away long enough to relieve me of dread, then they trooped back, lean, yellow-backed, white-finned wolves.

"We ought to have a rifle," I said. "Sharks won't stay to be shot at, whether hit or not."

It developed that my swordfish had leaped too often and run too swiftly to make an extremely long fight. I had expected a perceptible weakening and recognized it. So did Peter, who smiled gladly. Then I taxed myself to the utmost and spared nothing. In another hour, which seemed only a few minutes, I had him whipped and coming. I could lead him. The slow strokes of his tail took no more line. Then he quit wagging.

"Clear for action, Pete. Give John the wheel . . . I see the end of the double line . . . There!"

I heaved and wound. With the end of the double line over my reel I screwed the drag up tight. The finish was in sight. Suddenly I felt tugs and jerks at my fish.

"*Sharks!*" I yelled, hauling away for dear life.

Everybody leaned over the gunwale. I saw a wide shining mass, greenish silver, crossed by purple bars. It moved. It weaved. But I could drag it easily.

"*Mauu! Mauu!*" shrilled the natives.

"Heave!" shouted Peter, as he peered down.

In a few more hauls I brought the swivel of the leader out of the water.

"By God! They're on him!" roared Peter, hauling on the leader. "Get the lance, boathook, gaff—anything. Fight them off!"

Suddenly Peter let go the leader and jerking the big gaff from Jimmy he lunged out. There was a single enormous roar of water and a sheeted splash. I saw a blue tail so wide I thought I was crazy. It threw a six-foot shark into the air!

"Rope him, Charley," yelled Peter. "The rest of you fight the tigers off."

I unhooked the harness and stood up to lean over the gunwale. The swordfish rolled on the surface, extending from forward of the cockpit to two yards or more beyond the end. His barred body was as large as that of an ox. And to it sharks were clinging, tearing, out on the small part near the tail. Charley looped the great tail and that was the signal for the men to get into action.

One big shark had a hold just below the anal fin. How cruel, brutish, ferocious! Peter made a powerful stab at him. The big lance head went clear through his neck. He gulped and sank. Peter stabbed another underneath, and still another. Jimmy was tearing at the sharks with the long handled gaff, and when he hooked one he was nearly hauled overboard. Charley threshed with his rope; John did valiant work with the boathook, and Bob frightened me by his daring fury as he leaned far over to hack with the cleaver.

We keep these huge cleavers on board to use in case we are attacked by an octopus, which is not a far-fetched fear at all. It might happen. Bob is lean and long and powerful. Also, he was angry. Whack! He slashed a shark that let go and appeared to slip up into the air.

"On the nose, Bob. Split his nose! That's the weak spot on a shark," yelled Peter.

Next shot Bob cut deep into the round stub nose of this big black shark—the only one of that color I saw—and it had the effect of dynamite. More sharks appeared under Bob, and I was scared so stiff I could not move.

"Take that! . . . And that!" sang out Bob, in a kind of fierce ecstasy. "You will try to eat our swordfish!—Dirty, stinking pups! Aha! On your beak, huh! Zambesi! . . . Wow, Pete, that sure is the place!"

"Look out, Bob! For God's sake—look out!" I begged, frantically, after I saw a shark almost reach Bob's arm.

Peter swore at him. But there was no keeping Bob off those cannibals. Blood and water flew all over us. The smell of sharks in any case is not pleasant, and with them spouting blood, and my giant swordfish rolling in blood, the stench that arose was sickening. They appeared to come from all directions, especially from under the boat. Finally I had to get into the thick of it, and at that armed with only a gaff handle minus the gaff. I did hit one a stunning welt over the nose, making him let go. If we had all had lances like the one Peter was using so effectively, we would have made short work of them. One jab from Peter either killed or disabled a shark. The crippled ones swam about belly up or lopsided, and stuck up their heads as if to get air. Of all the bloody messes I ever saw that was the worst.

"Makes me remember—the war!" panted Peter, grimly.

And it was Peter who whipped the flock of ravenous sharks off. *Chuck!* went the heavy lance, and that was the end of another. My heart apparently had ceased to function. To capture that glorious fish only to see it devoured before my eyes!

"Run ahead, Johnny, out of this bloody slaughter-hole so we can see," called Peter.

John ran forward a few rods into clear water. A few sharks followed, one of them to his death. The others grew wary, and swam around and around.

"We got 'em licked! Say, I had the wind up me," said Peter. "Who ever saw the like of that? The bloody devils!"

Bob took the lance from Peter and stuck the most venturesome of the remaining sharks. It appeared then that we had the situation in hand again. My swordfish was still there, his beautiful body bitten here and there, his tail almost severed, but not irreparably lacerated. All around the boat wounded sharks were lolling with fins out, sticking ugly heads up, to gulp and dive.

There came a letdown and we exchanged the natural elation we felt. The next thing was to see what was to be done with the monster, now we had him. I vowed we could do nothing but tow him back to camp. But Peter made the attempt to lift him on the boat. All six of us, hauling on the ropes, could not get his back half out of the water. So we tied him fast and started homeward.

* * *

We arrived at the dock about three o'clock to find all our camp folk and a hundred natives assembled to greet us. Up and down had sped the news of the flags waving.

I went ashore and waited impatiently to see the marlin hauled out on the sand. It took a dozen men, all wading, to drag him in. And when they at last got him under the tripod, I approached, knowing I was to have a shock and prepared for it.

But at that he surprised me in several ways. His color had grown darker and the bars showed only palely. Still they were there and helped to identify him as one of the striped species. He was bigger than I had ever hoped for. And his body was long and round. This roundness appeared to be an extraordinary feature for a marlin. His bill was three feet long, not slender and rapier-like, as in the ordinary marlin, or short and bludgeon-like, as in the black marlin. . . . Singularly, he had a small head, only a foot or more from where his beàk broadened to his eye, which, however, was as large as a broadbill swordfish. There were two gill openings on each side, a feature I had never observed before in any swordfish, the one toward the mouth being considerably smaller than the regular gill opening. From there his head sheered up to his hump-back, out of which stood an enormous dorsal fin. He had a straight under-maxillary. The pectoral fins were large, wide, like wings, and dark in color. . . . His body, for eight feet, was as symmetrical and round as that of a good big stallion. According to my deduction it was a male fish. He carried this roundness back to his anal fin, and there further accuracy was impossible because the sharks had eaten away most of the flesh from these fins to the tail. On one side, too, they had torn away enough meat to fill a bushel basket. His tail was the most splendid of all fish tails I have observed. It was a perfect bent bow, slender, curved, dark purple in color, finely ribbed, and expressive of the tremendous speed and strength the fish had exhibited.

This tail had a spread of five feet two inches. His length was fourteen feet two inches. His girth was six feet nine inches. And his weight, as he was, 1040 pounds.

VIII

Australia

The big sharks will interest the overseas fishermen. Every last one of them will want to capture a huge tiger shark. Personally, I don't see anything lacking in this tiger to make him a prize. He is a strong, heavy, mean fighter. He is full of surprises. He is huge and frightful, beautiful and savage in the water, and terrible out of it. If, in any particular case, there is something lacking in this tiger shark, it is more than made up for by the fact that he is a killer and will eat you. In my mind that is a feature formidable and magnificent.

The savagery of the sea is exemplified in the fierce, swift action of sharks. I hate sharks and have killed a thousand, and have an inkling that I'll add another thousand to my list here.

from AN AMERICAN ANGLER IN AUSTRALIA

The possibilities of Australian big gamefishing intrigue me and excite me more and more, as I fish myself, and receive more and more word from different and widely separated places on Australia's grand coast of thirteen thousand miles.

I expected to find Australia and New Zealand somewhat alike, and the fishing also. They are totally different. In any fishing trip, such as I call worthy of the name, there are many considerations that make for the ultimate success and memorable record. The beauty and color of the surrounding country, the birds and snakes and animals, the trees and hills, the long sandy beaches, and the desolate ragged shorelines, the lonely islands—all these and many more appeal to me as much as the actual roaming the sea, in rain or shine, in calm and storm, and the catching of great gamefish.

One of the pleasantest experiences I have ever had, and one the joy of which will grow in memory, was to be awakened in the dusk of dawn by the kookaburras. That was unique. The big mollyhawks of New Zealand, the laughing gulls of California, that awaken you at dawn and are things never forgotten, cannot compare with these strange and homely and humorous jackasses of the Australian woods.

We ran our score of big fish caught up to twenty-one in seven weeks, which list, considering that half this time the weather was too bad to fish, and that it included my black marlin record of four hundred and eighty pounds, two of the same around four hundred pounds, and a really rare fish, the green Fox thresher, must be considered very good indeed.

[My last day off Bermagui] was an unusually beautiful day for any sea. The morning was sunny, warm and still. There seemed to be the balminess of spring in the air. We got an early start, a little after sunrise, with the idea of running far offshore—'out wide,' the market fishermen call it—into the equatorial stream.

I had been out in this current several times off Montague Island, but not very far, and not to study it, particularly. . . . Bait was easy to catch and quite abundant, which fact always lends an auspicious start to a fish day. The boys yelled in competition as they hauled in yellowtail (king fish), bonito, and salmon. Shearwater ducks were wheeling over the schools of bait, and the gannets were making their magnificent dives from above. A gannet, by the way, is the grandest of all sea-fowl divers. . . .

We ran thirty miles by noon. No fish sign of any kind—no birds or bait or splashes or fins—just one vast heaving waste of lonely sea, like a shimmering opal.

After lunch I told the outfit that I guessed it was up to me to find some kind of fish, so I climbed forward and stood at the mast to scan the sea. This was an old familiar, thrilling custom of mine, and had been learned over many years roaming the sea for signs of tuna or broadbill swordfish. In the former case you see splashes or dark patches on the glassy sea; in the latter you see the great sickle fins of that old gladiator *Xiphias gladius*, surely the most wonderful spectacle for any sea angler.

In this case, however, all I sighted was a hammerhead shark. His sharp oval fin looked pretty large, and as his acquisition might tend to good fortune, I decided to drop him a bait and incidentally show my camera crew, who had been complaining of hard battles with sharks, how easily it could be done.

Using a leader with a small hook, I had the boatman put on a small piece of bait, and crossed the track of the hammerhead with it. When he struck the scent in the water, he went wild and came rushing up the wake, his big black fin weaving to and fro, until he struck. Hammerheads have rather small mouths, but they are easily hooked by this method. In a couple of minutes I had hold of this fellow.

After hooking him I was careful not to *pull hard* on him. That is the secret of my method with sharks, of which I have caught a thousand. They are all alike. They *hate* the pull of a line and will react violently, according to what pressure is brought to bear. If they are not 'horsed,' as the saying goes, they can be led up to the boat to the gaff. This means a lot of strenuous exercise for the boatman, but only adds to the fun. Shooting, as is employed here in Australia, and harpooning, as done in New Zealand, disqualify a fish.

I had this hammerhead up to the boat in twelve minutes, and I never heaved hard on him once. Emil, my still photographer, a big strong fellow, had a three-hour battle with one a little smaller, and he simply marveled at the trick I played on the shark, and him, too.

There was a merry splashing melee at the gaffing of this hammerhead, in which all the outfit engaged. It was the largest hammerhead I had seen in Australian waters, probably close to six hundred pounds. Off the Perlos Islands I have seen eighteen-foot hammerheads, with heads a third that wide. I understand the Great Barrier Reef has twenty-two-foot hammerheads. Australia is verily the land, or water, for sharks; and I am vastly curious to see what a big one will do to me. [An Australian angler] was four and a half hours on his nine hundred and eighty-pound tiger shark, and I have heard of longer fights. No doubt I am in for a good licking, but that will be fun.

*   *   *

One of my strong reasons for coming to Bateman Bay, if not the strongest, was the fact that this big shallow body of water was infested with sharks.

Salmon, bonito, yellowtail, taylor, mullet, which are the very best bait for any and all saltwater fish, inhabit this bay; and I am sure have a very great deal to do with the presence of sharks. . . .

Sometimes when it was windy outside we ran in to fish around the islands or along the shoal west shore of the bay. Straight across from camp there was a high bluff covered with heavy growth of timber. From this a flat rocky reef ran out into the bay. Our man, Bill Lawler, the market fisherman I had engaged, took us often to this particular spot to fish for sharks. Some of the shark tales he told were incredible. But I learned to credit all of them.

Why a school of gray nurse sharks should hang around that shoal reef was a mystery to me. It cleared up, however, and seemed as natural as any other thing pertaining to the sea. We went there several times and chummed, (burley, they call this way of attracting sharks by cutting up bait or fish), without getting a single bite. Bill said the cool rainy weather accounted for the lack of sharks, and I could well believe him.

One warm still afternoon we hit it just right; and that afternoon must be recorded in my memory and in my fishing notes as one never to forget. Fishing for sharks is one thing; fishing for man-eating sharks, one of the most ferocious species, is entirely another.

I had seen two gray nurse sharks in the aquarium at the Sydney Zoo. I had watched them for hours. They really had beauty, if line and contour lending speed and savagery, can have such a thing. To my surprise the gray nurse shark had a longer, sharper nose than even the mako. I made a bet with myself that he could move fast in the water. I found out, too. I was surprised, too, to see that the gray nurse had no gray color in the water. He was a dark greenish tan.

We anchored the *Avalon* over the ridge, about five hundred yards out from the shore, and began to chum. We had a couple of boxes full of fish that from its odor should have attracted sharks all the way from Sydney. Our other boat, the camera outfit, chose a spot a half mile below us, not a very good place, Bill said.

I put a bait over on my big tackle and settled myself comfortably to wait. It was very pleasant and grew more beautiful as the afternoon waned. Two hours passed, during which we chummed all the while without having a strike. An oily slick drifted away from our boat for a mile. I had about decided that there were no gray nurse sharks in the bay, when I had a bite. It was a gentle, slow pull, not at all what I expected from a notorious shark.

"It's a gray nurse," avowed Bill.

"Yeah?" I replied doubtfully. "Okay! We'll hand it to him."

Whereupon I laid back with my heavy tackle for all I was worth. I hooked a fish all right and made ready for a run. But this one did not run. He came toward the boat. The men hauled up anchor and started the engine. We drifted while I most curiously applied myself to whipping this shark, if it were one. He was heavy and strong and quick as a flash. But he did not try to go places. He kept around and under the boat.

In due course I hauled him up, and what was my surprise when I saw a long symmetrical silver gray shark shape. He looked about eight feet long and fairly thick. Presently I had a good look at his head and then his eyes. I have had fish see me from the water, but this fellow's gaze was different. Pure, cold, murderous cruelty shone in that black eye. It made me shiver. I did not fool any longer with him.

Peter gaffed the gray nurse and held him while Bill slipped a rope over his tail. For his size, about three hundred pounds, he surely made a commotion in the water. After a bit Peter untied my leader from my line and let it hang. The shark hung head down, rolling and jerking.

"Pete, if these gray nurse sharks don't run away after being hooked, this tackle is too heavy," I said.

"Right-o. I was figuring that. The Coxe nine and thirty-thread line ought to do."

"Well," added Bill grimly, "I can tell you they don't run away."

We went back to our anchorage and I went on fishing with a lighter rig while the men chummed. Suddenly Bill saw one in the water. I thought I, too, caught a gray shadow flash. But in a moment after that I had another of those queer slow gentle strikes.

"Gosh!" I exclaimed. "I'll bet this bird doesn't work so slow when he's after a man."

"Quick as lightning!" replied Bill.

The shark swam under the boat. I hooked him, and he acted precisely as had the first. But with the lighter tackle I could handle him better. He turned out to be heavy and strong, making it necessary for me to put on my harness. Then we had it out, hard and fast. Nevertheless I was able to do little with him. Had he chosen to run off we would have had to up anchor and go after him. But he chose to circle the boat and swim under it, giving me plenty of trouble. When I discovered the gray nurse wouldn't run I put on some drag and pitched into him. Several times I had a glimpse of something long and gray, like a ghost of a fish. In half an hour I had him coming. I did not see him clearly, however, until Peter had heaved on the leader. Then—what a thrill and a start! This one appeared a monster, eleven feet long, thick as a barrel, huge fins all over him, veritably a terrible engine of destruction. He would have weighed eight hundred pounds. Peter held the leader while Bill gaffed him. Then there was hell. The shark threw the gaff and bit through the leader in what appeared a single action.

"Oh, Peter," I protested, in grievous disappointment. "He wasn't ready. Why didn't you let him go?"

Peter looked mad. Bill said not to mind, that there were more. This reassured me, and I asked for another leader. They were all twenty feet or more long, too long, but we had to use them.

"Look down there!" called Bill as I threw out my bait.

I did not look because my bait had hardly sunk to the bottom, which was only three fathoms, when I had another of those slow electrifying tugs. When I hooked this gray nurse shark he nearly jerked the rod away from me and the rod socket. By this time I was getting angry. I went after this one hammer and tongs. His action induced me to think he was trying to get to the boat and kill me. He never swam a dozen yards from where I sat. I put the wood on him, as we call hauling hard with the rod and eventually whipped him and brought him up to the gaff. He nearly drowned me. And the boys were ringing wet and mad as wet hens. When Peter tied this one alongside the other, they began to fight.

We rigged up another leader and I went at it again. This time Bill saw one before I threw my bait in.

"Look down," he directed and pointed.

By peering over into the green water I saw long wavering shapes. Sharks! Gray nurse sharks, some of them nearly twelve feet long, swimming around over the chum we had distributed.

"My word! What a sight!" I ejaculated.

"Be careful the next one doesn't jerk you overboard," warned Bill.

"What'd they do?"

"Tear you to pieces!"

I well believed that, and I proceeded to fasten the snap below the reel so the rod could not be pulled away from the chair. In less than ten seconds after my bait disappeared I had a strike, and in another second I was fast again. It required about a quarter of an hour to lick the next one, around three hundred pounds in weight. We got him, tied him alongside his comrade; and his arrival started another fight.

The next two severed my leader, one at the gaff and the other was cut clean about the middle of the fight. That required other new leaders. This last was put on by Bill and my bait thrown overboard, when we heard a hard thumping behind us. Peter, the scalawag, had dropped a hook down on a heavy cord, and he was fast to a shark. He got the end of the leader up. The shark was a whopper and he roared around the surface and banged against the boat.

"Help! Help!" yelled Peter.

Bill ran to his assistance just as I had another strike.

In a twinkling I was hooked to my heaviest gray nurse. He gave me a very hard battle. I needed my heavy outfit on him. But I was getting him under control when Peter's shark swam under the boat and fouled my leader with his. In the melee that followed Peter's shark broke away. I worked on mine awhile longer before I trusted him to Pete and Bill whose blood was up and who had a lust to kill these man-eaters. No doubt mine was up too, because I would have caught those devils until I was used up. This gray nurse was my largest to land. He weighed about five hundred pounds. When they tied him, head down, tail up, next to the other three, there was another convulsion. The boat canted over and I had to hold on. Four gray nurse sharks in a row! And all possessed of devils. They did not appear to be sick or weak. They just fought.

"Peter, for Pete's sake let up on that hand-line stuff," I begged.

"Like hob I will," replied my boatman.

"But you'll only foul my line."

"No matter. We'll ketch 'em."

And he had hold of another one in less than ten seconds. This time I watched. And I grasped that Peter would not give the sharks an inch of line. He sweated and swore and held on like grim death. The hook pulled out. Then I stood up to peer over the gunwale. Sharks thick as fence pickets! But I could not see clearly. A few were small and many were about ten feet long, and several were very large. I wanted one of the biggest. My next was a smaller one, however, and I soon dragged him up. Peter had one on too and could not help us. Bill held the leader and the shark while I gaffed it. What a strange, all-satisfying feeling as the steel went in! But of course I was wholly primitive at the moment. The shark gave a wag, and the gaff handle hit me on the head. I went down, not for the count, but to bounce up furious.

"Put a rope over his tail," yelled Bill.

"Don't do that," ordered Peter, aghast.

"Mind your own business," I replied. "Looks like you have your hands full."

Grasping up a tail rope, I widened the noose and bent over the gunwale to try to lasso that sweeping tail. I got the noose over, but before I could draw it tight he flipped it off. He bit at my hands and swept them aside as if they were paper. I was drenched to the skin. Then he hit me a re-sounding smack on the cheek and temple. Hurt? I was never so hurt in my life. Nor mad! I bent lower, grim and desperate.

"Look out!" yelled Bill. And before I could move he let go of gaff and leader and dragged me up. I had a glimpse of a gray flash, a cruel pointed nose. One of the devils had made a pass at me.

"My God! . . . Bill did that shark . . . ?" I gasped.

"He did. Grab the rod and pull your shark back. Afraid I've lost the gaff."

While I was pumping and winding my shark back, Peter broke the heavy cord on the one he had hooked. That made him madder than ever. Bill ran forward to recover the gaff which came out of the shark and floated up.

"I'll get one or bust," sang out Peter.

"This is a swell way to get rid of leaders," I replied. "But go to it. This will never happen again."

In less than a minute I was fast to another, and Pete's yell assured me he was, too.

Then things happened so quickly, and I was so confused with blood lust to kill sharks and the excitement of the sport, that for a space I could not tell what was going on. There was tremendous exertion and much hoarse shouting, and especially a terrific slashing maelstrom when both my shark and the one Peter had hooked got tangled up with the four wicked ones we had tied to the boat.

That was a mess. It must be understood that the four live sharks were tied on the opposite side of the boat from which I was hanging on to the one I had hooked. My rod was bent double, mostly under the water. I had hold of my line with both my gloved hands.

The men saved my shark, a good ten-footer, and lost Peter's, which he said was a whale. This time Peter cut his hand on the leader and therefore let up on his handline stuff. He had lost four. This helped matters somewhat, for the next and sixth one I hooked was not so hard to land. When he had been tied up on my side of the boat, the men tried to call me off. I indeed was spent and panting.

"Not on your life!" I yelled. "Not while they'll bite and I can lick 'em."

"They're thinning out," said Bill, gazing deep into the water. "But there's a big one, if you can get hold of him . . . "

Marvelous to relate, I did, and he felt as if he were the granddad of that school of gray nurse sharks. He kept away from the boat for a while. He even came up so that I could see his wonderful silver-gray shape, his many fins, his gleaming eye and terrible shining teeth. This one was close to being twelve feet long. He circled the stern, weaved to and fro, went under us time and again; in fact, he tried everything but to swim away. That was the strange thing. I could not understand it, unless he wanted to stay there and kill the thing which had him.

The sun was setting gold and blazing behind us on the wooded bluff. There were glorious lights and shadows on the Toll Gates. The water had a sheen of red, beautiful, though very significant of that afternoon's fight with man-eaters.

I was sure of this big one—which conceit was foolish. I worked hard on him. I stopped him, or thought I had, time and again. All of a sudden when he was almost under me, he made a quick lunge. I heard snaps. I felt released from a mighty pull. My tip, line and harness strap all broke at once, and I fell back into the cockpit.

Next morning we hung my six gray nurse sharks on our tripod on the beach. I never felt such satisfaction and justification as that spectacle afforded me.

They were sleek, shiny gray, lean and wolfish, yet somehow had a fascinating beauty. The largest two weighed nearly five hundred pounds each.

* * *

The third morning dawned warm and still, with a calm ocean and blue sky. Starting early, we trolled for bait along the bluffs as far south as Point Bondi. I had engaged the services of Billy Love, market fisherman and shark catcher of Watson's Bay, to go with us as guide to the shark reefs. We caught no end of bait and soon were trolling off Bondi. We ran ten miles out and then turned north and ran until opposite Manly Beach, where we headed in again to run past that famous bathing beach where so many bathers had been attacked by sharks, and on down to Love's shark grounds directly opposite the harbor entrance between the [Sydney] Heads, and scarcely more than a mile outside the Heads.

We put down an anchor, or 'killick,' as our guide called it, in about two hundred feet of water. A gentle swell was moving the surface of the sea. The sun felt hot and good. Putting cut bait overboard, we had scarcely settled down to fishing when we had a strike from a small shark. It turned out to be a whaler of about three hundred pounds.

Love was jubilant over its capture.

"Shark meat best for sharks," he avowed enthusiastically. "Now we'll catch a tiger sure!". . . .

For my bait Love tied on a well-cut piece of shark, about two pounds in weight, and added what he called a fillet to hang from the point of the hook. I was an expert in baits and remarked that this one looked almost good enough to eat.

Then he let my bait down twenty-five fathoms without float or sinker. This occurred at noon, after which we had lunch, and presently I settled down comfortably to fish and absorb my surroundings.

The sun was hot, the gentle motion of the boat lulling, the breeze scarcely perceptible, the sea beautiful and compelling, and there was no moment that I could not see craft of all kinds, from the great liners to small fishing boats. I sat in my fishing chair, feet on the gunwale, the line in my hand, and the passage of time was unnoticeable. In fact, time seemed to stand still.

The hours passed, until about mid-afternoon, and conversation lagged. Emil went to sleep . . . Peter smoked innumerable cigarettes, and then he went to sleep. Love's hopes of a strike began perceptibly to fail. He kept repeating about every hour that the sharks must be having an off day. But I was quite happy and satisfied.

I watched three albatross hanging around a market boat some distance away. Finally this boat ran in, and the huge white and black birds floated over our way. I told Love to throw some pieces of bait in. He did so, one of which was a whole bonito with its sides sliced off. The albatross flew towards us, landed on their feet a dozen rods away, and then ran across the water to us. One was shy and distrustful. The others were tame. It happened, however, that the suspicious albatross got the whole bonito, which he proceeded to gulp down, and it stuck in his throat.

He drifted away, making a great to-do over the trouble his gluttony had brought him. He beat the water with his wings and ducked his head under to shake it violently.

Meanwhile the other two came close, to within thirty feet, and they emitted strange, low, not unmusical cries as they picked up the morsels of fish Love pitched them. They were huge birds, pure white except across the back and along the wide spreading wings. Their black eyes had an oriental look, a slanting back and upwards, which might have been caused by a little tuft of black feathers. To say I was in seventh heaven was putting it mildly. I woke Emil, who, being a temperamental artist and photographer, went into ecstasies with his camera. "I can't believe my eyes!" he kept exclaiming. And really the lovely sight was hard to believe for Americans who knew albatross only through legend and poetry.

Finally the larger and wilder one that had choked over his fish evidently got it down and came swooping down on the others. They then engaged in a fight for the pieces our boatman threw them. They ate a whole bucketful of cut bonito before they had their fill, and one of them was so gorged he could not rise from the surface. He drifted away, preening himself, while the others spread wide wings and flew out to sea.

Four o'clock found us still waiting for a bite. Emil had given up; Peter averred that there were no sharks. Love kept making excuses for the day and like a true fisherman kept saying: "We'll get one tomorrow." But I was not in a hurry. The afternoon was too wonderful to give up. A westering sun shone gold amid dark clouds over the Heads. The shipping had increased, if anything, and all that had been intriguing to me seemed magnified. . . .

My companions obviously gave up for that day. They were tired of the long wait. It amused me. I remarked to Peter: "Well, old top, do you remember the eighty-three days we fished without getting a bite?"

"I'll never forget that," said Pete.

"And on the eighty-fourth day I caught my giant Tahitian striped marlin?"

"Right, sir," admitted Peter.

Love appeared impressed by the fact, or else what he thought was fiction, but he said, nevertheless: "Nothing doing today. We might as well go in."

"Ump-umm," I replied in cowboy parlance. "We'll hang a while longer."

I did not mention that I had one of my rare and singular feelings of something about to happen. My companions settled down resignedly to what seemed futile carrying-on.

Fifteen minutes later something took hold of my line with a slow irresistible pull. My heart leaped. I could not accept what my eyes beheld. My line slowly payed off the reel. I put my gloved hand over the moving spool in the old habit of being ready to prevent an overrun. Still I did not believe it. But there—the line slipped off slowly, steadily, potently. Strike! There was no doubt of that. And I, who had experienced ten thousand strikes, shook all over with the possibilities of this one. Suddenly, sensing the actuality, I called out, *"There he goes!"*

Peter dubiously looked at my reel—saw the line gliding off.

"Right-o, sir!"

Love's tanned image became radiant. Emil woke up and began to stutter.

"It's a fine strike," yelled Love, leaping up. "Starts like a tiger!"

He ran forward to heave up the anchor. Peter directed Emil to follow and help him. Then I heard the crack of the electric starter and the sound of the engine.

"Let him have it!" advised Peter, hopefully. "It was a long wait, sir . . . Maybe . . . "

"Swell strike, Pete," I replied. "Never had one just like it. He has taken two hundred yards already. It feels under my fingers just as if you had your hand on my coat sleeve and were drawing me slowly toward you."

"Take care. He may put it in high. And that anchor line is long."

When Love and Emil shouted from forward, and then came running aft, the fish, whatever it was, had out between four and five hundred yards of line. I shoved forward the drag on the big Kovalovsky reel and struck with all my might. Then I reeled in swift and hard. Not until the fifth repetition of this violent action did I come up on the weight of that fish. So sudden and tremendous was the response that I was lifted clear out of my chair. Emil, hands at my belt, dragged me back.

"He's hooked. Some fish! Get my harness," I rang out.

In another moment, with my shoulders sharing that pull on me, I felt exultant, deeply thrilled, and as strong as Samson. I quite forgot to look at my watch, which seemed an indication of my feelings. My quarry kept on taking line even before I released the drag.

"Run up on him, Pete. Let's get close to him; I don't like being near these anchored boats."

There were two fishing boats around, the nearer a little too close for comfort. Peter hooked up the engine and I bent to the task of recovering four hundred yards of line. I found the big Kovalovsky perfect for this necessary job. I was hot and sweating, however, when again I came up hard on the heavy weight, now less than several hundred feet away and rather close to the surface.

I watched the bend of my rod tip.

"What kind of fish?" I asked.

"It's sure no black marlin," answered Peter, reluctantly.

"I couldn't tell from the rod," added Love. "But it's a heavy fish. I hope a tiger."

Emil sang out something hopeful. I said: "Well, boys, it's a shark of some kind," and went to work. With a medium drag I fought that shark for a while, watching the tip, and feeling the line, to get what we call 'a line' on him. But it was true that I had never felt a fish just like this one. One instant he seemed heavy as a rock, and the next light, moving, different. Again I lost the feel of him entirely, and knowing the habit of sharks to slip up on the line to bite it, I reeled like mad. So presently I was divided between the sense that he was little, after all, and the sense that he was huge. Naturally I gravitated to the conviction that I had hooked a new species of fish to me, and a tremendously heavy one. My plan of battle therefore was quickly decided by that. I shoved up the drag on the great Kovalovsky reel to five pounds, six, seven pounds. This much had heretofore been a drag I had never used. But this fish pulled each out just as easily as if there had been none. I could not hold him or get in any line without following him. So cautiously I pushed up the drag to nine pounds, an unprecedented power for me to use. It made no difference at all to the fish, wherefore I went back to five pounds. For a while I ran after him, wound in the line, then had the boat stopped and let him pull the line again.

"I forgot to take the time. Did any of you?"

"About half an hour," replied Emil.

"Just forty minutes," said Peter, consulting his clock in the cabin. "And you're working too fast—too hard. Ease up."

I echoed that forty minutes and could hardly believe it. But time flies in the early stages of a fight with a big fish. I took Peter's advice and reduced my action. And at this stage of the game I reverted to the conduct and talk of my companions and to the thrilling facts of the setting. Peter held the wheel and watched my line, grim and concerned. Love bounced around my chair, eager, talkative, excited. Emil sang songs and quoted poetry while he waited with his camera. Occasionally he snapped a picture of me.

The sea was aflame with sunset gold. A grand golden flare flooded through the gate between the Heads. Black against this wonderful sky the Sydney Bridge curved aloft over the city, majestic, marvelous in its beauty. To its left the sinking sun blazed upon the skyscraper buildings. The black cliffs, gold rimmed, stood up boldly far above me. But more marvelous than any of these, in fact exceedingly rare and lovely to me, were the ships putting to sea out of that illuminated gateway. There were six of these in plain sight. . . .

All this while, which seemed very short and was perhaps a half an hour, I worked on my fish, and I was assured that he knew it. Time had passed, for the lighthouse on the cliff suddenly sent out its revolving piercing rays. Night was not far away, yet I seemed to see everything almost as clearly as day.

For quite a space I had been able to get the double line over the reel, but I could not hold it. However I always tried to. I had two gloves and thumb stalls on each hand, and with these I could safely put a tremendous strain on the line without undue risk, which would not have been the case had I trusted the rod.

By now the sport and thrill had been superceded by pangs of toil and a grim reality of battle. It had long ceased to be fun. I was getting whipped and I knew it. I had worked too swiftly. The fish was slowing and it was a question of who would give up first. Finally, without increasing the strain, I found I could stop and hold my fish on the double line. This was occasion for renewed zest. When I told my crew they yelled wildly. Peter had long since got out the big detachable gaff, with its long rope.

I held on to that double line with burning, painful hands. And I pulled it in foot by foot, letting go to wind in the slack.

"The leader—I see it!" whispered Love.

"Whoopee!" yelled Emil.

"A little more, sir," added Peter, tensely, leaning over the gunwale, his gloved hand outstretched.

In another moment I had the big swivel of the leader in reach.

"Hang on, Pete!" I panted, as I stood up to release the drag and unhook my harness. "Drop the leader—overboard . . . Emil, stand by . . . Love, gaff this fish when I—tell you."

"He's coming, sir," rasped out Peter, hauling in, his body taut. "There! . . . *My Gawd!*"

Emil screeched at the top of his lungs. The water opened to show the back of an enormous shark. Pearl gray in color, with dark tiger stripes, a huge rounded head and wide flat back, this fish looked incredibly beautiful. I had expected a hideous beast.

"*Now!*" I yelled.

Love lunged with the gaff. I stepped back, suddenly deluged with flying water and blindly aware of a roar and a banging on the boat. I could not see anything for moments. The men were shouting hoarsely in unison. I distinguished Peter's voice. "*Rope—tail!*"

"*Let him run!*" I shouted.

Between the up-splashing sheets of water I saw the three men holding that shark. It was a spectacle. Peter stood up, but bent, with his brawny shoulders sagging. Love and Emil were trying to rope that flying tail. . . . It beat any battle I recalled with a fish at the gaff. The huge tiger rolled over, all white underneath, and he opened a mouth that would have taken a barrel. I saw the rows of white fangs and heard such a snap of jaws that had never before struck my ears. I shuddered at their significance. No wonder men shot and harpooned such vicious brutes.

"It's over his tail," cried Love, hoarsely, and straightened up with the rope. Emil lent a hand. And then the three men held that ferocious tiger shark until he ceased his struggles. They put another rope over his tail and made fast to the ring bolt.

When Peter turned to me his broad breast heaved, his breath whistled, the corded muscles stood out on his arms; he could not speak.

"Pete! Good work. I guess that's about the hardest tussle we've ever had at the gaff."

We towed our prize into the harbor and around to the dock at Watson's Bay, where a large crowd awaited us. They cheered us lustily. They dragged the vast bulk of my shark up on the sand. It required twenty-odd men to move him. He looked marble color in the twilight. But the tiger stripes showed up distinctly. He knocked men right and left with his lashing tail, and he snapped those terrible jaws. The crowd, however, gave that business end of him a wide berth. I had one good long look at this tiger shark while the men were erecting a tripod; and I accorded him more appalling beauty and horrible significance than all the great fish I had ever caught. . . .

Doctor Stead, scientist and official of the Sydney Museum, and Mr. Bullen of the Rod Fishers Society weighed and measured my record tiger shark. Length, thirteen feet ten inches. Weight, one thousand and thirty-six pounds!

IX

Mexico

A fisherman has many dreams, and from boyhood one of mine was to own a beautiful white ship with sails like wings, and to sail the lonely tropic seas.

Sometimes dreams, even those of a fisherman, come true.

Zihuatanejo Bay

It took almost two weeks for the *Fisherman* to reach Zihuatanejo Bay [about a hundred miles up the coast from Acapulco]. We had to lay outside all night, as it was impossible to see the narrow entrance to the bay, or even the single black rock that stands about a mile offshore.

I was up at five o'clock, when the darkness seemed to be moving away across the ocean, before the gray light from the east. Magnificent dark mountains loomed above the dim mystic shore. When daylight came we found the black rock and then the entrance to the bay. The sun rose red over the range, flooding a scene of unparalleled beauty and wildness.

Zihuatanejo Bay opened out into a round, placid expanse of water, blazing with the gold and red of morning. The colored slopes ran down to the curved white beach and the lines of coconut palms. . . . We ran in for a mile and anchored about the center of the bay, with the white beach stretching on each side of us. Deep coves marked the extreme ends of the bay, and along the shore of the left one nestled the primitive dwellings of the natives—colored houses and shacks of thatched palm and whitewashed adobe. Columns of blue smoke rose lazily upwards. Natives in white patrolled the beach, watching the ship. The place was exquisitely beautiful, yet melancholy with something I could not grasp.

While we were putting the launches overboard we saw seven sailfish leap out beyond the mouth of the bay, and if it were needed this was enough to rouse us to the highest pitch of enthusiasm for this out-of-the-way spot.

* * *

Morro Rocks were some miles up the coast from Zihuatanejo Bay, about as far north as were the White Friars to the south.

But no other similarity existed, unless it might have been that the same felicitousness of name so characteristic of the Spaniards held true. They were rugged, gray, upheaved masses of stone, crowned with grass and low brush, and worn and serrated at the base by the ceaseless wash of the swells that piled and broke upon them.

When we ran by the first rock we were surprised by a loud squawking of parrots; and soon we discerned numbers of macaws flying with the flocks of boobies. They were large green birds, with very long tails of deep blue, and a red top-knot. What a clamor they raised! It was decidedly new and unique to fish under flocks of screaming macaws that manifestly resented our presence. Evidently they had their nests on these high rocks.

In the heavy currents and white boiling backwash from the cliffs we found the *gallo*, or roosterfish.

My first strike was a smash so swift that I saw only a flash of green. My tackle was light, of course, but as heavy as we thought proper. Nevertheless, I could not even stop this first fish. He ran around the jagged rocks, and once he was high in a swell above us. Soon he broke off. Then Captain Mitchell had a fine strike from a fish we plainly saw. His broad silver side and his raised black fin, like streamers of ribbon, betrayed him. He hit the spoon but missed the hook, and he did not come back.

We were using No. 6 Wilson spoons, which we had found the most attractive there for all these inshore fish. We hooked many redsnapper, crevalle, mackerel, and grouper, which no doubt kept us from hooking more gallo. It was strenuous work. A forty-pound red snapper took time and labor. But we figured out that the fast roosterfish usually had the first strike in any given place. When he hit the spoon he shook his head fiercely like a bulldog and usually shook free. We were some time learning this.

The windward side of the second Morro Rock was a turbulent place of seething green and white. A strong current ran in here and the swell crashed to ruin on saw-tooth ledges. As we ran past the outside rock, a yellow treacherous thing, I saw deep blue-green depths and amber shadows. When my shining wavering spoon reached this point, I had a solid strike at the instant I saw a black-and-white fish shape. I leaped up to the singing of the reel. My line sped out probably swifter than any time I remembered. At the end of a two hundred-yard run the fish came out. It would not be correct to say he leaped or jumped; he flew, like a silver, black-winged bird. He was a big, powerful, fierce fish, and surely gave me thrills and fears.

Meanwhile, Captain Sid got the launch turned, and we chased him full speed, both engines. And then we were just in the nick of time. This fish headed round the corner of the island, beyond the ragged rocks to deep water, where the magnificent swells heaved out of the green and crashed up the ledges. Then as the bottom of the sea seemed to drop, a deep roaring gulf slanted from our boat to the green shell encrusted rock, down which white waterfalls were pouring, from tiny streams to heavy torrents.

It was a place I would never have risked myself in a boat containing only one engine. But this little craft had two, and our risk was small.

My roosterfish ran into that caldron. The heavy swell caught him, lifted and carried him high. All the while he was fighting after the manner of a steelhead trout. I had not the slightest hope of saving him. Suddenly, he shot out again, close to us, so that we saw him clearly. He was broad, heavy, white and black; his tail was curved, his eyes seemed large and bold, his open jaws massive. And he shook himself in the air. Right then I fancied I saw in this *gallo* traces of yellowtail, amberjack, pompano, and especially the permit, which is as great if not as rare as the roosterfish.

He ran along the whole length of that island, through the thundering surges; and by some miracle of good fortune I led him out into the channel, where I soon subdued him.

When he lay on the floor of the boat I had opportunity to grasp the reality of a new, strange, wonderful fish. But how almost impossible to tell why this was true! The dorsal fin appeared to be a succession of black silk ribbons, broad at the base, tapering to the end of a full foot length. He was massive all over, from huge head to wide tail, the most dazzling silver hue I ever found in any fish. In the sunlight his back was green; in the shadow it was dark. From under the skin changing gleams of pearl seemed to shine.

Always the ocean was yielding some more superlative quality of beauty. Always the beauty! It seemed such a mystery to me. But perhaps nature required beauty as well as other attributes in its scheme of evolution.

When we ran back to the place from which I had lured my roosterfish, Captain Mitchell hooked another and a larger one. What a rush! Out he flashed twice, and then on the crest of a mighty swell, he limned his beautiful shape against the sky. That was enough for me. I felt unutterably rewarded. But the captain was of another mind and grimly held on to the job of catching this one. And after a tussle of a half an hour, now lifted aloft on a huge wave, and anon dropped into the hollow of the sea, with the boom and crash and windy spray all around us, and above the screaming macaws, he finally did it, too.

We tried the two other islands and were rewarded with several strikes. I hooked one that had too much speed and weight, and with a parting leap out of a patch of white foam he tore loose.

By this time our tackle was practically ruined, the most of which was due to the heavy snappers that we could not avoid. So we called it a day and said good-bye to the noisy macaws.

On the fifth day of our sojourn at Zihuatanejo we decided to run far offshore and see if we could locate sailfish or swordfish. I saw one fin that I was positive belonged to a sailfish. Captain Mitchell had two strikes from fish we could not see, but their manner of tugging at the bait, letting go, and coming back to tug again, convinced me that these were sailfish also. They were finicky strikers and hard to hook. Captain Mitchell thought he got hold of one of them, but I was inclined to doubt this.

The sun was roasting hot, and seven hours out there burnt us black. I did not suffer from sunburn, but the glare hurt my eyes. When we came in my sight was blurred by dots and hazy patches. What relief the sunset, and later the cool of night! I sat out upon deck listening to the roar of the slow swell around the bay. It was a moving and changing sound, tremendous at times, like the storm wind in the pines, and at others low, deep, melancholy, with a strange note.

Next morning I was rested and eager as ever. The day was cool, fresh, with a faint breeze rippling the water. Before the sun rose the sky was deep blue, and the shadows on the water were reflections of the rosy clouds. The red sun soon changed all that.

We left as early as usual and trolled along the rocky points for mackerel for bait. I hooked a roosterfish that ran off with my leader and spoon. We could not catch any mackerel. R.C. had gone out to Black Rock and was trolling around it.

There was a slow high swell running, very beautiful to see, and the motion was fascinating, but I had learned that such a swell was bad for fishing. My first strike came from a shark that leaped fiercely, turning in the air head forward like the revolution of a steel projectile. He made half a dozen of these wheeling leaps and then threw the hook. Captain Mitchell caught several crevalle, and I caught a yellowtail. R.C. ran by us and hailed us with good news. He had seen sailfish on the way out to the rock. We wasted a good deal of valuable time trying to catch bait, and at last gave up and headed out to sea.

We had covered a couple of miles when Sid sighted a sailfish on the horizon. He leaped nine times, enough for us to see he was big. With both engines at full speed we ran out and were soon somewhere in the vicinity. R.C. followed us closely.

I saw another sailfish way to the eastward, and then, as we began to troll again, I espied a big black sail coming out of a glassy patch not far away. We ran for it. Soon it disappeared, and we could only guess where to fish.

Captain Mitchell was trolling with a silver tarporeno, and I was using a strip of yellowtail. We were running at a pretty fast clip, after the method at Long Key. Soon I saw a sailfish leap, a mile away, and not long afterwards one came out within a couple of hundred yards. He leaped twice, curving out sidewise, and showing himself clearly. He was not very long, but pretty broad. I saw his tail several times, and we circled to get in front of him.

I was looking everywhere, except at out baits, when Captain Mitchell said calmly, "He's got it!" And as I looked he gave a slight jerk. Then followed a crash on the surface. A heavy sailfish came half out as he threw the tarporeno plug high in the air. In my excitement and disappointment I was blunt in telling the captain that he should have struck instantly with all his might.

While we ran on we talked about this fish, and the only thing we agreed upon was that it really was a sailfish. Perhaps a half an hour later, while we were running parallel with the other boat, we saw R.C. get a strike and hook a fish. Three times R.C. swept the rod back powerfully. I reeled in my bait in frantic haste and dove for my camera. As I came up with it the sailfish sent the water flying white and leaped out of it. He was long, black, sharp, with an enormous spread of sail that flapped like a huge wing. Down he crashed, to pitch aloft again; and that was the beginning of a series of a dozen or more jumps. Out of all I photographed five, and two that I secured were of his spectacular performances. Then he sounded.

In due time R.C. brought him to the boat, and we ran near to get a good view. While they were securing the fish he threshed and lashed the water white. What struck me most, when they drew him aboard, was the extraordinary length. I went on R.C.'s boat to get a better look at this sailfish. He was indeed a wild, strange creature from the deep. His color was a dark amber, very rich and glossy, and dim bars showed along the sides. The sail was black, with spots. His tail was magnificent, very wide and forked, with the lobes tapering to a point. His pectoral fins were truly striking, being two long rapier-like appendages, straight, and black as coal. The extreme delicacy and fineness of all the features about this sailfish were commented upon by all of us. He was certainly a different species from that of the Gulf Stream. His length was nine feet four and a half inches, which was fourteen inches longer than any Atlantic sailfish I had ever seen measured, including the record. The estimated weight was a hundred pounds, very light indeed for his length.

This good fortune fired us anew with zeal, and we went to trolling again. It was my fortune to see a sailfish come shooting back of my bait, his sail half out. I yelled thrillingly, so that all might see. He tapped my bait, took it swift as a flash, sped away. I let him have too much line. Still I was not slow. But he was a wary fish, and as I leaned forward to strike he let go of my bait and did not come back for it.

For a while my chagrin and disappointment were intense. My first sailfish strike in six days—missed! But after a while the selfish feelings wore away, and the day ended for me with a keen sense of pleasure. In all we had sighted sixteen sail-fish, several of them very large. R.C. assured us he had seen a marlin swordfish that was a five hundred-pounder. Chester verified this, and as he was standing on top of the deck, looking down at the swordfish coming for the teaser, his opinion was trustworthy.

That afternoon and evening we spent hours talking and conjecturing, working over tackle, and preparing for the next day. It dawned somewhat cloudy, and the cooler and fresher for that. The sunrise over the mountains was a burst of rose and gold through broken trade wind clouds. We were off before six-thirty, Captain Mitchell in the small launch with one of the sailors, Romer on R.C.'s boat, and I went alone with Sid and Heisler, one of the mates. We lost no time in getting out to Black Rock. A mighty surge was booming and we could not fish as close as usual; nevertheless, we soon caught all the bait we needed. Captain Mitchell went to the westward, while we headed out to sea.

About a mile off Black Rock we espied an Indian canoe with a singular figure in it. Upon near approach we found a young man squatting in one end of the canoe, which was drifting. We had imagined he was fishing. But he was not doing anything but crouching there in a strange, dejected posture. He was nude. We hailed him, but all the response we got was the raising of his head. Naturally we thought the Indian was drunk or crazy, and we went on our way. It did not appear to be our business to interfere with his peculiar way of being happy.

As we sped out to sea we kept a keen watch for leaping sailfish. Not a sign! The morning was perfect, and we were surprised and disappointed not to find the dark ripply water broken by an occasional white splash.

The boobies followed us in flocks, and when we tried to troll a bait they made it impossible. I jerked my bait away from what seemed a thousand. How they could dive! I amused myself by observing their accuracy. They could dive as true and straight as a rifle bullet. Every time I refrained from jerking my bait they hit it squarely. But if I made a quick jerk, just as they dove, they always hit just back of it, to their evident amaze[ment] and anger. Some wise old boobies, after a few ineffectual attempts, sailed aloft ahead of the moving bait, and they shot down with wings closed. But every time I frustrated this. After a while I grew tired and reeled in my bait until this particular flock of boobies gave up.

About ten o'clock R.C. and Romer had strikes, both of which they missed. We ran nearer to call inquiries and learned that Romer had missed the same striking sailfish five times, and R.C. once.

"Romer, you've got to be on the job to hook these birds," I called back.

A little later I felt a quick hard rap at my bait. It gave me a thrill, yet I looked sharp, expecting to see a boobie come up from a dive, as I had a thousand times more or less that morning. But no boobie showed. Another rap! Then my bait was snatched by a voracious sailfish, and my reel whizzed. I performed my part correctly, according to our practice, but I missed him. He took hold of my bait again, and in spite of my speed he let go before I could hook him.

This was all right. I was beginning to appreciate the swiftness, the sagacity, the delicate attack of these Pacific sailfish.

It added more zest to the pursuit. After that I stood up most of the time, watching my bait; and as luck would have it, inside of another hour, I saw the amber flash of a sailfish as he hit my bait. I let him turn and shoot away before I struck. I felt a solid, irresistible weight. Then the water cracked and the sailfish came out with arrowy swiftness. He looked green-gold-white. The bronze bars shone brightly. He waved an enormous blue sail.

I turned to locate R.C.'s boat and saw it quite a distance off, coming fast. But I felt they would arrive too late for pictures. My sailfish was out of the water more than in it; only once, however, did he leap high, as had R.C.'s fish. He made twelve jumps, all thrilling and beautiful, then sounded. I settled down to fight him then and in due time had him exhausted. Towards the end of the battle he stood up on his tail three times, all of which performances Chester photographed. My swordfish tackle was hardly fair to this size fish. When we brought him aboard, we all decided he was larger than R.C.'s.

Wind and sea came up, and by noon it was rough. We ran back to the ship. Captain Mitchell had not returned. My sailfish was nine feet five inches long and weighed one hundred ten and a half pounds. The spread of his tail was two feet ten inches. The grace and symmetry, the wonderful muscular power, seemed beyond description.

R.C. reported two strikes, and Romer had to confess to the five from one sailfish. About three o'clock Captain Mitchell arrived with a tale of woe. He could not raise a fish with cut bait, so he used the tarporenos again. He reported three sailfish strikes and another from a marlin or broadbill swordfish. This fish charged the tarporeno and rushed off with it. Captain Mitchell avowed he struck with all his might. The fish lifted head and shoulders out of the water, showing the red tarporeno stuck in the side of his jaw. He had a massive bronze head and a long bill. He sounded and deep down got rid of the offensive hooks.

We were at a loss what to be sure of. I inclined to the conviction that it was a marlin. In all my experience, only one broadbill even charged my bait.

Regarding the sailfish strikes, however, we were unanimous in our admiration for the remarkable speed and dexterity with which they were made. These Pacific sailfish were very much larger and faster and wiser than their Atlantic brothers. Considering, then, that I had always declared the sailfish of the Gulf Stream to be the finest gamefish for light tackle, these of the Pacific began to loom in amazing and bewildering proportions. How could we catch them, if that were possible? How large did they grow? What did they feed on? Where was their range? No angler before R.C. and me had ever wet a line along this lonely coast. It was as wild as the Galapagos. The native Indians went out in canoes hewn from logs, and, hugging the protected part of the shore, they speared small surface fish for food. We fished from five to ten miles offshore, and when we turned shipward after the day's sport was over, we had a magnificent panorama to gaze at all the way in. . . .

The White Friars shone like creamy snow, kneeling on the blue floor of the ocean. Beyond them began the first low shore range, burned brown by the heat, and this reached to the higher ranges, veiled in smoky haze, that were mere foothills to the grand black Sierra Madres, standing clear and bold above the heat palls. They lifted their peaks to the vast belt of cumulous cloud, the thunderheads so often seen above the Mojave Desert of California. Vast columns, pillars, temples of gods in the blue sky! They were white and gold, formed with the convolutions of smoke, standing motionless and sublime above the mountains. They were creations of the intense heat of the sun, and they had lodged against the peaks.

On March 22 all morning the sea was a dark, glooming, heaving expanse, gray under the soft clouds. It was such delightful weather that almost I did not care whether or not I saw any fish. But I had two strikes and missed both. I got a jump out of each fish, which Chester photographed, before they threw the hook. The last sailfish was most exasperating.

I saw him coming behind my bait and leaped to my feet. His sail cut the water, standing above the surface quite distinctly. His color was a bronze-purple. He did not weave behind the bait after the manner of a cunning marlin; he just sailed straight at the bait and hit it and took it. As he turned away I clipped on the drag and jerked. Pulled the bait out of his mouth! Releasing the drag I slacked a little line. He pounced upon the bait again. And again I missed hooking him. This time it was necessary to let back a good deal of line before he snapped the bait once more. Then I gave him considerable line. Nevertheless, when I did strike, the hook held only long enough to fetch him out in a beautiful leap.

That was the extent of my connection with sailfish this memorable day. To R.C. belonged the credit of making it memorable. I had Captain Sid run my boat close to R.C. all the morning; and that was how I happened to be a witness to his extraordinary experience.

We saw a sailfish leap near Black Rock, and we ran to troll our baits round the spot. R.C. raised this fish, hooked him, and got a high tumbling leap out of him before they parted.

An hour later, some miles out, we heard a yell that turned us quickly. A long ragged purple fin was shooting behind R.C.'s bait, which was perhaps fifty feet in the rear of the boat. R.C. duplicated my performance of missing him three times, and he beat it with a fourth miss. The fifth time, however, with three hundred feet of line out, he finally hung this sailfish solidly. With all that line out there was bound to be a circus. I ran round in my boat, camera in hands, while this gamefish leaped thirty-three times. When he was brought to the boat, we were all out of breath, especially Chester. We were also beaming, especially Chester, who had photographed every leap.

Not a great while after that Sid's yell made me wheel in time to see another sailfish on R.C.'s line. Its record leap was marvelous—a clean, lofty spring, a turn in the air, with great sail flying, and a dive back. My camera caught the third jump, and my eye began to appreciate the extraordinary length of this fish. We danced around R.C. in our little boat while his sailfish cleared the water some twenty-odd times. After he quit jumping it appeared he took a good deal of hard punishment. We ran close to see the finish. The sailfish came up tail first, apparently entangled in the leader, something that R.C. and I abominate. I saw the broken leader standing out of its mouth. We were to learn presently that the swivel on the leader had cut into the tail, and stuck there, after the leader broke. I not only gasped at R.C.'s announcement of the facts of the case but also at the wonderful length and slim beauty of this sailfish. He was black with light bars and a purple fin.

But that was not all! In less than thirty minutes R.C. had another big fin behind his bait. He had to tease this fish to bite and only hooked it after many slackings back of the bait.

White spurts of spray! A lean wagging wild birdlike shape in the air! Sid sped my boat up to get back of the sailfish, and I missed a chance at some spectacular leaps. I also lost his location.

Suddenly, close to R.C.'s boat, there was an enormous splash, and a heavy sailfish, wiggling and waving, clove the air. At the same instant the sailfish on R.C.'s hook leaped splendidly, so close to our boat that Sid had to throw the wheel hard to port. What was our utter amazement then to see, in another leap near R.C.'s boat that he had *two* sailfish on his line. Sid yelled, "Am I seeing things?" And I yelled back, "You sure are."

Just what was actually transpiring I could not understand; still I knew it was actual and incomparable.

I lost track of the sailfish on R.C.'s hook and kept my eye keen for the one tangled up in his line. It leaped repeatedly, so quickly that I was never quite ready. My boat rocked and the excitement was intense. I saw Chester winding the crank of his motion picture machine, and that afforded me infinite satisfaction. This sailfish quieted down quickly, as far as surface work was concerned, and went to plugging deep. However, in perhaps a quarter of an hour more, R.C. brought it to the boat. Bob got hold of the tangled line, drew the fish close, and grasped its bill. There was some threshing and flying spray.

The minds of all of us then reverted to the sailfish that had been on R.C.'s hook. It was gone. So was the leader.

We ran close, and R.C. said: "Did you ever see the beat of that? Never again can I jolly myself with hard luck stuff! This blooming sailfish ran past the boat, right at my line, *and began to bite it.* Then the sailfish on my hook made a quick leap, twitching my line over the bill of this one. I saw it happen. He made a lunge, came out, turned over, and twisted up in my line."

I waved to my red-faced and beaming brother. I salaamed to him. I doffed my fishing helmet.

"R.C., you win!" I called. "The plush-lined pajamas are yours. Henceforth I must fish alone."

Remarkable as were all the facts of this capture, it was my opinion that the fact of the sailfish biting at R.C.'s line was the most wonderful. We had seen the same act performed by sailfish in the Gulf Stream. I had not the slightest doubt that it was caused by the instinct of the sailfish to free its mate.

R.C.'s first fish measured nine feet two inches and weighed one hundred and nine pounds; the second nine feet ten inches long and weighed one hundred and thirteen pounds; and the third fish, nine feet three inches over all, tipped the scales at one hundred and eighteen pounds. If the long slim specimen had been fat instead of lean, he would have reached two hundred.

Fishermen, no matter what supreme good fortune befalls them, cannot ever be absolutely satisfied. It is a fundamental weakness of intellect.

Byme-by-Tarpon

To capture a fish is not all of the fishing. Yet there are circumstances which make this philosophy hard to accept. I have in mind an incident of angling tribulation which rivals the most poignant instant of my boyhood, when a great trout flopped for one sharp moment on a mossy stone and then was gone like a golden flash into the depths of the pool.

Some years ago I followed Attalano, my guide, down the narrow Mexican street of Tampico to the bank of the broad Panuco. Under the rosy dawn the river quivered like a restless opal. The air, sweet with the song of blackbird and meadowlark, was full of cheer; the rising sun shone in splendor on the water and the long line of graceful palms lining the opposite bank, and the tropical forest beyond, with its luxuriant foliage festooned by gray moss. Here was a day to warm the heart of any fisherman; here was the beautiful river, celebrated in many a story; here was the famous guide, skilled with oar and gaff, rich in experience. What sport I would have; what treasure of keen sensation would I store; what flavor of life would I taste this day! Hope burns always in the heart of a fisherman.

Attalano was in harmony with the day and the scene. He had a cheering figure, lithe and erect, with a springy stride, bespeaking the Montezuma blood said to flow in his Indian veins. Clad in a colored cotton shirt, blue jeans, and Spanish girdle, and treading the path with brown feet never deformed by shoes, he would have stopped an artist. Soon he bent his muscular shoulders to the oars, and the ripples circling from each stroke hardly disturbed the calm Panuco. Down the stream glided long Indian canoes, hewn from trees and laden with oranges and bananas. In the stern stood a dark native wielding an enormous paddle with ease. Wildfowl dotted the glassy expanse; white cranes and pink flamingoes graced the reedy bars; red-breasted kingfishers flew over with friendly screech. The salt breeze kissed my cheek; the sun shone with the comfortable warmth northerners welcome in spring; from over the white sand dunes far below came the faint boom of the ever-restless Gulf.

We trolled up the river and down, across from one rush-lined lily-padded shore to the other, for miles and miles with never a strike. But I was content, for over me had been cast the dreamy, care-dispelling languor of the south.

When the first long, low swell of the changing tide rolled in, a stronger breeze raised little dimpling waves and chased along the water in dark quickening frowns. All at once the tarpon began to show, to splash, to play, to roll. It was as though they had been awakened by the stir and murmur of the miniature breakers. Broad bars of silver flashed in the sunlight, green backs cleft the little billows, wide tails slapped lazily on the water. Every yard of the river seemed to hold a rolling fish. This sport increased until the long stretch of water, which had been as calm as St. Regis Lake at twilight, resembled the quick current of a Canadian stream. But it was also particularly exasperating, because when fish roll in this sportive, lazy way, they will not bite. For an hour I trolled through this whirlpool of flying spray and twisting tarpon, with many a salty drop on my face, hearing all around me the whipping crash of breaking water.

"Byme-by-tarpon," presently remarked Attalano, favoring me with his first specimen of English.

The rolling of the tarpon diminished and finally ceased as noon advanced.

No more did I cast longing eyes upon those huge bars of silver. They were buried treasure. The breeze quickened as the flowing tide gathered strength, and together they drove the waves higher. Attalano rowed across the river into the outlet of one of the lagoons. This narrow stream was unruffled by wind; its current was sluggish and its muddy waters were clarifying under the influence of the now fast-rising tide.

By a sunken log near shore we rested for lunch. I found the shade of the trees on the bank rather pleasant and became interested in a blue heron, a russet colored duck, and a brown and black snipe, all sitting on the sunken log. Nearby stood a tall crane watching us solemnly, and above in the treetop a parrot vociferously proclaimed his knowledge of our presence. I was wondering if he objected to our invasion, at the same time taking a most welcome bite of lunch, when directly in front of me the water flew as if propelled by some submarine power. Framed in a shower of spray I saw an immense tarpon, with mouth agape and fins stiff, close in pursuit of frantically leaping little fish.

The fact that Attalano dropped his sandwich attested to the large size and close proximity of the tarpon. He uttered a grunt of satisfaction and pushed out the boat. A school of feeding tarpon closed the mouth of the lagoon. Thousands of mullet had been cut off from their river haunts and were now leaping, flying, darting in wild haste to elude the great white monsters. In the foamy swirls I saw streaks of blood.

"Byme-by-tarpon!" called Attalano, warningly.

Shrewd guide! I had forgotten that I held a rod. When the realization dawned on me that sooner or later I would feel the strike of one of these silver tigers, a keen, tingling thrill of excitement quivered over me. The primitive man asserted himself; the instinctive lust to conquer and to kill seized me, and I leaned forward, tense, and strained with suspended breath and swelling throat.

Suddenly the strike came, so tremendous in its energy that it almost pulled me from my seat; so quick, fierce, bewildering that I could think of nothing but to hold on. Then the water split with a hissing sound to let out a great tarpon, long as a door, seemingly as wide, who shot up and up into the air. He wagged his head and shook it like a struggling wolf. When he fell back with a heavy splash, a rainbow, exquisitely beautiful and delicate, stood out of the spray, glowed, paled, and faded.

Five times he sprang toward the blue sky, and as many he plunged down with a thunderous crash. The reel screamed. The line sang. The rod, which I thought stiff as a tree, bent like a willow wand. The silver king came up far astern and sheered to the right in a long, wide curve, leaving behind a white wake. Then he sounded, while I watched the line with troubled eyes. But not long did he sulk. He began a series of magnificent tactics new in my experience. He stood on his tail, then on his head; he sailed like a bird; he shook himself so violently as to make a convulsive, shuffling sound; he dove, to come up covered with mud, marring his bright sides; he closed his huge gills with a slap and, most remarkable of all, he rose in the shape of a crescent, to straighten out with such marvelous power that he actually seemed to crack like a whip.

After this performance, which left me in a state of mental aberration, he sounded again, to begin a persistent, dragging pull which was the most disheartening of all his maneuvers;

for he took yard after yard of line until he was far away from me, out in the Panuco. We followed him and for an hour crossed to and fro, up and down, humoring him, responding to his every caprice, as if he verily were a king. At last, with a strange inconsistency more human than fishlike, he returned to the scene of his fatal error, and here in the mouth of the smaller stream he leaped once more. But it was only a ghost of his former errors—a slow, weary rise, showing he was tired. I could see it in the weakening wag of his head. He no longer made the line whistle.

I began to recover the long line. I pumped and reeled him closer. Reluctantly he came, not yet broken in spirit, though his strength had sped. He rolled at times with a shade of the old vigor, with a pathetic manifestation of the temper that became a hero. I could see the long slender tip of his dorsal fin, then his broad tail, and finally the gleam of his silver side. Closer he came and circled slowly around the boat, eyeing me with great, accusing eyes. I measured him with a fisherman's glance. What a great fish! Seven feet, I calculated, at the very least.

At this triumphant moment I made a horrible discovery. About six feet from the leader the strands of the line had frayed, leaving only one thread intact. My blood ran cold and the clammy sweat broke out on my brow. My empire was not won; my first tarpon was as if he had never been. But true to my fishing instincts I held on morosely; tenderly I handled him; with brooding care I riveted my eye on the frail place in the line, and gently, ever so gently, I began to lead the silver king shoreward. Every smallest move of his tail meant disaster to me, so when he moved it I let go of the reel. Then I would have to coax him to swim back again.

The boat touched the bank. I stood up and carefully headed my fish toward the shore, and slid his head and shoulders out on the lily pads. One moment he lay there, glowing like mother-of-pearl, a rare fish, fresh from the sea. Then, as Attalano warily reached for the leader, he gave a gasp, a flop that deluged us with muddy water, and a lunge that spelled freedom.

I watched him swim slowly away with my bright leader dragging beside him. Is it not the loss of things that makes life bitter? What we have gained is ours; what is lost is gone, whether fish . . . or love, or name, or fame.

I tried to put on a cheerful aspect for my guide. But it was too soon. Attalano, wise old fellow, understood my case. A smile, warm and living, flashed across his dark face as he spoke:

"Byme-by-tarpon."

Which defined his optimism and revived the failing spark within my breast. It was, too, in the nature of a prophecy.

X

The Galapagos

*The hazard of this fishing game in the tropics did not on
the moment seem as fascinating as I had imagined it might
be. Perhaps that was because I felt responsible for everybody, especially my boy Romer, and his pal, and R.C.*

*This thought led me to another danger, and that was to risk
a ship more than five hundred miles out of the track of
steamers and sailing craft. I felt terribly alone. We did not
fear storms, for they were rare in this latitude. The thought
of fire on board was appalling. I had never been placed in
quite such an insecure situation. It would have appealed
more to me if I had been without responsibility for others.
The lure of virgin seas was irresistible, but it had its draw-
backs, such as I now faced. Thought and intelligence have
considerable power over the primitive in man. That is the
hope of progress in the world.*

The Galapagos

Facts are often inimical to romance, but they are very important when it comes to distance. We had been told at Balboa that Cocos Island lay anywhere from one hundred and fifty to three hundred miles off the mainland. As a matter of fact the chart and the log made it over five hundred and forty. The same inaccuracy applied to the distance between Cocos Island and the Galapagos. When we left Cocos the chart showed that we had four hundred and fifty to run.

The wide waste of blue waters appalled me, especially at night, when the moon soared blazing and white, surrounded by pale-green effulgence. Hour after hour the sails flapped, the booms creaked, the dark waters glided by; and yet we seemed never to be getting anywhere.

The solemn days were easier to bear because of the clear white light of day, and the hope of seeing bird or fish life, even if there were none. For two days the ocean seemed barren of life. But how beautiful in its vivid blue, its gentle swell, its solitude and tranquility!

Then we began to see bonita darting ahead of the bow, and splashes on the distant horizon, and unknown sea birds, and schools of porpoises. Once we ran across the smooth oil track—slick it is called—of a whale that had sounded. I saw a booby, white as snow, with black-tipped wings. Flying fish arose occasionally, scattering after they rose.

We ran across a school of dolphin, long and slim, and more agile than the northern species. They leaped often, sometimes lifting lazily and high, and at others shooting out, to cavort in the air, twisting like steel projectiles, and then to hit the water with a sharp splash.

In the afternoon we had the rare good fortune to pass within a few hundred yards of a school of porpoises, small and short and black, feeding on the surface. Boobies were hovering over them, darting down. And big silver-white tuna were smashing the water into the familiar sharp spurts and leaping high to dive down. This species was neither the yellow-fin nor long-fin, so it must have been the blue-fin. R.C. and Bob, Captain Mitchell and Sid and I all identified this tuna, as well as it could possibly be done, as the blue-fin. We were exceedingly pleased.

When the ship reached a point about two hundred yards behind the porpoises and tuna, and somewhat to their left, they suddenly ceased feeding and began to leap and plunge away from us, charging in almost a solid line, churning the water white. It was so extraordinary and new a spectacle that we loudly exclaimed our delight. For a few moments tuna showed here and there in that splashing formation; then they vanished to give place to porpoises. These kept up the leaping, almost with a straight front, for fully a quarter of a mile. Then they slackened their leaps, and slowed down, and sounded. We could only conclude that this mixed school of fishes and porpoises had taken fright at the near approach of the ship.

Our intention had been to strike our first anchorage in the Galapagos Archipelago at Tagus Cove, in Albemarle Sound. But we decided later to head for Conway Bay on [Santa Cruz] Island, and altered our course to this end.

The change gave us the advantage of the light breeze, and we glided along over a summer sea at eight knots. On all sides above the horizon trade wind clouds shone pearly white in the bright sunlight. Their regular formation and level bottoms reminded me of the trade wind clouds over the Gulf Stream. They added not only beauty but comfort to our ride down the Pacific under the tropic skies. The early still morning had been very hot and humid, so that any effort was disagreeable, but at three o'clock, with the breeze freshening, the air grew delightful, even cool, and sailing was most enjoyable. I seemed to lose track of the days. The immensity of trackless lonely seas lay behind me.

The night of the full moon I remained on deck late, unable to resist the enchantment of the marvelous silver orb and the immense white track it cast upon the radiant sea. All seemed magnified—the starry dome above, the wide circle on the horizon, the dark ocean with its moon-whitened road, broad as a great river. There was a dancing ripple on the water. This watching and feeling of mine augmented the sense of immeasurable distance.

We expected to sight the first island of the Galapagos group sometime in the early hours of the morning. Navigation had been perplexing, owing to inaccuracies of the chart, and the influences of tides and currents. The first twenty-four hours out from Cocos Island we drifted over two score miles off our course; the next day ten; and the following, when our navigators made allowance for this drift, there was no perceptible change at all.

I went on deck at three o'clock in the morning. The moon had paled and diminished somewhat, and was sloping away from its zenith. Broken trade wind clouds covered the sky, and low down on the horizon they were dark and vague.

I spent hours on the bow with the lookout, peering through the opaque silvery gloom, over the black waters, to sight land. Once I saw a huge bird, bow-winged, silent and uncanny, that sailed across our ship, silhouetted against the moon. It reminded me of the albatross of the Ancient Mariner.

Dawn came gray, shadowy, with a freshening, cool breeze. The trade wind clouds in the east took on a tinge of rose. The horizon brightened. Red and gold burned on the level bottoms of the clouds. And when the fiery disk of the sun peeped up from the underworld I realized that I was gazing at my first sunrise on the equator. The difference seemed too great for me to grasp.

Shortly after sunrise I sighted the land that the mate had seen from the masthead. A dim, low mound, as illusive and vague as a cloud! But it grew. My sensations were indescribable. I could only gaze until my eyes dimmed. Galapagos!

The blur on the horizon lifted, spread, darkened, took shape, and at last merged into an island with a high peak, a range of hills to the south, and to the north an endlessly long slope, going down into the sea. An hour later we identified it as Marchena (Bindlowe) and another to the west as Pinta (Abingdon).

When we approached close enough to Marchena to distinguish color and nature, I saw it to be a desert island, iron-hued and gray, ghastly, stark, barren, yet somehow beautiful. How incredible the change between Cocos and Marchena, only a little over four hundred miles apart! It recalled to me long ridges of Arizona desert land, and there was a thrill in the familiarity. This tropic island excited emotions of awe and grandeur. Forbidding and inhospitable, it seemed to warn the mariner to pass on down the lanes of the sea.

Beyond Marchena a low dark rambling cloud above the horizon soon took on the stability of land. Another island of the Galapagos Archipelago! We were uncertain as to which island this was, but inclined toward the opinion that it was San Salvador (James I).

While nearing the coast of Marchena I saw a ragged line of white surf along the bronze shore, and high on the dark slopes patches and squares of pale green verdure, probably brush and cactus.

A most welcome surprise was the delightful cool weather and exhilarating air. While approaching the equator we had expected it to be torrid. The sea was violet, ruffled with white caps.

Darwin's *Voyage of H.M.S. Beagle* has for many years been one of my favorite books, and became so long before I entertained the remotest dream of ever visiting the Galapagos. This great naturalist's account of his visit to the islands was as fascinating to me as fiction . . . and through it I came to learn considerably about this archipelago . . . .

There are ten or more islands in the Galapagos Archipelago, five of them large; and geologically they are of recent (geographically) volcanic origin. Darwin records no less than two thousand craters on the islands. One of these was smoking in 1830, during his visit.

The islands lay on the equator and are washed by the Humbolt Current, a strange river of the sea similar to the

Gulf Stream. It runs up out of the Antarctic Ocean, along the South American shore, and somewhere off Peru swings west to touch the Galapagos. It has a temperature fifteen to twenty degrees colder than the surrounding hot ocean waters. Between the Galapagos Islands are channels from one to twenty miles wide through which set strong currents, running sometimes two and a half knots. These currents and the depth of water account partially for the isolation and independence of various species of plants and living creatures.

*   *   *

The nearer we approached Santa Cruz the more we realized that it could not be appreciated from a great distance. The sea leagues were as deceitful as the open wastes of the desert.

From five miles out the color and lines of the island assumed properties that could be defined. Both east and west ends, perhaps thirty miles apart, sloped up from the sea level in a most wonderfully gradual and graceful sweep to the black peaks, against which a mass of pearl and purple cloud had lodged. These slopes were almost without a break in their smooth, exquisitely pale-green contour. Here and there red outcroppings of lava made the color and grace more emphatic by contrast. This green was a low thick brush streaked with dark stems that must have been cactus. White crescent beaches gleamed in the sun; black rough shorelines were encroached upon by green swells breaking to white. Huge rocks, islands in themselves, like immense fortresses, loomed up on all sides.

The Galapagos

We ran slowly into Conway Bay and dropped anchor behind Eden Island, a pyramid-like rock that would have been a mountain in less colossal surroundings.

Bold dark islands, large and small, hugely near and dimly far, heaved up out of a sunset sea; and over them rolled mass on mass of amber and purple clouds, brightening to silver toward the west. Strange new world this Galapagos Archipelago! It baffled me. It was nothing like what I had dreamed of myself or imagined from the descriptions of Darwin . . . .

Desert and sea together, both of which I knew singly, had combined to magnify each other's peculiar characteristics. I had sailed four thousand miles to fish the virgin seas that embraced these islands. Sight alone of the volcanic slopes and cones and the purple channels that washed their shores would have been ample reward for the long journey.

The bigness of the Pacific seemed to lend atmosphere; and then the strangeness of the equatorial regions invested the land and water, cloud and verdure, with something I could feel but not grasp.

* * *

The breeze we had hoped for did not spring up, and the heat was torrid. Nevertheless we went out fishing in force, taking the three launches. A few miles from the ship loomed the several huge blocks of lava, islands they might have been, around the rugged shores of which the white seas lunged and crawled and fell away in waterfalls. On the way out we were interrupted twice by tuna that insisted on attaching themselves to R.C.s hook. They were of the yellow-fin variety and about fifty and sixty-five pounds, respectively. I looked for fish but did not let out my line.

The water was smooth in patches, and again lightly rippled, of a most intensely vivid blue color. Romer and Johnny at once began to hook fish, so fell behind. Turtles basked in the sunshine; rays flapped the tips of their fins like wings in awkward yet efficient swimming motion; small shearwater ducks flitted about us; several great white-and-black boobies riding the sea allowed us almost to run them down before flying; the twinkling, dimpling motion of the water, such as is caused by a school of fish under the surface, crossed our bows. I stood on deck in the hope that I might espy a sailfish leap or swordfish fins.

We ran up to the yellow and black lava rocks which now towered high in the air. Seals and iguana lay side by side on the shelves just above the thundering surges. The green billows piled up on the ledges and, turning white, burst into spray.

R.C. interfered with my observations by hooking another pretty hard-fighting fish. It turned out to be another yellow-fin, larger than the others. I remembered that I had come to these far distant seas to fish. Still, even with a bait overboard and rod in hand, I had to look everywhere.

I saw a black and white boobie sailing off the summit of the nearest rock, fold its wings, and plunge down like an arrow to go clear out of sight.

R.C. let out a yell, and I turned to see a beautiful flashing silver cloud of fish go leaping over the blue water. How they made the water roar! Behind them showed vicious splashes, proving that some gamefish were in pursuit.

"They're big ballyhoo," declared Bob.

Indeed they were big, and by far the fastest leaping fish we had ever seen. They almost flew across the water, blazing silver in the sunlight. Then they sounded. I was gazing here and there, hoping to see them again, when I had an electrifying strike that almost jerked me back off the seat. My line whizzed out. I heard a cracking splash, but as I was gazing straight into the glare of the sun, I could not see. R.C., however, yelled that I had hooked a whale of a dolphin.

We had come round to the windward of the rocks, into a wonderful place where the sea boomed against black walls and seals barked and gulls sailed over us and green white-fringed channels ran between the islands.

Here I fought and landed the largest dolphin I had ever seen—fifty pounds. It was five and a half feet long, a blunt-headed, arrow-tailed fish with body almost a solid gold color. What a blaze it made in the water! R.C. was so long in photographing the dolphin to his satisfaction that I nearly lost it.

"Say, I was afraid a shark would get him," I ejaculated.

"It sure is good to fish where you don't have a million sharks after you," declared R.C.

Bob said he had seen several sharks, two of them hammer-heads. But during our fishing around these rocks we were not handicapped [by sharks]. I had one more strike, a most strenuous and solid tug on my line, but the hook did not catch.

At five o'clock a little breeze began to fan our heated faces. We turned for the ship and presently came upon Romer and Johnny in their boat with Captain Mitchell. They reported a most successful afternoon and showed us tuna, bonita, grouper and several great cero-mackerel. These last named were very welcome to us, for they are the best of food fish . . . . These fish have gold spots and seemed to be identical with the cero-mackerel of the Gulf Stream. According to the boys they exhibited wonderful fighting qualities.

Upon arriving once more at the ship I found myself pretty well exhausted. It had been a busy day, but would have been nothing unusual for me had it not been for the heat. I felt better after a shower-bath, my first in the Humbolt Stream water . . . .

When I came on deck the sun was setting in magnificent gold and purple splendor. Away to the north a vast bank of salmon-pink cloud shone refulgently. Over the endless green slope of Santa Cruz masses of gray clouds had congregated, and they had encompassed the peaks. Dark veils of rain were hanging from the under edge, making a bar against the violet sky beyond. The *Fisherman* at anchor in an opal sea; the strange entrancing islands all around, varied, beautiful; the soaring of long-tailed frigate birds; the low moan of the surf; and lastly a school of rays, gigantic bat-winged creatures of the sea, flopping along the surface of the tranquil water, showing their kite-shaped white barred forms and hawklike heads—all these things thrilled me, revived my joy in one of the wildest and lonesomest places in all the Seven Seas.

* * *

Other hot days contributed to the growing appreciation that the pleasant weather conditions under which we had sailed down into Conway Bay had passed us by. The pitch oozed out of the deck, and the rail was too hot to touch. The staterooms were antechambers of the torrid zone. I found a woolen shirt, after the ordeal of putting it on, to be cooler than thin cotton ones. We all burned black. Romer and Johnny might have gone into motion pictures as savages. In fact, they almost reverted.

Nevertheless, we fished morning and afternoon, made raids on the beach, ate sparingly and drank water copiously, fought the sticky flies by day and the hungry mosquitoes by night, and had a perfectly wonderful time.

I, more noticeably than any of the others, began to grow a little thin. Romer was affected, too, though at the same time he appeared to be growing taller. Sometimes I was exhausted, but I began to stand the heat better than at first. When the sky clouded over, which happened before noon every day, the weather was bearable. At night it was cool on deck. Direct contact with the sun, however, between nine and five, was something to remember. It reminded me that I had always been a sun-worshipper, like an Indian, and that for once in my life I had begun to dream of tinkling ice in pitchers of crystal water, and the sleet and snow of New York, which I had always hated. Experience develops. Sometimes I wonder why Ulysses, the Homeric wanderer, did not learn to stay home.

The brush covering Santa Cruz Island was as impenetrable as a wall, and infinitely more cruel. Rhododendron thickets along Pennsylvania trout streams, mangrove swamps in the Everglades of Florida, manzanita copses in the Tonto Basin of Arizona, have at different times tortured me. The cholla cactus on the slopes of the Pinacate have turned me back. But I never saw a worse place than the jungle of this particular Galapagos island. No doubt the intense heat supplied the last and most implacable barrier. My explorations were limited to a mile of the coast near where the ship lay at anchor.

On the sea, however, we ranged near and far, as fishermen must range to find fish. Our launches were fast and could cover long distances. Around the small islands and the monument-like rocks we found fish in abundance, with only an occasional shark to harass us, but out in the open channels, in the deep water, where the great gamefish, such as sailfish, swordfish, spearfish, should be found, we had not yet had a strike or seen a telltale fin.

* * *

R.C. and Bob complained that my fish sense, as they termed it, was not operating—that when I did not go out early and stay late and keep a bait in the water while always watching the sea, it was a pretty good indication that the great gamefish were not there. Faced with this evidence, and made to think of its significance, I had to confess there was something in it.

Swordfish, marlin, sailfish, tarpon, tuna, barracuda, always make their presence known to the alert and experienced fisherman. But on the other hand, fish did not surface in this tropical sea. The schools of small fish stayed down deep. I could not bring myself to believe, however, that the great gamefish inhabited these waters and never showed themselves.

"Let's take a long run," suggested R.C.

"That's my idea," added Bob. "It's a cinch we can't ketch any settin' heah thinkin' of Catalina an' Nova Scotia an' Florida."

"We may be here at the wrong season," I said. "Swordfish and sailfish are always on the move."

"We don't see any mullet or anchovies or skipjack," complained Bob. "If we hadn't seen that bunch of ballyhoo I'd swear there wasn't any bait fish heah."

Perhaps we arrived at a pretty accurate estimate of fishing around the Galapagos. Nevertheless it was a splendid proof of our long experience, and the innumerable mistakes we had made, that we did not absolutely trust our judgments and believed that in the last analysis the way to find out about the fishing was to keep everlastingly at it. Moreover, we taxed our ingenuity to devise untried means to attract fish, and pondered over baits, lures, spoons. None of us took much stock in the artificial baits. Bob, being a Florida fisherman, was partial to the cut bait, which was a long thin strip of fresh fish, cut skillfully, and attached to the hook in such a way that it would troll straight and smooth through the water. For sailfish this was the best bait. But I did not like the cut bait for all kinds of fishing. My favorite was a whole flying fish or mullet, hooked so that it would troll perfectly. This, of course, was not a suitable bait for the small fish.

The experience of Captain Mitchell, Romer and Johnny best illustrated the fact that artificial baits were sufficient in these waters. They had great fishing with whatever they happened to put on their hooks. The captain was partial to spoons; Johnny liked the solid metal Catalina minnows; and Romer used tarporenos, squids, jigs, and whatever was nearest at hand. Whenever we happened to look in their direction, with glass or naked eye, we always found one or more of them pumping away on fish. What an enormous quantity of tackle they did consume!

Now there was a valuable lesson for me in their experience, for it represented what Galapagos fishing would be at its best, for nine hundred and ninety-nine out of a thousand anglers who might visit the islands. To say the Galapagos fishing was not wonderful would be unfair and untrue. It certainly was great. The fact that it was disappointing to R.C. and me was very little against it. We were always seeking the great gamefish, the fighters that took hours to subdue; we always dreamed of strange new waters, of huge unconquerable denizens of the deep. But despite this fact I believed that we were both singularly appreciative of any kind of fishing, always enthusiastic and keen, and grateful for good luck, philosophical over the bad, and especially trained by experience to see everything and learn everlastingly.

"We'll take the big launch and fish together for a change," I decided. "Let's use medium-light tackle, the six-ounce Murphy rods, and twelve-thread lines. And have heavy-tackle ready with baits, in case we see a real fish."

It was a beautiful summer morning, with fleecy clouds in the sky and a refreshing breeze. Impossible to believe we were on the equator! I feared my senses had become sort of stultified, and that I could no longer realize where I was or what I saw.

Seals barked at us from the ledges of Eden Island. The water was gently ruffled in some places and glancingly smooth in others. Green turtles showed in unusual numbers. A single frigate bird soared high above the island.

We ran full speed round the corner of [Santa Cruz] and did not wet a line until we were in waters we had not fished before.

I espied a school of tuna on the surface and stood up on the deck while we circled it. R.C. had a strike long before we got near the dark rippling patch on the water.

"Zowie! Look at my line go," exclaimed R.C. "Now I'll have to wind all of it back."

The task was accomplished eventually, and the tuna, a yellow-fin of forty pounds, was freed. Then we ran on, making a wide turn until we were headed toward San Salvador. In order to cover the distance rapidly we were running too fast for trolling. All the same, R.C. kept a bait out, and he had one grand strike that made us thrill. But the fish, whatever he was, missed the hook. We circled back over where he struck, but to no avail.

Close toward San Salvador the numerous rocks and channels looked attractive, and also rather hazardous. As we neared the island, however, I neglected searching the sea for fish and had eyes only for this marvelous mountain rising so austere and grim. It appeared much higher than Santa Cruz, and infinitely harder, wilder, more rugged and barren. The slopes were red lava, except where the cloud shadows rested, and there they were purple. Patches of green stood out against this stark background. The proportion of verdure appeared very slight, and showed here and there in squares or blocks, very much like fields of green alfalfa in a desert setting. San Salvador seemed a thousand times more forbidding than Santa Cruz. It did not deceive. There was no soft, fresh, green mantle to waylay the sight. We had read that wild dogs and wild burros roamed this island. It did not seem that anything except lizards could exist on such a desolate place.

Some few miles offshore we struck fish, small yellow-fin tuna, and in the hope of happening on a big one we trolled faithfully and worked hard. Sixty-five pounds, however, was the largest, and this fell to R.C.'s rod. So about the middle of the forenoon we headed northeast across the channel in the direction of the Seymour Islands, great colored monuments of lava that were landmarks even at a long distance.

It took over an hour, with both engines running full speed, to get within distance of these strange islands. The northeast end of Santa Cruz was a long low strip of green that ran out interminably into the sea. It must have been level for miles before it showed a perceptible slope toward the distant summit of the mountain. This cape of green was what brought out the amazing contrast of the Seymours. They were colossal monuments, one round and sloping, red in color, and the other blunt and square, with precipitous sides, black as coal. They were very high, and the latter at least was insurmountable. Even the sea fowl seemed to shun them. And the green swells beat ceaselessly and resentfully at their iron bases.

In the channel between them and the open water toward Santa Cruz flocks of birds were circling, telltale signs of fish on the surface; and white splashes further attracted our attention. Soon we distinguished blackfish rolling, and giant rays leaping out, flapping their wings. We seemed to be a long time running over to this ground, but at last we attained it, and R.C. got his bait out first.

I saw a green flash and R.C. yelled. Smash! It was a churning white strike. How the line whistled off the reel!

"Wahoo," I said, with satisfaction, "and he might be big."

"Nix. It's a tuna," averred R.C., easing on the drag.

"No, that's a wahoo. See, he's on the surface ... Now your line is tight and then it's slack. Strange he doesn't leap. Wahoos are great jumpers."

It was indeed a pleasure to fish without the dread certainty of sharks. R.C. soon had his quarry stopped and on the way to the boat. I was afforded no little satisfaction at the sight of the long sharp blazing outline of a wahoo. Then, wonderful to see, a whole colony of fish came along with him. They were swimming too deep to permit classification, but I was certain no sharks were among them.

R.C.'s wahoo had to be handled gently, so that he might live when released, and in consequence we did not get the best estimate of his size. But I had no doubt that he was the largest we had caught, something over forty pounds. This was most encouraging.

When I let my bait drift back some yards, a short chunky brown fish appeared. He had long saberlike fins. Albacore! When I hooked him he showed the well-known sounding, fighting proclivities of this species. I did not have an easy task bringing him in. In shape he was indeed an albacore, but the warm tints, the gold tones, the mother-of-pearl iridescence belonged to the fish of hot seas.

While I was getting ready again R.C. had a sounding smack at his bait; then a splash and a nodding rod and screeching reel told of another hooked fish.

"Business is shore pickin' up," said Bob, with satisfaction.

From behind us came a heavy sousing splash. I wheeled in time to see a great green boil of foam on the surface.

"That was a ray an' a buster," declared Bob.

Before I could move to get my camera a brown mass loomed up out of the green. The water opened with a roar to let out an enormous black creature, as large as the boat and with wings like a bat. These limber, curved wings waved. I heard the swish, saw the spray fly from them. Then the huge thing flipped clear over, turning uppermost its silver-white underside, and fell back into the water with a tremendous crash. The splashing water went twenty feet high.

"Oh, what a picture!" I cried, coming out of my paralysis, and I dove for my camera.

But this ray did not come up again. Others, however, were leaping around us, on all sides. In the hope of getting a marvelous photograph I stood ready with camera, eyes roving to and fro. Patience is the prime requisite in getting pictures of game or fish. This was an exceedingly wonderful opportunity, which I was not slow to grasp. Bob ran the boat, and R.C. trolled. Every little while they would be stopped by a fish, but I kept on watching for a giant ray to leap. There was no way to calculate when and where they would come out. Many leaped too far away. Twice there were leaps close behind me, one of which splashed water over my arm. I stood up in the rocking boat until I was tired, during which time R.C. caught two tuna, one wahoo, three mackerel, one dolphin, and a fifty-pound grouper, almost red in color, truly a remarkable fish.

"Some class to this!" declared R.C., his face beaming.

"I'd say so, if we'd only slam into a big sailfish," added Bob.

"We ought to be ashamed," I said. "There are millions of fishermen who'd think this the grandest sport. And it *is*. The place is enough."

We ran close under the looming black wall of the great fortresslike island, and out of the blue depths a white flash shone behind my bait. It might not have been a broad shield-shaped fish, for water is deceiving, but it certainly looked like that. I had no time to jerk or do anything but cling to the rod. The fish was swift, and he gathered speed as he went. What was more, he took three hundred yards of brand-new line with him.

"Well! Now look who was here," I ejaculated, as I reeled in the limp line that was left.

"Big tuna," said R.C., complacently.

"No. He didn't sound. He ran off high. Whew! That was a strike."

"Wouldn't surprise me to ketch a buster round these rocks," declared Bob. "Looks good to me. You ought to have had him on your big tackle."

R.C. took his turn trying to photograph the rays. They kept on leaping all around us, close and far away. I finally saw one come out with a tussle of his flat body and throw a remora yards into the air. This was the secret of their leaping, to fling the sucking fishes from them. I had seen sharks, sailfish, swordfish leap to get rid of the tenacious little remoras, and now I had the pleasure of watching the giant rays do it.

Then followed several sharp tugs at my bait, a lightning-swift strike, a curling splash, and a tumbling blaze of gold in the air.

"Dolphin!" yelled R.C.

"Now you're shoutin'," verified Bob.

How quickly we responded to the action of a gamefish on the surface! This dolphin bounced out as if he were a rubber fish. It was incredible the way he leaped, apparently without long enough time in the water to generate such remarkable energy. He really did not leap, but tumbled up backwards, over and over, sideways and headlong. The only elegance about him was his beauty. His action was that of a bull terrier with a rat. Part of the time I had a tight line, but mostly it was slack. The sun was shining from behind me down upon this beautiful fish, and the background was the purple sea and those two grand monuments of lava.

I brought him in finally and let him go unhurt, not wholly sure in my mind that he was smaller than my first dolphin. As he turned over, gaping with wide jaws, his great broad side like the golden shield of Achilles, I experienced a quick feeling of regret, common to me in such moments. Suppose he was exhausted and fell prey to sharks! But he sheered away in a curve and suddenly shot like a ray of light down into the blue depths.

"Wasn't he a beauty, R.C.?" I queried. "Seems to me he ought to have a better name than dolphin. Or at least one that would distinguish him from the dolphin beloved by sailors."

On this trip into tropic waters we had seen many of the dolphin so well known to the ancients. It takes a keen eye to detect the difference between a real dolphin and a porpoise, when they are playing on the surface at a distance. Both are mammals, and the dolphin appears to me to be a smaller, slimmer, more graceful creature, lighter in color. The fish dolphin, the golden creature I had just caught and released, should be given a name other than that of the mammal. Its scientific name is *coryphene*.

R.C.'s next catch was the largest mackerel I ever saw, one of the golden-spotted variety that I had first taken to be cero-mackerel, and it weighed all of twenty-one pounds. Mackerel are usually slim fish, but when they get heavy they take on the breadth that makes them very handsome.

We caught over a dozen fish between the Seymour and Guy Fawkes Islands. When we reached these latter islands the sun was burning gold and red in the clouds above Albemarle, and the afternoon was far spent.

Boobies were plunging down from the cliffs into the water. I never saw one of these incomparable fishers come up without a luckless little fish in his bill. . . . The tide was full, the swells rose white over the ledges where the seals lolled, the iguanas stood high on their short legs with their fringed crowns and backs plainly visible.

I struck a tuna too heavy for the light tackle in hand, and after a hard effort, vainly expended, I lost him.

"Well, I guess that'll be about all," I remarked, laying aside the rod.

Sources

Page 3:   "The Lord of Lackawaxen Creek" appeared in *Tales of Freshwater Fishing*, Harper and Brothers, 1928.

Page 19:   "Two Fights with Swordfish" appeared in *Tales of Fishes*, Harper and Brothers, 1919.

Page 35:   "Tuna at Avalon, 1919" appeared in *Tales of Swordfish and Tuna*, Harper and Brothers, 1927.

Page 43:   "Bonefish" appeared in *Tales of Fishes*.

Page 57:   "Rivers of the Everglades" appeared in *Tales of Southern Rivers*, Harper and Brothers, 1924.

Page 67:   "Some Rare Fish" appeared in *Tales of Fishes*.

Page 77:   "Giant Nova Scotia Tuna" appeared in *Tales of Swordfish and Tuna*.

Page 105:   "At the Mouth of the Klamath" appeared in *Tales of Freshwater Fishing*.

Page 122:   "Rocky Riffle" appeared in *Tales of Freshwater Fishing*.

Page 132:   "Down River" appeared in *Tales of Freshwater Fishing*.

Page 141:   "Black Marlin" appeared in *Tales of the Angler's Eldorado, New Zealand*, Harper and Brothers, 1926.

Page 156:   "The Tongariro River and The Dreadnaught Pool" appeared in *Tales of the Angler's Eldorado, New Zealand*.

Page 179:   "Nato Fishing" appeared in *Tales of Tahitian Waters*, Harper and Brothers, 1931.

Page 182:   "Marlin!" appeared in *Tales of Tahitian Waters*.

Page 199:   The Australia chapter is excerpted from *An American Angler in Australia*, Harper and Brothers, 1937.

Page 223:   "Zihuatanejo Bay" appeared in *Tales of Fishing Virgin Seas*, Harper and Brothers, 1925.

Page 238:   "Byme-by-Tarpon" appeared in *Tales of Fishes*.

Page 245:   "The Galapagos" appeared in *Tales of Fishing Virgin Seas*.